Best Hikes Salt Lake City

The Greatest Vistas, Waterfalls, and Wildflowers

SECOND EDITION

Lori J. Lee

FALCONGUIDES

GUILFORD, CONNECTICUT

For all those who love the land, who preserve our public lands,
and who feel a stewardship over protecting and caring for these places
that feed our souls and nourish our lives.

FALCONGUIDES®

An imprint of The Rowman & Littlefield Publishing Group, Inc.
4501 Forbes Blvd., Ste. 200, Lanham, MD 20706

Falcon, FalconGuides, and Make Adventure Your Story are registered trademarks of The Rowman &
Littlefield Publishing Group, Inc.
Distributed by NATIONAL BOOK NETWORK

British Library Cataloguing-in-Publication Information Available

Library of Congress Cataloguing-in-Publication Information Available

ISBN 978-1-4930-3012-5 (paperback)
ISBN 978-1-4930-3013-2 (e-book)

∞™ The paper used in this publication meets the minimum requirements of American National Standard
for Information Sciences—Permanence of Paper for Printed Library Materials, ANSI / NISO Z39.48-1992.

Printed in the United States of America

The author and The Rowman & Littlefield Publishing Group, Inc., assume no liability for accidents
happening to, or injuries sustained by, readers who engage in the activities described in this
book.

Contents

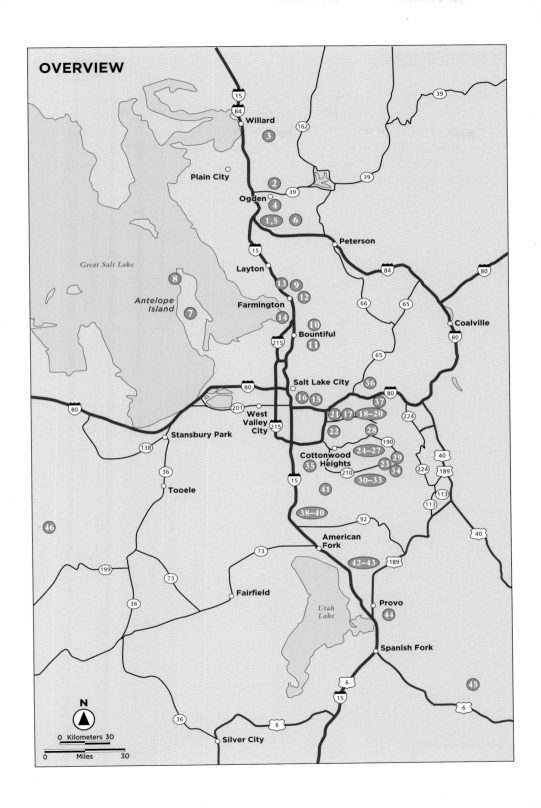

OVERVIEW

Acknowledgments

In appreciation to all who helped me complete this second edition with updates and new hikes. Thank you to Mike Scalora for his help with my maps. Thank you to Sherry Holmes, William Barba, Robert Bunkhall, Marc Fletcher, Mike Scalora, Ethan Howell, and Matt Thalman for sharing their photographer's eye and their beautiful photos. Thanks to Greg Hilbig at Draper City Parks and Recreation for his time and insights into the Corner Canyon area. Thanks to those who manage and care for the trails we all love so much.

Introduction

Hikes are pilgrimages. We do them to find solace, because others have done them, to mark them off our life list, because they are recommended, to prove something, to stay fit, to connect with the spirit of nature, and sometimes just because they are there. Hikes build memories with families and friends. They feed our souls and give us time for reflection and solitude. As John Muir said, "In every walk with nature one receives far more than he seeks."

Each hiking trail near Salt Lake City offers its own treat. Climbing Mount Timpanogos and other 11,000-foot peaks provides 360-degree views across mountain ranges, the vast Salt Lake Valley, the Great Salt Lake, the cities that lie between, and a hundred other scenic details you will never see from your couch. Hiking Albion Basin offers visual candy—such as prolific wildflowers, some found only in the Wasatch. The Lake Blanche area takes you to glacially carved lakes that sit below a sundial-shaped formation. The hike to Donut Falls is an easy jaunt to a doughnut-shaped hole in the rock and the waterfall that pours through it. Each hike offers its own reward, and with this book you can begin to discover what each has to offer you: a personal treasure hunt. In this second edition we have added four additional trails that absolutely rank as some of the best hikes near Salt Lake City. Ben Lomond Peak, one of the tallest peaks in northern Utah, provides a notch on any hiker's belt. The Catherine Pass and Sunset Peak hike has become one of my new favorites with its astounding views and gorgeous hiking experience. The Lakeside Trail on Antelope Island provides phenomenal views of the Great Salt Lake along a trail that is an easy stroll. And finally, the trail to Dog Lake via Mill D trailhead is a Big Cottonwood Canyon classic that shouldn't be left out of any hiking book. Enjoy these new additions.

The heart of Salt Lake City beats with business, culture, education, traffic, and all the accoutrements of metropolitan living. But unlike most other metropolitan areas, lush, beautiful mountains and canyons sit on the very borders of the city and offer hiking opportunities within minutes of its hustle and bustle. These trails lead into the depths of the glorious, green mountains and the respite they offer. The outdoor lifestyle available in Utah draws many to the area. Being able to take a quick hike or bike ride before or after work, get to a ski resort in half an hour, sit atop 11,000-plus-foot peaks outside your back door—proximity is but one of the reasons the outdoor lifestyle thrives in Utah. Each of the trails described in this guide lies within an hour of Salt Lake City, most much closer.

The Wasatch Mountains make up Salt Lake City's eastern border and then continue north, bordering other northern Utah cities and up into Idaho. The range supports lush alpine forests, waterfalls, rushing streams, quiet lakes, grassy meadows dotted with wildflowers, and belt-notch-worthy peaks.

Just a glance at the Wasatch Range can leave visitors as well as locals in awe. Though I have driven past the range my entire adult life, I still can't make it through the Salt Lake Valley without exclaiming on the majesty and beauty of the mountains.

Considered the western edge of the Rocky Mountains, the Wasatch Range stretches 246 miles from southeast Idaho to central Utah. Its slopes reach 73 miles from east to west. The range comprises three sections: The Northern Wasatch includes the mountains around Brigham City, the Bear River mountains in Cache Valley, and they top out in Idaho. The Southern Wasatch is home to the highest peak in the range—11,928-foot Mount Nebo—and ends approximately at the city of Nephi. The Central Wasatch Range, the primary focus of this book, runs along the Wasatch Front (the populated east side of the Wasatch Range) from Ogden Canyon to American Fork Canyon and makes its way into the Park City area known as the Wasatch Back.

Original inhabitants of the Salt Lake Valley included such Native American peoples as the Shoshone, Paiute, Goshute, and Utes. The Indian Trail via Cold Water Canyon (see Hike 4) is one of the trails established by Native Americans as they forged a route past the waters of what is now called Ogden Canyon.

The Wasatch was first viewed by Europeans in 1776 when priests Francisco Atanasio Dominguez and Silvestre Velez de Escalante traversed the range. These were the first non–Native American explorers to lay eyes on much of New Mexico, Colorado, Utah, and Arizona. In the 1820s fur trappers and traders discovered the area and established trading posts and trapping systems to provide beaver pelts for the beaver-fur hats then in fashion. The trapping industry brought Peter Ogden, William Ashley, Jedediah Smith, Etienne Provost, and Jim Bridger—men for whom national forests, cities, and sections of land were named. You'll recognize their names as you explore the area. Fur interests throughout the West dwindled in 1840 when silk replaced beaver fur as the height of fashion, and mining moved into Utah.

In 1847 the first Mormon pioneers came to the valley. Their leader and prophet Brigham Young declared it "The Place," and the Mormons began to establish their respite from the religious persecution that had tormented them in the East. Members of the LDS Church came from across the world to settle in the Salt Lake Valley. The hike up Mormon Pioneer Trail (Hike 36) revisits the last climb for the Mormon pioneers and their first view of the valley. The trek to Ensign Peak (Hike 16) takes you to the viewpoint from which the Mormon leaders decided upon the city's layout. During the Civil War, Col. Patrick Connor and his Third California Infantry entered Utah to establish Fort Douglas in Salt Lake City.

Californians prospected for minerals in the Wasatch and other areas near Salt Lake, and by the 1860s these prospectors had discovered silver, lead, and zinc deposits in the canyons and mountains southeast of Salt Lake City, particularly in Big Cottonwood, Little Cottonwood, and Parley's. The now-abandoned mines still sit within these canyons. You will pass old mines and tailings piles on many trails, though they are often unrecognizable. At Lake Solitude (Hike 29) the trail takes you to the east side of the lake, where you can feel a breeze blowing through one of the old mine shafts that has been mostly filled in.

View from the Ogden Overlook (Hike 6)

By 1870 towns like Alta and Park City had sprung up with all the usual mining town establishments. At one time Alta supported twenty-six saloons and six breweries, while Park City derived the majority of its revenues from saloon licenses and fines for prostitution. Today former brothels are used as homes, and in the Park City area, these small shanties cost a pretty penny. The trail to Cecret Lake and Albion Basin (Hike 33) and the trail option to Catherine Pass and Sunset Peak on Brighton Lakes Tour (Hike 23) explore the beautiful scenery and stark views surrounding Alta.

The Wasatch area is rich in history, natural resources, scenery, tall peaks, and the natural respite of trees, streams, mountain lakes, and wildlife. Whatever your personal reason for placing your feet upon the trails of the Wasatch Range, you are bound to find more than you seek.

Weather

The Salt Lake area has four distinct seasons with an average annual snowfall of 56.9 inches and average annual rainfall of 14.7 inches. Utah is considered desert and has low humidity. The air is dry, and temperatures are predictable. Spring (March–May) is often wet, and snow in the upper elevations does not melt some years until June or July. In April trails often tend to be muddy and wet as the snow finishes its melt.

Hiking season officially begins in the lower elevations in May. By May the trees have filled in with green and the temperatures are in the 60-to-70-degree range.

July and August are the hottest months of the year, with temperatures ranging from 80 to 100 degrees. These are great months to hike the higher elevation because of the coolness to be found there. By this time the snow has melted out and the trails are dry and hospitable.

September is the ideal time for scenic fall hikes at all elevations. The temperatures drop into the 60-to-70-degree range, and the changing leaves turn the trails into bright, colorful routes. The Aspen Grove area (Hikes 42 and 43) is renowned as a scenic byway thanks to the array of leaf color over the incredible Timpanogos area. By October the leaves have usually fallen and the alpine scenery has become barren in preparation for winter, but many hiking trails are still usable.

Trail use is not restricted, and trails are available year-round. During winter, when temperatures can range from 0 to 40 degrees, snowshoes can be used on many trails. However, the Wasatch Range holds some steep mountains, so check avalanche conditions before heading out for a winter hike.

Flora and Fauna

The flora and fauna of Utah is as diverse as the state. Change mountain ranges and you change flora and fauna. The hike to Deseret Peak is in the Stansbury Range west of Salt Lake Valley, while the hike to Frary Peak is on Antelope Island in the Great Salt Lake. Most of the trails near Salt Lake City are in the Wasatch Range east of the city, but each of these areas has its own distinctive flora and fauna.

Antelope Island in the Great Salt Lake (Frary Peak, Hike 7, and the Lakeside Trail, Hike 8) is home to a herd of bison introduced in 1893, antelope, and millions of migrating shorebirds such as white-faced ibis, gulls, trumpeter swans, and pelicans, to name only a few. The desertlike flora consists of grasses, sage, cacti, and juniper. The Farmington Bay Waterfowl Management Area (Hike 14) also is ideal for birding. This area boasts as many as 400 bald eagles during winter and is set up for viewing a large variety of birds.

The canyons of the Wasatch Front are filled with trees and shrubs such as box elder, willow, aspen, scrub oak, maple, and chokecherry. Higher up reside Douglas fir, limber pine, white fir, and Utah's state tree, the blue spruce. At higher elevations (10,000 to 11,000 feet) in the Wasatch Range, spruce, bristlecone pines, and subalpine fir bravely live out their gnarled lives.

Twelve hundred species of wildflowers splash the Wasatch with bright hues all summer long, depending on elevation. Flowers begin to peak at lower elevations in April and May, and during August trails like Albion Basin to Cecret Lake, Catherine Pass and Sunset Peak, and the Brighton Lakes hikes are in full and glorious bloom. According to the Cottonwood Canyons Foundation, there is one flower found only along the Wasatch. The Wasatch shooting star was known to grow only in a 1-square-mile area in Big Cottonwood Canyon until 2008, when populations were located in

Wildflowers along the trail to Mount Raymond (Hike 26)

Little Cottonwood Canyon. This flower grows nowhere else in the world. A wild-flower festival is held each summer in the Cottonwood Canyons.

Mountain animals tend to stay out of sight and out of the way of humans, but as we encroach upon their habitat, more human-animal encounters are inevitable. Though mountain lions are elusive and seldom seen, they live throughout the Wasatch Mountains. Black bears are the only bear species left in Utah, and though they're relatively common in mountain forests, I have never personally run into one on these trails, though sightings have been more prevalent recently. Moose sightings are very likely, especially on the trails where boggy, wet areas and streams abound. Moose are not usually aggressive, but they can be very dangerous. Feel free to take photos, but keep your distance.

Rattlesnakes are common in all five areas covered in this guide. They prefer the dry, south-facing foothill slopes and often sun themselves on rocks. Rattlesnakes don't desire contact with humans and in most cases will slither out of your way. Other animals you may see include squirrels, chipmunks, pot guts, deer, coyotes, fox, elk, and mountain goats in the cliff areas such as White Pine Lake (Hike 30), Ben Lomond Peak (Hike 3), and the cliffs in Little Cottonwood Canyon.

In all cases respect the circle of life, prepare for your safety, and don't ever feed or touch wild animals—not even the cute, fluffy ones that beg for food.

Adams Canyon Waterfall (Hike 9)

Wilderness Restrictions/Regulations

Along many of the trails in this guide, including Red Pine Lake, Maybird Lakes, Deseret Peak, and Mount Timpanogos, you will cross into wilderness areas.

The majority of the trails near Salt Lake City lie within the majestic peaks and rugged backcountry of the Uinta-Wasatch-Cache National Forest. Encompassing nearly 2.1 million ecologically diverse acres, including seven wilderness areas, the forest is strewn with trails for exploring. These forests and wilderness areas hold the Wasatch Front watershed, which provides water for more than 75 percent of Utah's population. Because the wilderness areas have also been designated to protect natural resources, certain use restrictions apply. For example, wilderness areas are closed to motor vehicles, commercial enterprises, roads and structures, the landing of aircraft or hang gliders, the use of motorized equipment, and motor or mechanical support. Horses are allowed, but mountain bikes are not.

Each wilderness area has its own unique regulations, but general guidelines include:

- Stay on designated trails and don't cut switchbacks.
- Watch where you step to avoid trampling delicate plants.
- Group size is limited to ten.
- You are responsible for disposal of all debris, garbage, and waste.
- Campsites must be 200 feet from trails or streams, and campfires are not permitted in certain areas.

Specific guidelines for individual wilderness areas are available at www.fs.fed.us/r4/uwc/recreation/wilderness/restrictions.shtml. Watershed canyons require additional regulations for the safety of the community.

Sanitation and the Wasatch Front Watershed

Since the earliest days of settlement, the majority of Utah's population has chosen to settle along the range's western front. Here numerous river drainages exit the mountains, and in a desert with a giant salt-saturated lake, these freshwater sources are the hub of life. Guarding these resources is a watershed plan that encompasses the seven major canyons of the Wasatch Mountain Range (the Wasatch Canyons) and their drainages. From north to south these drainages are City Creek, Red Butte Creek, Emigration Creek, Parleys Creek, Mill Creek, Big Cottonwood Creek, and Little Cottonwood Creek. Draper City has also designated the Corner Canyon area as watershed. The Salt Lake City watershed comprises the waters of these creeks, the surrounding lands that support these water sources, and the groundwater recharge areas for the Salt Lake Valley.

Watershed restrictions are enforced in the following canyons: Little Cottonwood, Big Cottonwood, Parley's north and east of Mountain Dell Reservoir, Little Dell (toward East Canyon), Lambs, Corner Canyon, and City Creek. Domestic animals such as dogs and horses are not allowed in the watershed canyons. Camping is permitted in developed campgrounds only, and backcountry campsites must be 0.5 mile from any road and 200 feet from any water source.

When getting rid of human waste in these watershed canyons, follow a few simple rules:

1. Use restrooms when available.
2. If restrooms are not available, never urinate next to or above a stream or other water source; move at least 200 feet away.

3. Defecate before you leave home, or bring a small hiking shovel to bury your waste and a zippered plastic bag to carry out your toilet paper. Bury solid waste 6 inches deep, and make sure you don't leave toilet paper stuck in the brush.

Leave No Trace

Trails along the Wasatch Front are heavily used, especially during summer and fall. We, as trail users and advocates, must be especially vigilant to make sure our passage leaves no lasting mark. Here are some basic guidelines for preserving trails in the region:

- Use maps to navigate (and do not rely solely on the maps included in this book).
- Remain on the established route to avoid damaging trailside soils and plants. This is also a good rule of thumb for avoiding trailside irritants like poison ivy.
- Pack out all your own trash, including biodegradable items like orange peels. Also consider packing out garbage left by less-considerate hikers.
- Help keep water sources clean by using outhouses at trailheads or along the trail.
- Don't pick wildflowers or gather rocks, antlers, feathers, and other treasures along the trail. Removing these items will take away from the next hiker's experience, plus it's against the law on most federally protected land.
- Be careful with fire, and build campfires only where permitted. Use an existing fire ring and keep your fire small. Remember to burn all the wood to ash and be sure the fire site is completely cold before leaving.
- Use a camp stove for cooking.
- Don't approach or feed any wild creatures—the ground squirrel eyeing your snack food is best able to survive if it remains self-reliant.
- Control pets at all times.
- Be considerate of other visitors. Remember that you share the trail with others, and don't make loud noises while hiking or camping.
- Yield to other trail users when appropriate.

Getting Around

The Utah Transit Authority, or UTA, manages TRAX, a light rail system; the bus system; and the Front Runner, a train that connects Salt Lake City with surrounding counties. Park-and-ride lots are located across the Wasatch Front in conjunction with the TRAX, bus, and train stations for parking and carpooling. Buses make daily runs into the Cottonwood Canyons. For information on schedules and locations, go to www.rideuta.com or call (801) RIDE-UTA (743-3882).

How to Use This Guide

This guide contains just about everything you'll ever need to choose, plan for, enjoy, and survive a hike near Salt Lake City. Packed with useful Salt Lake area information, *Best Hikes Salt Lake City* features forty-six mapped and cued hikes. Here's an outline of the book's major components:

Each section begins with an introduction to the particular region, county, or canyons in which you're given a sweeping look at the lay of the land. Each hike then starts with a short summary of the trail's highlights. These quick overviews give you a taste of the hiking adventures to follow. You'll learn about the trail terrain and what surprises each route has to offer. Following the overview you'll find the **hike specs:** quick, nitty-gritty details. Most are self-explanatory, but here are some details:

Distance: The total distance of the recommended route—one way for loop hikes, the round-trip on an out-and-back or lollipop hike, point-to-point for a shuttle. Some hikes have options that increase or reduce the total distance.

Hiking time: The average time it will take to cover the route. It is based on the total distance, elevation gain, and condition and difficulty of the trail. Your fitness level will also affect your time.

Difficulty: Each hike has been assigned a level of difficulty. The rating system was developed from several sources and personal experience. These levels are meant to be a guideline only, and hikes may prove easier or more difficult depending on personal ability and physical fitness.

- Easy hikes have minimal elevation gain and are on paved or smooth-surfaced dirt trails.
- Moderate hikes are on trails with moderate elevation gain and potentially rough terrain.
- Strenuous hikes are on trails with considerable elevation gain and rough and/or rocky terrain.

Trail surface: General information about what to expect underfoot.

Best season: General information on the best time of year to hike.

Other trail users: Others you might meet on the trail, such as horseback riders, mountain bikers, and people in wheelchairs.

Canine compatibility: Know the trail regulations before you take your dog hiking with you. Dogs are not permitted on several trails in this guide due to watershed restrictions. Tickets and fines may be levied if you end up with your dog in the wrong canyon.

Land status: National forest, county open space, wilderness, etc.

Schedule: If there are hours, road closures, or other scheduling you should be aware of regarding access to the trail, you will find it in this area.

Nearest Town: This will list the nearest town to help you gain general bearing and to know where you can go for emergency contact or last minute needs.

Fees and permits: Whether you need to carry any money with you for park entrance fees and permits.

Maps: A list of other maps to supplement the maps in this book. US Geological Survey (USGS) maps are the best source for accurate topographical information, but the local park map may show more recent trails.

Trail contacts: Location and contact information for the local land manager(s) in charge of the trail. If you have questions about trail access or need to report a problem on the trail, contact this agency.

Special considerations: Specific trail hazards or other important information, such as a lack of water on the trail and hunting seasons.

Other: Additional information that will enhance your hike.

Finding the trailhead gives you dependable driving directions from Salt Lake City to where you'll want to park, including GPS coordinates for the trailhead.

The Hike is the meat of the chapter. Detailed and honest, it's a carefully researched impression of the trail. It also often includes area history, both natural and human.

Under **Miles and Directions**, mileage cues identify significant trail splits, bridges, or other items of note to help you stay on the correct trail. Options are provided for many hikes to make your journey shorter or longer, depending on the amount of time you have.

The **Hike Information** section provides information on local events and attractions, hiking organizations, and area campgrounds.

Don't feel restricted to the routes and trails mapped here. Be adventurous, and use this guide as a platform to discover new routes for yourself. Enjoy your time in the outdoors, and remember to pack out what you pack in.

How to Use the Maps

Overview map: This map shows the location of each hike in the area by hike number.

Route map: This is your primary guide to each hike. It shows all the accessible roads and trails, points of interest, water, landmarks, and geographical features. It also distinguishes trails from roads and paved roads from unpaved roads. The selected route is highlighted, and directional arrows point the way.

Trail Finder

Hike No.	Hike Name	Best Hikes for Waterfalls	Best Hikes with Children	Best Hikes with Dogs	Best Hikes for Views	Best Hikes for Peak Baggers	Best Hikes for Easy Access	Best Hikes for Lake Lovers	Best Hikes for History Buffs	Best Trails for Mountain Bikes
1	Waterfall Canyon	●	●	●						
2	South Skyline Trail: North Ogden Divide to Skyline Ridge									
4	Indian Trail to Nevada Viewpoint				●				●	
5	Malan's Peak and Basin				●				●	
6	Ogden Overlook									●
7	Antelope Island: Frary Peak				●	●				
9	Adams Canyon	●					●			
10	Holbrook Canyon						●			
11	Mueller Park to Elephant Rock			●			●			●
12	Farmington Creek Trail 11.1 (Sunset Trail)		●				●			
13	Kays Creek Parkway		●				●			
14	Farmington Bay Waterfowl Walk		●							
15	The Living Room				●					
16	Ensign Peak		●		●				●	

Hike No.	Hike Name	Best Hikes for Waterfalls	Best Hikes with Children	Best Hikes with Dogs	Best Hikes for Views	Best Hikes for Peak Baggers	Best Hikes for Easy Access	Best Hikes for Lake Lovers	Best Hikes for History Buffs	Best Trails for Mountain Bikes
17	Pipeline Trail						●			●
18	Wasatch Crest Trail									●
19	Dog Lake from Mill Creek			●	●					●
20	Little Water—Great Western Trail Loop			●						
21	Grandeur Peak			●			●			
22	Desolation Trail to Salt Lake Overlook		●					●		
23	Brighton Lakes Tour		●							
24	Lake Blanche						●	●		
25	Willow Heights Trail		●							
26	Butler Fork to Mount Raymond				●	●				
27	Donut Falls	●	●							
29	Silver Lake, Lake Solitude, and Twin Lakes							●		
30	White Pine Lake							●		
31	Red Pine Lake							●		
32	Maybird Lakes							●		

Hike No.	Hike Name	Best Hikes for Waterfalls	Best Hikes with Children	Best Hikes with Dogs	Best Hikes for Views	Best Hikes for Peak Baggers	Best Hikes for Easy Access	Best Hikes for Lake Lovers	Best Hikes for History Buffs	Best Trails for Mountain Bikes
33	Cecret Lake from Albion Basin							●		
35	Ferguson Canyon to Big Cottonwood Canyon Overlook						●			
36	Mormon Pioneer Trail								●	
38	Ghost Falls	●	●				●			
39	Canyon Hollow/Ghost Falls Trail						●			●
40	Clark's Trail/Canyon Hollow Trail Loop						●			●
41	Bell Canyon to Lower and Upper Waterfalls	●					●			
42	Mount Timpanogos from Aspen Grove				●	●				
43	Stewart's Cascades (Stewart Falls)	●								
44	Squaw Peak						●			
45	Diamond Fork Hot Springs: Fifth Water Trail					●				
46	Deseret Peak				●					

MAP LEGEND

Symbol	Description	Symbol	Description
5	Freeway/Interstate Highway	Bench	Bench
50	US Highway	Bridge	Bridge
49	State Highway	General Point of Interest	General Point of Interest
00	County/Other/FR	Campground	Campground
Gravel Road	Gravel Road	Cavern/Cave/Natural Arch	Cavern/Cave/Natural Arch
Unpaved Road	Unpaved Road	Mountain / Peak	Mountain / Peak
Railroad	Railroad	Ranger Station	Ranger Station
Featured Trail	Featured Trail	Parking	Parking
Trail or Fire Road	Trail or Fire Road	Picnic Area	Picnic Area
Paved Trail	Paved Trail	Restroom	Restroom
Steps/boardwalk	Steps/boardwalk	Scenic View/Viewpoint	Scenic View/Viewpoint
National Forest	National Forest	Ski Resort	Ski Resort
State/County/Local Park	State/County/Local Park	Spring	Spring
Small Pond/Lake	Small Pond/Lake	Trailhead	Trailhead
Swamp / Marsh	Swamp / Marsh	Visitor/Information Center	Visitor/Information Center
River or Creek	River or Creek	Waterfall	Waterfall
Intermittent Stream	Intermittent Stream		

North of Salt Lake City

Two counties lie north of Salt Lake City, Weber County (furthest north) and Davis County (closest to Salt Lake City). Weber County is home to Ogden Canyon and Weber Canyon where scenic trails crisscross this section of the Wasatch Range. The trails highlighted for Weber County are a mix of historic, scenic, and the most popular for the county. Davis County is made up of Antelope Island to the west (in the Great Salt Lake) and a handful of cities that run along the foothills of the Wasatch. The trails I have chosen for Davis County are the most popular trails in the area. I have chosen the best trails from each area of the county rather than an accumulation in any one city. In both counties access is easy and the trails lead into the small side canyons that make up this north section of the Wasatch Range.

Adams Canyon waterfall
ROBERT BUNKHALL

1 Waterfall Canyon

Short and strenuous, this poorly signed trail is a rugged scramble over rocks and roots to a dramatic 200-foot waterfall. The trail follows the stream that descends from the falls, and in spring and summer the waterfall can be gushing; wading may be necessary in spots. Fall hikers will find a much smaller waterfall and a trickling stream. Revered for its scenic view down into the valley as well as the luscious waterfall, this hike is often tackled by children as well as adults. A moderate fitness level is suggested.

Start: 29th Street trailhead
Distance: 2.6 miles out and back
Hiking time: About 1.5 hours
Difficulty: Strenuous due to elevation gain
Elevation gain: 1,010 feet
Trail surface: Sandy gravel, rock and boulders, bridge
Best season: Late spring through early fall
Other trail users: Bikers on lower portions of the trail
Canine compatibility: Leashed dogs permitted
Land status: Private land
Nearest town: Ogden

Fees and permits: No fees or permits required
Schedule: Trail closes 1 hour after sunset and opens 1 hour before sunrise
Maps: USGS Ogden; Weber Pathways trail map available by calling (801) 393-2304
Trail contacts: Weber Pathways, PO Box 972, Ogden 84402, (801) 393-2304, www.weber pathways.org; Land owner: Chris Peterson
Special considerations: Don't be tempted to climb up the rocks around the waterfall. It is illegal, and several hikers have fallen to their death.

Finding the trailhead: From Salt Lake City head north on I-15 to US 89 near Lagoon Amusement Park in Farmington (exit 324). Drive south on US 89 toward Ogden for 12.5 miles to Harrison Boulevard. Turn right onto Harrison Boulevard and continue to 30th Street. Turn right onto 30th Street, then turn left onto Polk and go to 29th Street. Turn right onto 29th Street and follow it to its end. Take a right into the trailhead. There is parking for forty cars but no restrooms. The trail is accessed from the south side of the parking lot and the trailhead shelter. This trailhead services a handful of trails, so make sure you start out on the correct one. **GPS:** N41 12.672' / W 111 55.909'

The Hike

The trail up Waterfall Canyon is one of many that set out from the popular 29th Street trailhead shelter. The trail begins at the south side of the shelter and is the trail on the far left (north). Head up the hill. Within the first 0.1 mile, the stands of Gambel oak open to a view of Weber Valley to the west and the trail makes a horseshoe curve and climbs to the first intersection.

At 0.2 mile the trail intersects the Bonneville Shoreline Trail; a rather confusing wooden trail marker signals the various directions. Though the arrows on the sign are unclear, take the horseshoe curve and head right (south) up the trail. The doubletrack trail continues toward the canyon and forks near a set of old water tanks. Take the upper trail that continues to wind into the canyon.

The public has used this trail for more than 150 years, but the land on both sides of the trail is privately owned. Be sure to stay on the designated trails. Lined with sage, scrub oak, juniper, and rocks, the trail enters the canyon and the protection of the trees at 0.8 mile. Here the trail narrows to a rocky singletrack and begins to follow the stream up the canyon. Shortly you cross a wooden bridge.

A hundred feet after the bridge crossing, reach a T junction. In front of you is a forest alcove where rock training is done. Bright green sheriff storage boxes are secured in the area. The trail appears to curve easily to the right, but this branch leads away from Waterfall Canyon and out along the face of the mountain. Instead turn left and start the rocky climb up to the waterfall.

From this point the trail is a jumble of medium-size boulders and roots that must be climbed up and over to reach the top. The trail follows the stream, and at 1.2 miles

The rocky canyon walls from which the waterfall cascades MARC FLETCHER

The waterfall ROBERT BUNKHALL

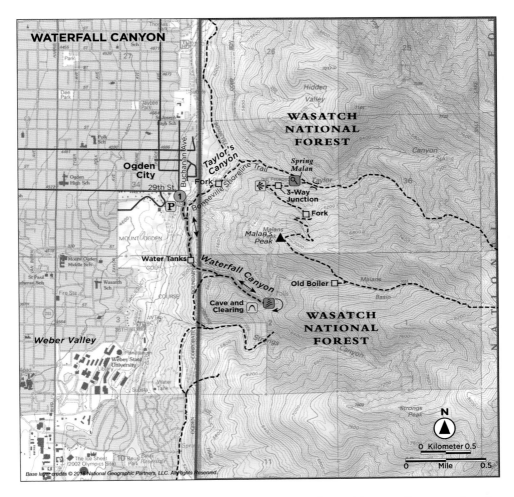

a clearing on the south side of the stream, complete with a small cave, makes for an interesting picnic spot. The waterfall cascades just up the trail from here. During spring and early summer wading may be required in a few places as the trail crosses the stream. The 200-foot waterfall is a cooling experience as well as a fascinating sight. There are plenty of rocks available for sitting on and snacking while you enjoy the view. Return the way you came.

Miles and Directions

0.0 Start at the 29th Street trailhead.

0.2 Come to a trail intersection that crosses the Bonneville Shoreline Trail; turn right (south).

0.6 The trail forks by water tanks; take the upper trail.

0.75 The trail enters the canyon.

0.8 Come to a T junction; turn left and head farther into the canyon.

The waterfall MARC FLETCHER

1.2 Reach a cave and clearing.

1.3 Arrive at the waterfall. Retrace your route to the trailhead.

2.6 Arrive back at the trailhead.

Hike Information

Local information: Ogden Nature Center, 966 West 12th St., Ogden 84404-5410; (801) 621-7595; open weekdays 9 a.m. to 5 p.m., Sat 9 a.m. to 4 p.m.

Organizations: Weber Pathways, PO Box 972, Ogden 84402; (801) 393-2304; www.weberpathways.org; e-mail: wp@weberpathways.org

> **Bonneville Shoreline Trail (BST).** The BST runs down the Wasatch Range and when complete is planned to span from Logan in the north to Provo in the south. The BST intersects and often links several trails that cross it and ascend east into various Wasatch canyons. You will cross the BST on your way up Waterfall Canyon.

2 South Skyline Trail: North Ogden Divide to Skyline Ridge

South Skyline Trail to the ridge is about the view, but it also boasts a climb amidst maples, subalpine and white fir, Gambel oak, and seasonal wildflowers. From North Ogden Divide the trail switchbacks to the top ridge of the mountain. Where vegetation falls away, the ridge view opens up down both sides of the mountain range: Weber Valley to the west, Ogden Valley and Pineview Reservoir to the east, and the towering view of Ben Lomond Peak to the north. As you hit the ridge the trail eases into an easy ridgeline, the Skyline that connects North Ogden Divide to Ogden Canyon in the south. This may be one of the best trails for enjoying fall's color display.

Start: North Ogden Divide trailhead
Distance: 5.4 miles out and back
Hiking time: About 2.5 hours
Difficulty: Moderate
Elevation gain: 1,870 feet
Trail surface: Dirt and rock path
Best season: Summer and fall
Other trail users: Mountain bikers, horses, off-road vehicles
Canine compatibility: Dogs permitted
Land status: Uinta-Wasatch-Cache National Forest
Nearest town: Pleasant View
Fees and permits: No fees or permits required

Schedule: Open year-round
Maps: USGS Huntsville (UT)
Trail contacts: Weber Pathways, PO Box 972, Ogden 84402, (801) 393-2304, www.weber pathways.org; Ogden Ranger District, 507 25th St., Ogden 84401, (801) 625-5112
Special considerations: The mountain wildflowers usually hit their peak from the last week in July to approximately the second week in August. If winter and spring have been wet, be prepared for more ticks, mosquitoes, and deerflies. Snakes and birds will be more prolific as well.

Finding the trailhead: Heading north on I-15, take the 2700 N/Farr West exit. Head east along 2700 N to Washington Boulevard. Turn left onto Washington Boulevard and go to 3100 N. Turn right at the light and follow this road for 4 miles to the North Ogden Divide pass. The trailhead sits right at the pass with plenty of parking, a restroom, and trailhead markers. **GPS:** N41 19.211' / W111 53.953'

The Hike

In 1852 when the area was first settled, three boys made the first recorded ascent to the peak. Sixty years later the peak was named Lewis Peak in the youngest boy's honor. Today the route to Lewis Peak and the Skyline Ridge it sits on involves a set

South Skyline Ridge

of switchbacks that climb up the North Ogden Divide. At the ridge of the mountain crest, the lush alpine environment falls away to grasses, dirt, and long, clear views.

This trail is called the Skyline Trail because it literally walks the line between sky and mountain. The view along the ridge is a destination in itself. Additional trail options include following the Skyline Ridge all the way to Lewis Peak or continuing south along the ridge into Ogden Canyon, but South Skyline Ridge provides a spectacular full-bodied view, often from one vantage point, down the range and across the communities on both sides.

From the North Ogden Divide trailhead, the first section of the trail is socked in with Gambel oak, maples, fir, and plenty of undergrowth. Your first viewpoint occurs at 0.7 mile, where the trail allows a peek into Weber Valley, North Ogden, Pleasant View, and other communities to the west. At 1.2 miles, while you are still switchbacking up the mountain, the trail forks. The right fork is a small jaunt of 100 feet to a lookout point. The left fork continues up the trail.

The trail winds to the east side of the mountain, and at 1.3 miles the east side view opens down the other side of the mountain into Ogden Valley. To the north you can see the Wellsville Mountains; to the southeast is Pineview Reservoir. The trail curves around the mountain and back to the west, where it hits the skyline and the views open up. At 1.6 miles you can stand on the Skyline Ridge and look both east and west down the Wasatch Range.

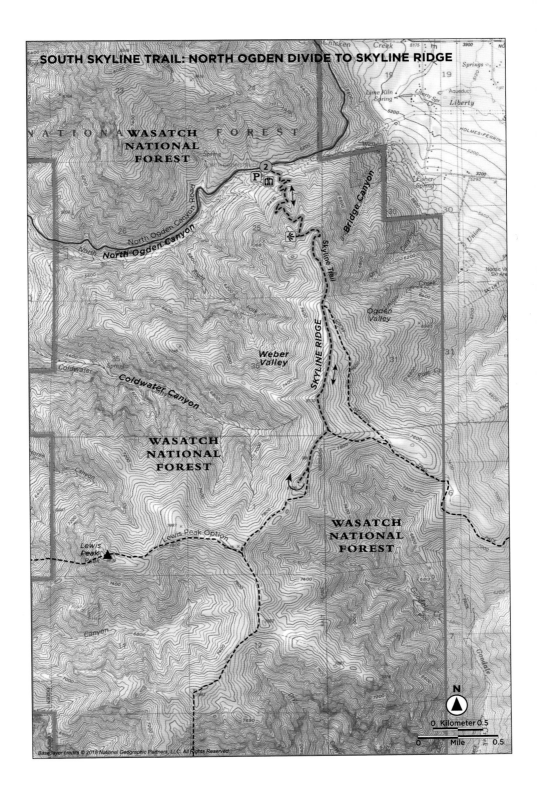

SOUTH SKYLINE TRAIL: NORTH OGDEN DIVIDE TO SKYLINE RIDGE

Trail runners on Lewis Peak

The Skyline Trail is part of the Great Western Trail (GWT)—a corridor of braided trails covering 4,455 miles through Utah, Arizona, Idaho, Montana, and Wyoming. It connects eighteen national forests and Native American, state, and Bureau of Land Management (BLM) lands and includes diverse geography, topography, and biosystems. The GWT links into many of the popular trails throughout the five states. Some segments of the GWT are open only to nonmotorized use, some are shared use, and other portions have been specifically developed for motorized use. In 1996 the GWT was designated Utah's Centennial Trail as part of the Statehood Centennial celebration.

Continue down the ridge for another mile, enjoying the views of the communities, Willard Bay to the west, and Pineview Reservoir to the east. Head for Overlook Knob 1 at 8,115 feet in elevation (**GPS:** N41 17.748' / W111 53.560'). This is a nice area to stop for lunch, take photos, and enjoy the view before your return. Return the way you came, or continue on to Lewis Peak or Pineview Reservoir. By all means, bring your camera.

Miles and Directions

0.0 Start at the North Ogden Divide trailhead.

0.7 The first views along the trail open up.

1.2 Come to a fork; go right for a quick overlook down into Weber Canyon. Return to the main trail and continue to the left.

1.3 First views to the east and into Ogden Valley open up.

1.6 Come to the Skyline Ridge.

2.7 Reach Overlook Knob 1, your turnaround point.

5.4 Arrive back at the trailhead.

View down the back side into Ogden Valley with glimpses of Pineview Reservoir
ROBERT BUNKHALL

Options

Lewis Peak Trail: Continue south from Overlook Knob to the Lewis Peak Trail. The signed trail is 5.5 miles long, climbing 1,847 feet in elevation as it climbs up and down along the ridge and then heads west out to the peak.

Skyline Trail to Pineview Reservoir: This route runs 9.5 miles to join North Ogden Canyon with Ogden Canyon. Defined trailheads sit at both ends. Trail users are the same as for the featured hike. During summer get an early start—the trail's southern exposure and minimal leaf cover make for a warm hike once you reach the ridge and head down toward Pineview Reservoir.

Hike Information

Local events and attractions: Weber Pathways often has a summer hike series with weekly guided hikes. Their website contains a calendar and schedule: www.weber pathways.org.

Organizations: Weber Pathways, PO Box 972, Ogden 84402; (801) 393-2304; www.weberpathways.org; e-mail: wp@weberpathways.org

Camping: Anderson Cove Campground, located on the south shore of Pineview Reservoir in Ogden Canyon (about 10 miles east of Ogden on UT 39). Group sites available and lots of open lawn. Open May 1 through September 20; gate locked the rest of the year. Campground is patrolled nightly by a Weber County sheriff's deputy or Forest Service law enforcement. For reservations call (877) 444-NRRS (6777).

North Fork Park Campground opens the first week in May and closes the last week of October. There are 181 individual campsites available on a first-come, first-served basis. There are six large group sites that can be reserved (801-399-8230). RV sites, tent sites, horse corral and stalls, running water, and flushing toilets are available.

3 Ben Lomond: North Fork to Cutler Basin to Ben Lomond Peak

Ben Lomond Peak is the best-known peak in the Ogden area. Named after a mountain in the Scottish Highlands, it also holds the distinction of being the logo for Paramount Pictures. It is said that William W. Hodkinson, the founder of Paramount and a native of the Ogden area, drew the image in a likeness of his home mountains. Loved by trail runners, mountain bikers, hikers, and riders on horseback, this 9,712-foot peak has four separate trailheads. The incredible views of Ogden, the Wasatch Range, Willard Bay, the Great Salt Lake, and surrounding peaks are just part of the allure. There are also fields of wildflowers, a great workout as you ascend over 3,700 feet in elevation, mountain goats, butterflies, dragonflies, marmots, and other wildlife that frequent this alpine heaven. The climb to the summit is a full and strenuous day and you will need plenty of water and snacks to keep you fueled. This route is one of the shortest (the others come in at 15–20+ miles), steepest, and often least crowded of the routes accessed from the Ogden Valley, but it also holds some of the most beautiful scenery in the area. The solitude is also a bonus on this route. Cutler Basin Trail is named after a scenic alpine basin formed by Ben Lomond and Willard Peaks.

Start: North Fork Park: Cutler Basin Trailhead

Distance: 10.4 miles out and back

Hiking time: About 7 hours

Difficulty: Strenuous

Best season: Summer and fall (during winter the area is used for backcountry skiing)

Other trail users: Horses, mountain bikes, motorbikes, and ATVs are not allowed access from this trailhead, but once the trails converge at the saddle you may find motorized recreation vehicles that have accessed the area from the North Ogden Divide/Skyline Trail.

Canine compatibility: Leashed dogs permitted

Land status: Uinta-Wasatch-Cache National Forest and Weber County land

Nearest Town: Eden

Fees and permits: None; North Fork Park is a fee area for campers

Schedule: Gates to North Fork Park are locked from 10 p.m. to 7 a.m. daily

Maps: USGS North Ogden

Trail contacts: Ogden Ranger District, 507 25th St., Ogden 84401, (801) 625-5112; Weber County Parks and Recreation, (801) 399-8491

Special considerations: Moose and other wildlife are often seen in this area. Remember to keep your distance and be respectful. Take lots of water.

Other: Other trailhead options include starting at North Ogden Divide, also known as the Skyline Trail. This route is more gradual but significantly longer. ATVs and motorbikes are allowed from this trailhead. The second route option starts from Willard Basin to the north. This is the shortest and easiest way to climb the mountain but requires a long drive on dirt roads south of Mantua and accessed from Sardine Canyon to the north. This route goes to the top of Willard Peak, the tallest peak in this northern section of the Wasatch Range, and then traverses across the ridge over to Ben Lomond. The third route starts from North Fork Park near the horse corrals, very close to the Cutler Basin route I am recommending here.

Finding the trailhead: From Salt Lake City take I-15 North to the Ogden 12th Street exit. Head east off the exit and follow it all the way into Ogden Canyon where the road turns into UT 39. Six miles up the canyon you come to Pineview Reservoir and a dam that holds the reservoir in place. Cross the dam and follow the signs toward Liberty. At a little under 4 miles you will go left at a Y in the road toward Liberty. In under a mile you will hit a stop sign; turn left here also. Travel 3 more miles to a T in the road and turn left onto 4100 North. Two-tenths of a mile from the T is 3300 East. Take a right here toward North Fork. At the next Y take a left onto North Fork Road and follow for another mile until you see the sign for the South Entrance and Ben Lomond Trailhead. Turn left here and follow it for another mile where you will enter the North Fork Park area. There are two Ben Lomond trailheads found within North Fork Park. One is by the horse corrals, but we will be starting from the Cutler Basin trailhead that is found 1.7 miles down the road inside North Fork Park. **GPS:** N 41.38292' / W 111.91963'

The Hike

Cutler Basin trailhead has an odd start as it may be gated. Per the directions to the trailhead, you will travel 1.7 miles within North Fork Park heading north on the road. At 1.7 miles you come to a small parking area that is often gated off and has a signed trailhead that can be mistaken for the Cutler Basin Trail. It is not. If the gate is closed, park here and walk the 0.2 mile down the gravel road to the actual singletrack trail that is the route to Ben Lomond. If the gate is not closed, you can drive 0.2 mile and park at the pullout near the trail that starts off to the west. There is a trail sign that says "Ben Lomond Trail" here.

The trail winds through wildflowers, grasses, tall evergreens, and brush. During spring runoff you may have water running down the path in places, and snow is often found on the upper sections of the trail well into July. Enjoy the scenic wandering as you climb up the basin toward Ben Lomond. The trail is well developed and easy to follow. There are no forks in the trail.

At 2.9 miles the trail forks and the right fork goes to a small, often swampy pond and to Cutler Spring. Take the left fork to stay on the Cutler Basin trail. The trail rounds a corner and you start to run into fire breaks cut across the mountain. Some of these look like forks in the trail, but stay on the main trail as it climbs up the mountain.

At 3.5 miles all three trails intersect at the saddle (North Ogden Pass, the Horse Corral route, and Cutler Basin). Here you are standing right beneath Ben Lomond Peak.

Head up the trail to the north and toward the summit. Immediately the trail forks again—stay left. The trail shortly opens up to a view of the Wasatch Range to the south and to all of Ogden and North Ogden below. Enjoy the magnificent view. The trail becomes a set of switchbacks as you make your way up this last push to the peak.

Cutler Basin

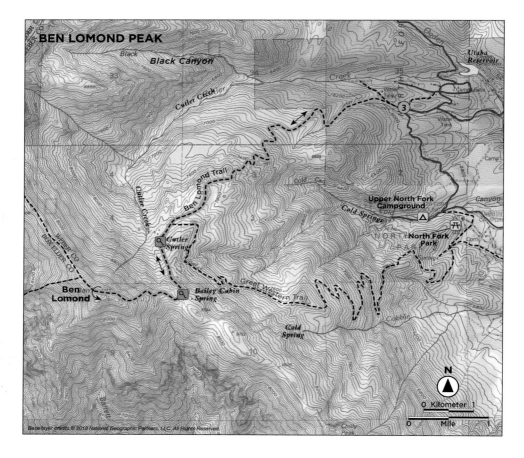

At 4.3 miles the trail forks—go right. The closer you get to the top the rockier the trail gets. At 4.7 miles the switchbacks open up to the tremendous view below again. Keep climbing to the summit where you will find a sign-in box and views of Willard Bay, the Great Salt Lake, as well as the cities and valleys below.

Return the way you came.

Miles and Directions

0.0 Gate and parking area.

0.2 Cutler Basin trailhead to Ben Lomond: trail begins.

2.9 Trail forks: Right fork goes to a small pond near Cutler Spring, left fork continues straight up the trail.

3.5 North Ogden Divide, Horse Corral Trail and Cutler Basin Trail all converge at the saddle for the climb to the peak.

4.3 Trail forks, go right to stay on the main trail.

Left: Sign-in box on the summit of Ben Lomond
Right: Trail up Cutler Basin

4.7 Switchbacks open to view of Ogden Valley, Great Salt Lake, Willard Bay, and the surrounding mountains.

5.2 Ben Lomond Peak and sign-in box.

10.4 Arrive back at the trailhead.

Hike Information

Camping at North Fork Park: North Fork Park Campground opens the first week in May and closes the last week of October. There are 181 individual campsites available on a first–come, first-served basis. There are six large group sites that can be reserved (801-399-8230). RV sites, tent sites, horse corral and stalls, running water, and flushing toilets are available.

Native American tribes lived in the Northern Wasatch Mountains near Ben Lomond. This area was known to the Shoshone, Ute, and Bannock Indians.

4 Indian Trail to Nevada Viewpoint

The Indian Trail was once used by the Shoshone to avoid high waters at the mouth of Ogden Canyon before the waters were dammed to form Pineview Reservoir. This hike covers half the Indian Trail and ends at Nevada Viewpoint overlooking Weber Valley, the canyon below, and on a clear day maybe even into Nevada. An old log shelter sits at the overlook and is often used by hikers. This is a great sunset hike and perfect during hot summer months, as the north-facing trail affords pleasant shade the entire way. A nice family hike, this easily accessed, well-maintained trail has something different to offer in each season of the year.

Start: Cold Water Canyon trailhead
Distance: 4.0 miles out and back
Hiking time: About 2 hours
Difficulty: Low end of moderate
Elevation gain: 1,230 feet
Trail surface: Dirt path, rock, and bridge
Best season: Spring for flowing streams; summer for great shade; fall for nice color
Other trail users: None
Canine compatibility: Dogs permitted

Land status: Uinta-Wasatch-Cache National Forest
Nearest town: Ogden
Fees and permits: No fees or permits required
Maps: USGS Snow Basin; Weber Pathways trail map available by calling (801) 393-2304
Trail contacts: Weber Pathways, PO Box 972, Ogden 84402, (801) 393-2304, www.weber pathways.org; Ogden Ranger District, 507 25th St., Ogden 84401, (801) 625-5112

Finding the trailhead: Ogden lies 30 miles north of Salt Lake City. Head north on I-15 to the 12th Street exit (exit 344). Take a right off the exit onto 12th Street/UT 39 and follow it for 6 miles through Ogden, into Ogden Canyon, and to the Cold Water Canyon trailhead, which sits on the south side of the road. The gravel parking area holds approximately ten cars. There is a Smokey Bear sign as well as other informational signs at the trailhead, which is located on the east side of the parking area. **GPS:** N41 14.409' / W111 5.243'

The Hike

Short, beautiful Cold Water Canyon was home to the Civilian Conservation Corps (CCC) in the 1930s during President Franklin D. Roosevelt's New Deal attempt to provide employment for those out of work during the Great Depression. A CCC camp (one of 1,500 nationwide) housed the men in this canyon as they stabilized hillsides, constructed paths, built bridges and buildings in the Ogden area, and funneled $52 million into Utah's depressed community. The area still has remnants of the camp and an old sawmill. A restored version of a large kiln sits at the trailhead.

Hikers climbing to Nevada Viewpoint

The trail leaves the east side of the parking area and quickly begins to switch back and forth, making large S's up the mountain beneath fir, oak, and spruce. These switchbacks are reinforced with wooden support walls to stop erosion and define the well-maintained trail. Hosting squaw bush, wild pink geranium, Oregon grape, and Gambel oak, the trail climbs the mountain and heads deeper into Cold Water Canyon.

There are a handful of backcountry fire rings and potential campsites along the trail, but no trash service is provided, so please pack out what you pack in.

At 0.4 mile the trail curves. The hairpin right takes you out 100 yards to a little overlook and camp area that overlooks the canyon. Continue straight.

The trail crosses a bridge over a running stream. The water in the canyon varies by season and runoff. There is a small fire pit and a bench next to the bridge, perfect for taking a break and enjoying the area. The first 0.75 mile of the trail wanders near a creek that runs during higher water times, making the trail all the more pleasant.

Once you are past the stream, the trail forks. The left-hand trail heads up the left branch of Cold Water Creek, takes you by an old sawmill, and ends at the base of the mountain. Take the right fork to continue up to Nevada Viewpoint. Over the next 0.5 mile fire pits and potential camping spots can be spotted from the trail.

At 1.5 miles the trail crosses a rock outcropping, after which the view from the trail opens as you break out of the trees. As the trail curves to the south, you can see

Sunset from the Nevada Viewpoint

the north face of the canyon and east into Cold Water Canyon with its amphitheater feel. The rocks, trees, and surrounding cliffs become visible for the first time. The trail drops immediately back into tree cover, heading south and then west. The trail crosses a talus field before you hike the final 500 feet to the top.

The trail reaches Nevada Viewpoint lookout and the old log shelter as you top the ridge. A log serves as a bench where you can sit and watch the sunset or ogle the valley and all the mountains to the west. Can you see all the way to Nevada?

To the west the Pilot Range, Newfoundland Mountain, Little Mountain, and Promontory Mountain all stake out their place on the planet. The trail continues hugging the mountain curves as it makes its way to the 22nd Street trailhead, but Nevada Viewpoint is your turnaround point for this hike.

Miles and Directions

0.0 Start at the Cold Water Canyon trailhead.
0.4 The trail forks; continue straight ahead.
0.5 Cross a bridge; pass a fire pit and bench.
0.8 The trail forks; stay right.
1.0 Pass a campsite.
1.5 Cross a rock outcropping.
2.0 Reach the Nevada Viewpoint and log shelter. Retrace your route to the trailhead.
4.0 Arrive back at the trailhead.

Option

The Indian Trail continues from Nevada Viewpoint past rocky narrow ledges and through more evergreen forest as it winds out of Ogden Canyon and continues south toward the 22nd Street trailhead in Ogden for a 4.3-mile shuttle hike or an 8.6-mile

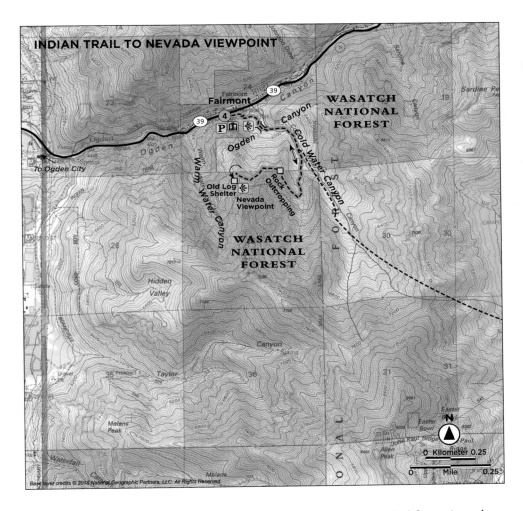

out-and-back. There are some sheer cliffs and interesting geological formations along the route. The 22nd Street trailhead is at the far east side of 22nd Street in Ogden.

Hike Information

Local events and attractions: Ogden Nature Center, 966 West 12th St., Ogden 84404; (801) 621-7595; www.ogdennaturecenter.org. The nature center is located just off of I-15 and the 12th Street exit in Ogden. You pass it on the way to Cold Water Creek trailhead. Visitors to this 152-acre nature preserve and education center are invited to explore trails, meet birds of prey, spot wildlife, and enjoy the quiet respite of the campus. The nature center is open year-round and offers educational programs for people of all ages.

Organizations: Weber Pathways, PO Box 972, Ogden 84402; (801) 393-2304; www.weberpathways.org; e-mail: wp@weberpathways.org

5 Malan's Peak and Basin

Pioneer trails dot the Wasatch Range, but this one was formerly a wagon road that switchbacked up the steep mountainside through cool, lush forests of Douglas fir to a resort and pioneer hotel built by the Malan family in the late 1800s. This hike is replete with history, natural springs, great views, and possible camping spots. The climb to Malan's Peak provides 360-degree views over Weber Valley to the west; Mount Ogden and Allen Peak to the east; Ben Lomond Peak to the far north; Taylor Canyon; and Waterfall Canyon to the south. The optional spur to Malan's Basin is only 0.6 mile farther and takes you to where the Malan Heights resort stood from 1893 to 1913.

Start: 29th Street trailhead
Distance: 5.8 miles out and back to Malan's Peak; 7.0 miles out and back to Malan's Basin
Hiking time: About 3.5 hours
Difficulty: Strenuous
Elevation gain: 2,134 feet
Trail surface: Dirt path, rock, bridge
Best season: Summer and fall
Other trail users: Bikes allowed in the area but not recommended for this trail
Canine compatibility: Leashed dogs permitted
Land status: Part of Ogden Trails Network; managed by the US Forest Service; privately owned
Nearest town: Ogden
Fees and permits: No fees or permits required

Schedule: Trail closes 1 hour after sunset and opens 1 hour before sunrise
Maps: Weber Pathways trail map available by calling (801) 393-2304
Trail contacts: Weber Pathways, PO Box 972, Ogden 84402, (801) 393-2304, www.weber pathways.org; Ogden Ranger District, 507 25th St., Ogden 84401, (801) 625-5112
Special considerations: A large portion of this trail is on private land with public access permitted. Please stay on the trails.
Other: This trail can be started at the 27th Street trailhead, which is less developed and has less parking. Begin on the Taylor Canyon North Trail.

Finding the trailhead: From Salt Lake City head north on I-15 to US 89 near the Lagoon Amusement Park. Take exit 324 and head north toward South Ogden for 12.5 miles to Harrison Boulevard. Turn right (north) on Harrison Boulevard and travel to 30th Street. Turn right (east) onto 30th Street then turn left (north) onto Polk and continue to 29th Street. Turn right (east) onto 29th Street and continue to where it dead-ends; turn right into the 29th Street trailhead parking lot. **GPS:** N41 12.672' / W111 55. 909'

The Hike

Named for Bartholomew Malan, Malan's Peak and Malan's Basin were first reached in 1892 when a road was carved up the mountain to access the upper section of Waterfall Canyon. Here the Malans built a resort retreat where pioneers could enjoy

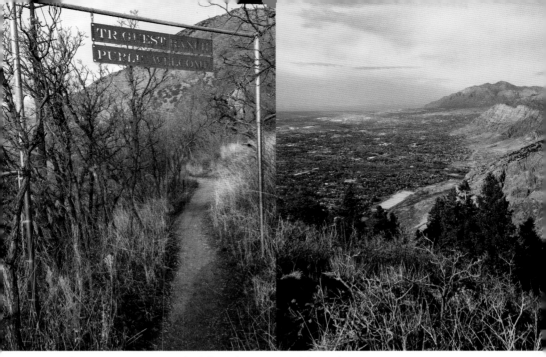

Left: Crossing into private land for a short section of the trail
Right: View from the lookout point

the panoramic views. The Malan family provided the transportation to the hotel, charging $1 per person for the ride. All that is left of this once-luxurious getaway is an old boiler that sits to the west of the basin, but you must dig through the overgrowth to locate the pieces. A historical plaque marks the basin. As you hike the trail, try to imagine the old wagons climbing the steep face and making the tight switchbacks. It must have been quite an adventure just getting there.

The trail to Malan's Basin begins at the 29th Street trailhead. Three trails take off from the kiosk, so make sure you get on the correct trail. From the south side of the trail kiosk, head east on the northernmost trail. Follow it as it curves up the mountain. At 0.15 mile up the trail it forks off to the left through a grove of Gambel oaks. Take this left fork. After a short walk through the Gambel oak grove you come to the Bonneville Shoreline Trail. Head north. A hundred feet up the Bonneville Shoreline a small trail intersects with BST on the right. Take this unassuming singletrack and head back into the trees. From here you are approaching private land. A metal archway with the sign "TR Guest Ranch" hangs from the archway—this is the entry into private land. Please stay on the trail. A few hundred feet later you will exit through a

Lake Bonneville was formed during the Late Pleistocene period (30,000 years ago) and once covered 20,000 square miles. The Great Salt Lake is all that remains of the prehistoric lake. Small shells from the ancient lake can be found along the Wasatch Range.

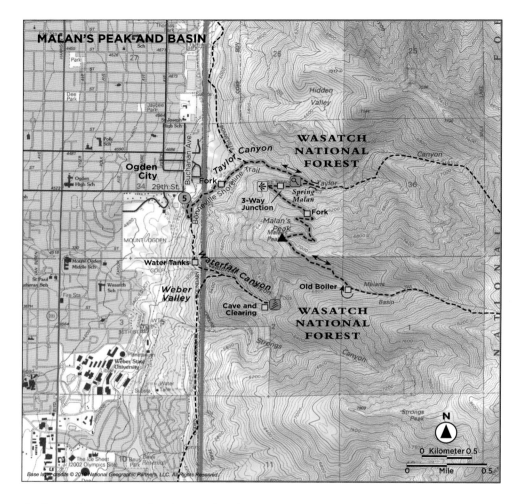

similar archway as you head toward Taylor Canyon. Five-hundredths of a mile later you will cross a service road and continue straight ahead, back into the oak. Stay on the single track. Another .05 mile later there is a signed trail junction.

Follow the signs to Taylor Canyon South Trail where the trail will round to the east and head up the canyon. Head up Taylor Canyon on the south side of the creekbed to a bridge. Cross the bridge over to the north side of the creekbed and continue upcanyon. Once you cross the bridge you transition from Taylor Canyon South Trail to Taylor Canyon North Trail. The trail follows the creekbed up the canyon. Depending on the time of year water may or may not be running in the streambed. During spring you will be accompanied by the sound of rushing water, while the stream is usually dry by fall. Despite many side trail branches that cross the creekbed, stay on the main trail until you reach a sign that tells you to cross for Malan's Basin. Cross the stream and head up the mountain. This is where the more serious climbing starts.

From here to Malan's Peak you are on a steady uphill climb. This section of the trail consists of a short span of rocky steps at the base of a rock cliff face. Farther up the trail you can look back at the bizarre rock formation with its caves. Views of the other side of Taylor Canyon appear as well.

As you climb stay on the main trail. At 1.8 miles you come to a wonderful lookout point that looks out over Ogden City and the valley below. This is a great spot to watch the sunset or stop for a rest. The trail continues to the east as it horseshoes over slabs of jutting rock to continue up the canyon.

The closer you get to Malan's Peak the taller the trees, and the shade can provide relief on a hot summer's day.

Look for small shells in the dirt, remnants of prehistoric Lake Bonneville. At 2.2 miles the trail forks; follow the bottom right fork. At 2.5 miles the trail opens to the north and you can see the funky rock formation, and across Taylor Canyon. To the right is Mount Ogden with its radio towers; Allen Peak is the peak farthest to the left. You hit the peak at 2.9 miles.

The trail to Malan's Basin leaves Malan's Peak from the southeast corner. The 0.6-mile (1.2 miles round-trip) stretch begins with continued open views down into Weber Valley for the first section of the trail, while the last 0.4 mile is under a canopy of scrub. Malan's Basin sits at 3.5 miles—a 15-minute side trip that's worth the small trek. In the basin there is a stream to the south that empties into the waterfall at the top of Waterfall Canyon. If you follow the footpath east, out of the basin, in a couple hundred feet you will find the boiler next to the stream. It is covered in grasses and plants, so you'll have to look for it.

The shaded, leisurely stroll up Taylor Canyon is a nice warmup for the steep set of long switchbacks that climb Malan's north face to the peak. A short scenic stroll to Malan's Basin from Malan's Peak rounds out the hike. Return along the same route.

Miles and Directions

0.0 Start at the 29th Street trailhead.

0.15 Trail forks to the left through the trees.

0.3 Exit the Bonneville Shoreline Trail on a footpath to the right.

0.35 Trail crosses into TR Guest Ranch.

0.6 Come to a fork; follow the signs to Taylor Canyon South Trail.

1.4 Cross the bridge and start the climb up and out of Taylor Canyon.

1.8 Reach the lookout point over the valley.

2.2 The trail forks; follow the bottom fork.

2.9 Reach Malan's Peak. Pick up the trail to Malan's Basin from the southeast corner. (**Option:** Turn around here for a 5.8-mile round-trip.)

3.5 Reach Malan's Basin. Return the way you came.

7.0 Arrive back at the trailhead.

Hike Information

Local events and attractions: Ogden Nature Center, 966 West 12th St., Ogden 84404; (801) 621-7595; www.ogdennaturecenter.org. The nature center is located just off of I-15 and the 12th Street exit in Ogden. Visitors to this 152-acre nature preserve and education center are invited to explore trails, meet birds of prey, spot wildlife, and enjoy the quiet respite of the campus. The nature center is open year-round and offers educational programs for people of all ages.

Organizations: Weber Pathways, PO Box 972, Ogden 84402; (801) 393-2304; www.weberpathways.org; e-mail: wp@weberpathways.org

Ogden Sierra Club: http://utah.sierraclub.org/ogden

Signs to Taylor Canyon

6 Ogden Overlook

Beginning at Snowbasin ski resort, the hike to Ogden Overlook sits in a high alpine environment complete with quaking aspen, a variety of conifers, maples, and abundant wildflowers in spring. The trail traverses the mountain on a number of switchbacks as it climbs to an overlook, complete with benches for viewing Ogden to the west, Cold Water Canyon directly below to the west, Sardine Peak and Ogden Canyon to the north, and surrounding mountains and cliffs to the east and south. You can even catch the tip of Ben Lomond Peak—one of the 11,000-foot peaks in the Wasatch Range. The trail switches between shade and sun as you climb up the mountain surrounded by nature at its finest and periodic views of Snowbasin to the south.

Start: Maples trailhead
Distance: 5.6 miles out and back
Hiking time: About 3 hours
Difficulty: Easy
Elevation gain: 900 feet
Trail surface: Gravel road, packed-dirt singletrack
Best season: Summer and fall
Other trail users: Horses allowed on the gravel road but not on the trail. Bicycles allowed after the trail is dry and officially opened for the summer.
Canine compatibility: Leashed dogs permitted
Land status: Uinta-Wasatch-Cache National Forest

Nearest town: Mountain Green
Fees and permits: No fees or permits required
Schedule: Hikers are asked to be off the mountain by dark.
Maps: USGS Snowbasin Ogden; Weber Pathways trail map available by calling (801) 393-2304
Trail contacts: Weber Pathways, PO Box 972, Ogden 84402, (801) 393-2304, www.weber pathways.org; Ogden Ranger District, 507 25th St., Ogden UT 84401, (801) 625-5112
Special considerations: Bring insect repellent
Other: Snowbasin has a system of hiking trails that can be accessed from their gondola. Trail maps are available online or at the resort.

Finding the trailhead: From Salt Lake City head north on I-15 to exit 324 (South Ogden) near the Lagoon Amusement Park. Head toward South Ogden on US 89 for 10.4 miles, then turn off on an unmarked exit to the right to head up Weber Canyon. Following signs to Snowbasin ski resort, go 4 miles to the Mountain Green/Huntsville exit (exit 92). Turn left off the exit; drive under the bridge and take your first right onto UT 167, continuing toward Mountain Green/Huntsville. Travel 1.4 miles and turn left at the Sinclair gas station onto Trappers Loop. The turnoff for Snowbasin is 5.2 miles from here, at the top of the loop. Turn left to Snowbasin and continue through the resort to parking lot 2. Maples trailhead is on the north side of the parking lot, just east of the bridge.
GPS: N41 13.112' / W111 51.776'

Left: Wildflowers along the Ogden Overlook Trail
Right: View of the Ogden Overlook trailhead

The Hike

The land around Snowbasin is a patchwork of private land owned by the ski resort and national forest land managed by the US Forest Service. Maples trailhead is located in the northwest corner below parking lot 2 behind a large metal gate. The first 0.8 mile of the trail follows the dirt road, heading north into what was once a picnic area. At 0.5 mile a small stream starts to parallel the road and adds its carefree gurgle to your hiking experience. At 0.7 mile the road forks; take the right fork. The road quickly forks again; this time take the left fork. At 0.8 mile the gravel road dead-ends at the Ogden Overlook trailhead. A Forest Service sign marks the spot as the single-track packed-dirt trail heads through a log fence and into a forest of singing birds, tall flowers, towering quaking aspen, and shady maple trees. Traffic is minimal on the well-maintained trail. Spring brings fields of wildflowers, and the trail switches between shade and sun as it climbs the mountain on easy switchbacks.

At 1.5 miles the trail opens to the south for views of Snowbasin ski resort. Enjoy the pleasant forest foray. At 2.8 miles you reach Ogden Overlook. A couple of benches provide a place to sit and take in the 360-degree views. Return to Maples trailhead following the same route.

Miles and Directions

0.0 Start at Maples trailhead and head out on the dirt road.

0.7 Come to two forks in the road in quick succession; head right at the first and left at the second.

0.8 Reach the Ogden Overlook trailhead on Forest Service land.

1.5 Views of Snowbasin ski resort open to the south.

2.8 Reach Ogden Overlook. Retrace your steps.

5.6 Arrive back at Maples trailhead.

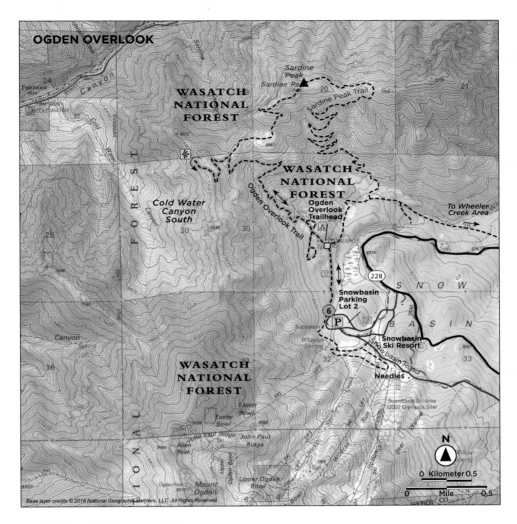

Hike Information

Local events and attractions: Snowbasin Resort hosts summer activities including lift-assisted biking with 26 miles of trails that hook into even more Forest Service trails for a total of 50 miles of biking fun; a summer concert series with live music on the mountain every Sunday; and weekly mountain bike races. Additional hiking trails on the resort's private land are also available. Visit www.snowbasin.com for more information.

7 Antelope Island: Frary Peak

Frary Peak is the highest point on Antelope Island—a thoroughly original state park that sits in the Great Salt Lake (second saltiest body of water in the world) west of Salt Lake City. The trail rises quickly and is unfettered by trees, so the views around the island and across the lake stretch before you from the beginning of the hike. The hike runs through sparse grass and sage on this desert island as well as fascinating rock that dates back 2.7 billion years. The views across the island and the Great Salt Lake, along with wildlife such as bison, antelope, and deer, propel this highest-peak notch to a must-do status. From the summit you get 360-degree views that open the entire island, even the southern section, where public access is limited. The trail offers very little shade, so hiking in the morning or evening will provide the most comfortable temperatures. Take plenty of water.

Start: Frary Peak trailhead on Antelope Island

Distance: 6.6 miles out and back

Hiking time: About 5 hours

Difficulty: Strenuous

Elevation gain: 2,100 feet

Trail surface: Dirt and rock path

Best season: Spring and fall

Other trail users: None. Horses are allowed all over the island, but it is unlikely you will find them on this trail.

Canine compatibility: Allowed on leash

Land status: State park

Nearest town: Syracuse

Fees and permits: Fee required to enter the state park gate, payable at the causeway.

Schedule: Antelope Island is open year round. Hours vary by season: During the summer the island is open from 6 a.m. to 10 p.m.; Nov through Mar the island is open from 6 a.m. to 6 p.m. The Antelope Island State Park Visitor Center, located on the north end of the island, is open year-round and offers restrooms, water, and exhibits and a video presentation to help you learn more about the island. The visitor center is open 9 a.m. to 6 p.m. Apr 15 through Sept 14; 9 a.m. to 5 p.m. Sept 15 through Apr 14.

Maps: USGS Antelope Island, Antelope Island North

Trail contacts: Antelope Island State Park, 4528 West 1700 South, Syracuse 84075; http://stateparks.utah.gov/parks/antelope-island. Entrance to the island: (801) 773-2941; Visitor Center (801) 725-9263; Utah State Parks and Recreation, 1594 West North Temple, Ste. 116, Salt Lake City 84116, (801) 538-7220, http://stateparks.utah.gov

Special considerations: Timing is crucial at Antelope Island. If you don't want to be barraged by the smell of rotting brine fly pupae, overrun by swarms of the annoying but harmless mature flies, or end up during the biting gnat hatch, it may be a good idea to check the website for updates. It's best to avoid this hike in July and August. This trail is closed for a month or more in spring during the bighorn sheep lambing season. Verify accessibility by calling (801) 725-9263.

View from the trail across the Great Salt Lake WILLIAM BARBA

Finding the trailhead: From Salt Lake City take I-15 north to Antelope Drive (exit 332) near Layton. Turn left (west) off the exit onto Antelope Drive. The road connects directly to the causeway on the far west side. There is a parking lot before the fee booth if you wish to carpool; otherwise each vehicle must pay the entry fee to cross the causeway. When you get to the island, head left along the east side of the island toward Fielding Garr Ranch. The Frary Peak trailhead is 5 miles down this road; watch for signs. You will turn right onto a dirt road and travel to an upper level of the island for the trailhead. The trail leaves from the south side of the trailhead; take the upper trail to the right. **GPS: N40 59621' / W112 12.153'**

The Hike

Frary Peak Trail is a hiking-only trail with the best views and photography opportunities on the island. Located on an island in the middle of the desert, this trail provides an escape into a unique ecosystem. Though the beach looks like any other, only algae, brine flies, and brine shrimp can withstand the high mineral levels in the water. However, these three life forms thrive here. In fact, the Great Salt Lake is the world's largest provider of brine shrimp. The brine shrimp and brine flies feast on the algae, while birds enjoy both the flies and the shrimp.

Bison grazing on Antelope Island WILLIAM BARBA

The lake and its islands are a crucial stopover point for millions of migrating waterfowl. Nearly 80 percent of Utah's wetlands surround the Great Salt Lake, making it one of the most important migratory points in North America. The area hosts 250 bird species each year. Birders can enjoy the largest lake west of the Mississippi and all the birds that use it as a crucial point on their life paths. The Great Salt Lake is a remnant of Lake Bonneville, a prehistoric freshwater lake that was ten times larger than the Great Salt Lake during the last ice age. The current lake size fluctuates with runoff but is about 75 miles long and 28 miles wide. The lake is typically three to five times saltier than the world's oceans.

The Frary Peak Trail affords a view across the island that often provides glimpses of the herds of bison. The top of Frary Peak is the only vantage point from which the entire island, including the south side, can be viewed.

The trailhead is a big gravel lot with plenty of parking and looks out over the Great Salt Lake. Two trails head out from the south side. Take the upper trail to the right, which quickly begins to climb the desert mountain. Views immediately open to the east over the lake. The trail is rimmed with grass and sagebrush, so the views

Artifacts on Antelope Island reveal more than 6,000 years of human habitation. Native Americans showed Jim Bridger the island in 1824, and John C. Fremont and Kit Carson made the first Anglo exploration of the island in 1845. They named the island after watching the abundant antelope graze the grasslands. Today the island hosts a managed herd of 500 bison. Each fall a giant roundup pulls horses and riders from all over the United States to bring in the herd for counting and maintenance. The island is also home to nearly 200 pronghorn antelope, 350 deer, and 160 bighorn sheep.

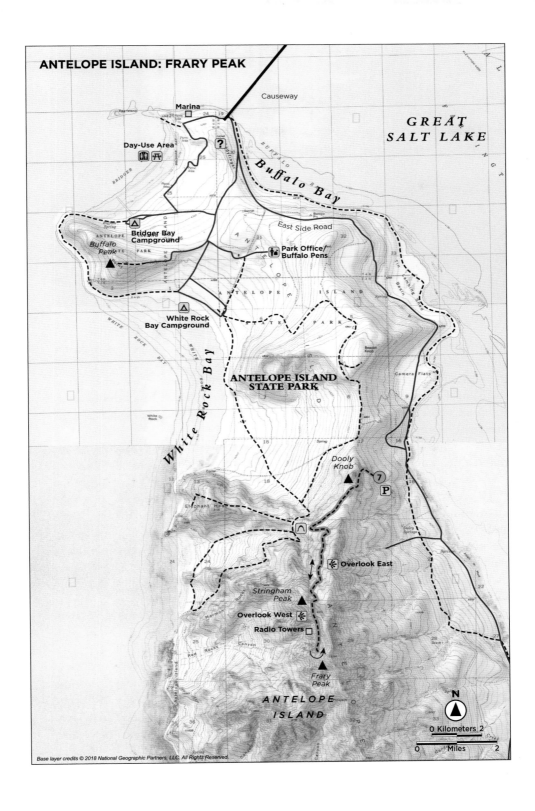

ANTELOPE ISLAND: FRARY PEAK

Causeway

Marina

Day-Use Area

GREAT SALT LAKE

Buffalo Bay

East Side Road

Bridger Bay Campground

Buffalo Peak

Park Office/ Buffalo Pens

White Rock Bay Campground

White Rock Bay

ANTELOPE ISLAND STATE PARK

ANTELOPE ISLAND STATE PARK

White Rock

Beacon Knob

Camera Flats

Dooly Knob

7

P

Elephant Head

Overlook East

Stringham Peak

Overlook West

Radio Towers

Frary Peak

ANTELOPE ISLAND

N

0 Kilometers 2

0 Miles 2

Resting at a viewpoint along the route WILLIAM BARBA

open wide across the island. The trail is also interspersed with interesting rock, and you find the first as you start your climb.

The trail forks at Dooly Knob junction. The right fork heads to the other side of the island. Follow the left fork as it continues straight (south). The trail climbs to the top ridge of the island and then drops down onto the west side, with views over the other side of the island and the lake to the west.

At 1.3 miles the trail passes under a set of boulders that create a shaded cave. The trail then continues to the right and then circles above the rocks to begin a set of steep switchbacks before an open climb through the grasses to get back up to the ridge of the island.

Atop the next ridge is a nice rock outcropping and lookout point to the south and east. From here the easy-to-follow trail again cuts around over the west side of the island and heads south. The southern two-thirds of the island contain some of the oldest rock found anywhere in North America. The Farmington Canyon Complex dates back 2.7 billion years, older than rocks found at the bottom of the Grand Canyon.

At 2.7 miles you reach another overlook ridge that affords interesting views down into White Rock Bay to the west. From this point you can also see to the east, with the Wasatch Front in full view.

A set of radio towers sit on top of the island. You'll reach these at 2.8 miles, and from here Frary Peak is only a short 0.5-mile climb to the south. Two trails leave the area south of the radio towers. The left (east) trail proceeds toward Frary Peak over the rocky cliff outcroppings you see before you. The right (west) trail drops back down 150 feet under the cliffs and then climbs back up to the peak. Choose the rocky route only if you're surefooted, unafraid of heights, and ready to climb over rocks using both hands and feet. If you choose the lower route, be prepared to lose elevation and then have to regain it to climb back out. There are nice views no matter which route you take.

Frary Peak is marked with a stack of rocks and a summit marker disk secured into the rock. The peak is a flat landing reached by climbing up and over the rocky surroundings, reaching the summit at 3.3 miles. The 360-degree views around the entire island, the Great Salt Lake, surrounding islands, the Wasatch Front, and the mountain ranges to the west are worth the climb. Forty miles to the southwest, Deseret Peak—highest peak in the Stansbury Range—is visible. Take some time to enjoy the fruits of your labor before retracing your steps.

Miles and Directions

0.0 Start at the Frary Peak trailhead.

0.8 Come to the Dooly Knob trail junction; take the left fork and continue straight.

1.3 The trail comes to a shaded rock cave.

1.6 Arrive at a southeast-looking viewpoint.

2.7 Arrive at the White Rock Bay overlook. There is an eastern view of the Wasatch Front as well.

2.8 Reach the radio towers.

3.3 Arrive at Frary Peak. Return the way you came.

6.6 Arrive back at the trailhead.

Hike Information

Local events and attractions: Great Salt Lake Bird Festival; www.greatsaltlakebird fest.com. The Antelope Island State Park Visitor Center is open year-round. Located on the north end of the island, the visitor center offers restrooms, water, and exhibits and a video presentation to help you learn more about the island. Visit https:// stateparks.utah.gov/parks/antelope-island/ for more information on the state park. Fielding Garr Ranch (801-510-7056) is accessible year-round on the southeast side of the island. Tours are available for those who want to explore the island's pioneer history, and horseback adventures depart from the ranch. The Antelope Island Marina at the north end of the island provides boat slips.

Camping: Primitive campgrounds are available on the island in addition to day-use picnic areas near the shores of the Great Salt Lake, where many like to take a dip in the salty waters that increase buoyancy. White Rock Bay group campground and Bridger Bay Campground provide picnic tables, fire pits, and vault toilets but no water or electricity. Reserve America handles all campsite reservations: (801) 322-3770.

8 Antelope Island: Lakeside Trail

Lakeside Trail is one of my favorite trails on Antelope Island because the trail is a scenic meander around the northwest tip of the island, and the route affords you views of the Great Salt Lake through the entire hike. The elevation gain is minimal, and bison often wander on the latter section of the trail. It's a trifecta of scenery, easy strolling, and wildlife. Antelope Island is a desert landscape, but the lake is a sapphire shining in the desert sun. Balm for the desert soul, the view of the lake is certainly the highlight sparkling and stretching out across the west desert. Antelope Island is home to the pronghorn antelope, which contributes to the exotic feel that makes the island seem like a remote getaway, while still being so close to millions of people just across the causeway. A trip to Antelope Island is a trip to another world, a unique ecosystem with high-salinity water that allows nothing but brine shrimp to survive. I recommend taking time to go to the visitor center to truly comprehend the wonder of this salty haven.

Start: West end of Bridger Bay campground; Lakeside Trail trailhead
Distance: 5.6 miles out and back
Hiking time: About 3 hours
Difficulty: Easy
Elevation gain: 154 feet
Trail surface: Gravel and packed dirt
Best season: The trail is usable year-round, but the hot days of July and August are not ideal times as the desert sun and exposed southern aspect of the trail can prove less pleasant. The trail is open and pleasant in the winter, though snowshoes or extra traction may be needed at times.
Other trail users: Horses, bikers
Canine compatibility: Leashed dogs permitted
Land status: State park
Nearest town: Syracuse
Fees and permits: Fee to enter Antelope Island State Park

Schedule: Antelope Island is open year-round. During the summer the island is accessible from 6 a.m. to 10 p.m.; Nov to Mar from 6 a.m. to 6 p.m.
Maps: USGS Antelope Island, Antelope Island North
Trail contacts: Antelope Island State Park, 4528 West 1700 South, Syracuse 84075; (801) 725-9263; http://stateparks.utah.gov/parks/antelope-island
Special considerations: The water of the Great Salt Lake is not potable. The high levels of salinity do not allow for drinking, so bring plenty of water. Remember that bison are wild and loose on the island, so only bring dogs you can control and who will not excite the wildlife. Late May or early June there is a biting gnat hatch. Check the websites for updates on the hatch.

Finding the trailhead: From Salt Lake City head north on I-15 to Antelope Drive, exit 332 in Layton. Turn left off the exit onto Antelope Drive (UT 108). Head straight west on this road for just over 6.5 miles where you will run into the fee booth that marks the entrance onto the causeway and Antelope Island State Park. There is a parking lot just before the fee booth for groups who may want to carpool onto the island. Cross the causeway, a 7-mile stretch to reach the island. At the island the road comes to a V split. Take the road to the left. At 1.1 miles from the V turn right. Follow this road straight into Bridger Bay Campground. Follow it through the campground to the far west side. You will come to the Lakeside Trail trailhead which is marked by a sign. Six parking spots are available in front of the sign. **GPS:** N41.03971' / W11.226314'

The Hike

This easy, pleasant trail begins at Bridger Bay Campground and curves around the northwestern tip of the island to White Rock Bay, meandering beneath Buffalo Point as it sweeps along the curve of the island, always looking out over the blue waters of the Great Salt Lake. Sage and rocks line the first section of the trail, the Bridger Bay area. At 0.8 mile the trail makes its way around the point. Once you turn the corner beneath Buffalo Point, the trail becomes grassy and open. This section of the trail is more exposed and open to the sun and wind. If you see bison on the trail, they will usually be in this area of White Rock Bay. Bison have been on the island for more than 100 years. Every year the bison are rounded up for veterinary checks, shots, and sale. About 150 are auctioned each year to control the size of the herd. There are between 500 and 700 bison on the island. From this south side you can see the highest point on the island, Frary Peak to the southeast, as well as more southern sections of the island. The trail makes a straight path along the island for another 2 miles where it ends at a circle turn-about that is marked by another Lakeside Trail sign. If

Lakeside Trail

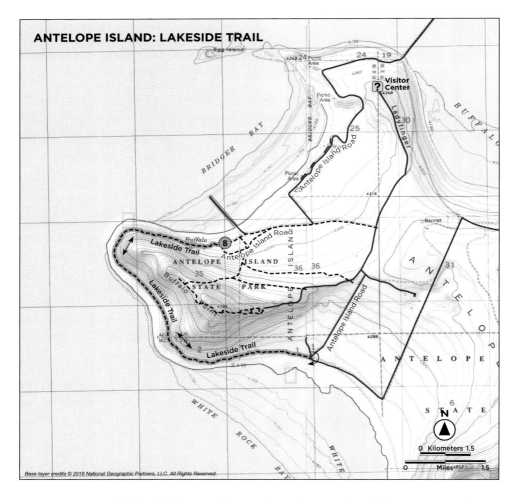

ANTELOPE ISLAND: LAKESIDE TRAIL

a restroom is needed, head left out of the circle, up the gravel road, for a quarter of a mile to a pit toilet. Turn around and follow the trail back to the parking area.

Miles and Directions

0.0 Start at the Lakeside Trail trailhead.

0.8 Trail rounds the corner of the island beneath Buffalo Point into White Rock Bay area.

2.8 Arrive at the other end of the Lakeside Trail. Return the way you came.

5.6 Arrive back at the Lakeside trailhead and parking area you started from.

John C. Fremont and Kit Carson made the first known Anglo exploration of Antelope Island in 1845. The island was named after the pronghorn antelope the explorers observed grazing across the island.

Rock formation along the Lakeside Trail. Antelope Island contains rock dated as old as 2.7 billion years old.

Hike Information

Local events/attractions: Great Salt Lake Bird Festival, www.greatsaltlakebirdfest .com.

The Antelope Island State Park Visitor Center is open year-round. Located on the north end of the island, the visitor center offers restrooms, water, and exhibits and a video presentation to help you learn more about the island. Visit https://stateparks .utah.gov/parks/antelope-island/ for more information.

Fielding Garr Ranch (801-510-7056) is accessible year-round on the southeast side of the island. Tours are available for those who want to explore the island's pioneer history, and horseback adventures depart from the ranch.

The Antelope Island Marina at the north end of the island provides boat slips and a place to launch watercraft.

Camping: Primitive campgrounds are available on the island in addition to day-use picnic areas near the shores of the Great Salt Lake, where many like to take a dip in the salty waters that increase buoyancy. White Rock Bay group campground and Bridger Bay Campground provide picnic tables, fire pits, and vault toilets but no water or electricity. All camping reservations are handled by Reserve America at (801) 322-3770.

9 Adams Canyon

It's safe to say that Adams Canyon is Davis County's most popular trail due to accessibility and the 40-foot waterfall at the end of the canyon. Adams Canyon was named for Elias Adams, an early pioneer, but today the trail is much more developed than it was in his day. The hike begins on a sandy, sun-exposed climb where barriers have been built to keep the trail from dissolving down the hillside. Once in the canyon, the trail is shaded and runs next to the north fork of Holmes Creek. You enjoy the sights, sounds, and coolness of the stream as you climb your way to the fresh and impressive waterfall at the top.

Start: Northeast corner of the parking lot
Distance: 4.0 miles out and back
Hiking time: About 2 hours
Difficulty: Moderate
Elevation gain: 1,247 feet
Trail surface: Dirt, stone, some rock scrambling, stream crossing
Best season: Summer and fall
Other trail users: None
Canine compatibility: Dogs permitted

Land status: Uinta-Wasatch-Cache National Forest
Nearest town: Layton
Fees and permits: No fees or permits required
Maps: USGS Kaysville
Trail contacts: Salt Lake Ranger District, 6944 South 3000 East, Salt Lake City 84121
Special considerations: In places the trail requires scrambling across rock faces and steep root inclines and may not be suitable for the less than fit. Watch for rattlesnakes.

Finding the trailhead: From Salt Lake City head north on I-15 to exit 324 near the Lagoon Amusement Park. Head south on US 89 toward South Ogden for 6 miles. Take your first right on a small road after the Oak Hills Drive stoplight and then another quick right onto a frontage road. The trailhead is 0.25 mile down this road. Parking is plentiful, but no water or restrooms are available at the trailhead. **GPS:** N41 03.980' / W111 54.565'

The Hike

Once within the canyon itself, the hike provides shade and pleasant traveling, but the first 0.5 mile—from the trailhead up to the Bonneville Shoreline Trail—is a sandy slog that climbs over 500 feet of switchbacks to line you up for entry into the canyon. At the top of this section you hit the Bonneville Shoreline Trail (BST), a trail that marks the old shoreline of prehistoric Lake Bonneville. From the BST you gain a viewpoint out across the valley below. Views open up of Antelope Island, the Oquirrh Mountains on the west side of the valley, and the Wasatch Front.

Adams Canyon Waterfall ROBERT BUNKHALL

Head right along the BST and continue straight into the canyon when the trail continues to the south. The trail then winds into Adams Canyon and drops into a shaded singletrack that follows the north fork of Holmes Creek through scrub oak and white pine. The well-defined trail is easy to follow, with the first creek crossing coming 1.6 miles into the hike. A bridge makes crossing easy, but once on the other side you quickly enter the last phase of the hike and the most difficult maneuvering over rock faces and a less-defined trail. Stick closer to the creek when you have the option rather than getting caught up in the talus and side trails up the right side of the mountain.

There are places along this last portion of the trail where you may wonder if you have hit the end of the trail, but keep going. You'll know the end—the waterfall is hard to miss. The trail and the creek curve to the left just before the waterfall, and here you must cross the stream. Plan to get your feet a little wet, as the crossing is shallow but 20 feet wide. Once you cross the creek and turn the corner, the waterfall appears out of nowhere. This is a perfect spot for a snack or lunch and a dip in the falls before heading back to the trailhead.

Miles and Directions

0.0 Start at Adams Canyon trailhead.

0.5 Hit the Bonneville Shoreline Trail; head right and continue straight into the canyon.

1.6 Come to a bridge crossing.

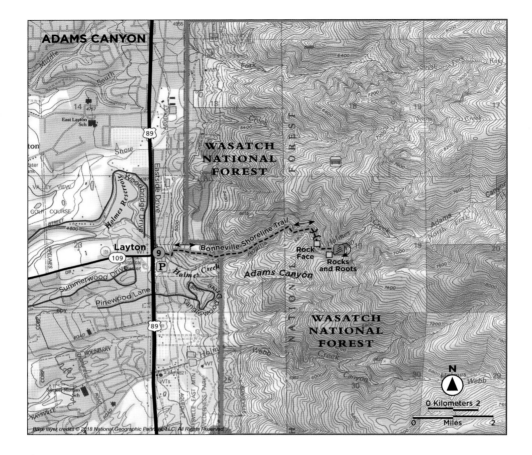

1.7 Reach a rock face that requires scrambling over or hiking up and over the top of the rock.

1.8 Come to a jumble of rocks and roots that must be scrambled up and over.

1.9 The trail appears to run into a talus slope. Follow the trail along the creek, or in the creekbed, to the waterfall that lies just around the corner.

2.0 Reach the waterfall. Return the way you came.

4.0 Arrive back at the trailhead.

Hike Information

Local information: Davis County Convention and Visitors Bureau, 1572 North Woodland Park Dr., Ste. 510, Layton 84041; (888) 777-9771; e-mail: info@davis.travel

Camping: There are a few fire rings in this canyon that indicate past campsites. Camping is permitted at these sites. No fee or registration required.

10 Holbrook Canyon

Holbrook Canyon begins and ends with cascading waterfalls, while the middle is more of the same. A wet hike, the trek up the canyon follows Holbrook Creek deep into the Sessions Mountains. The riparian area is lush with foliage, swampy sections, creek crossings, and the sound of the creek. Prepare for a long day, a steady grade, and wet feet, but you will also enjoy the shade of a deep canyon hike and the sound of Holbrook Creek the entire way. This trail is long, and bushwhacking is often the order of the day as you get deeper into the canyon. This trail has lots of burrs that can torment your canine friends, and it should only be attempted by older children who are hearty hikers. Shaded in many places, the hike up Holbrook Canyon can be a wonderful hike in summer and fall. Its proximity to local neighborhoods make it a hike that many people access intending to enjoy smaller sections of the trail, rather than topping out of Holbrook Canyon. The river crossings and groves along the way provide picnic space and stopping points for enjoying the stream.

Start: Holbrook Canyon/Sessions Mountain trailhead
Distance: 9.4 miles out and back
Hiking time: About 7 hours
Difficulty: Strenuous
Elevation gain: 2,233 feet
Trail surface: Doubletrack dirt road, singletrack packed dirt, bridges, stream crossings, marshy areas
Best season: Summer and fall
Other trail users: Horses
Canine compatibility: Dogs permitted

Land status: Uinta-Wasatch-Cache National Forest
Nearest town: Bountiful
Fees and permits: No fees or permits required
Maps: USGS Fort Douglas
Trail contacts: Bountiful City maintains the trailhead: Bountiful Parks Department, (801) 298-6178.
Special considerations: Hiking poles will be helpful during the many stream crossings, as will sturdy hiking sandals or hiking shoes you don't mind getting wet. Throw in the bug repellent as well.

Finding the trailhead: From Salt Lake City head north on I-15. Take the Bountiful 2600 South exit 315 and head east. Follow the road as it winds around to 1800 South and turn right (east). Continue through Bountiful to Bountiful Boulevard on the far east side of the city. Turn left onto Bountiful Boulevard and continue 0.8 mile to the trailhead, which sits off to the right. The paved parking area is just across the street and slightly south of the LDS Bountiful temple. There are restrooms at the trailhead. **GPS:** N40 52.902' / W111 50.662'

The Hike

A quick descent from the parking area down a doubletrack gravel road puts you immediately at the mouth of Holbrook Canyon. A waterfall meets you at the mouth as the trail heads east into the canyon. From your first steps into the canyon, the trail parallels Holbrook Creek and you are immediately immersed in a forested, riparian world. During spring runoff the creek will be higher and water crossings deeper, during early summer the foliage is thick and often encroaches on the trail in all its green glory, and in autumn the canyon is a patchwork of fall colors. At the higher elevations, the snow takes awhile to melt out; although you may be able to access the lower portions of the trail in late spring, you will not be able to make it to the top until later in the summer.

Within the first 0.5 mile the trail makes two quick forks. The second junction runs into the stream. Head to your left, slightly upstream, where the trail continues to a small bridge crossing. There are numerous stream crossings over the next 1.0 mile. Some are on established footbridges; others require rock hopping or cooling your feet in the water.

Left: Waterfall at the mouth of Holbrook Canyon
Right: Hikers enjoying the spring runoff waterfalls

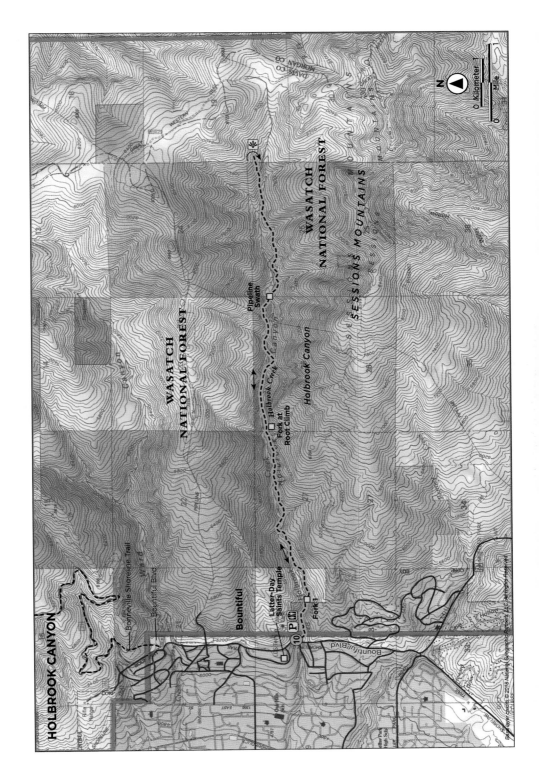

HOLBROOK CANYON

At 2.0 miles the trail runs into the stream. You must walk upstream a few yards to get back to the trail, which climbs up the mountain on a steep root bank. You can either follow that route and drop down again later or head right, cross the stream, and catch the trail up the canyon on the other side of the stream. If you climb up the root bank, a trail continues to a rock, where the trail disappears. At this point you would need to climb down below the rocks to hook up with the trail below, next to the stream. This is the halfway point and often used as a turnaround point.

This last section of the trail is traveled less and more overgrown. The footpath stays visible, but the foliage closes in more quickly around the trail. Be prepared for swampy areas and times of following stream rivulet trails as you proceed up the canyon.

At 3.3 miles a large natural gas pipeline, brought from Wyoming, crosses through this area of the Sessions Mountains on its way to California. The pipeline was cut through this trail in 2011; the hiking trail continues upcanyon on the other side of the cleared swath.

The climb out of Holbrook Canyon to the viewpoint is short and sustained. At 4.5 miles the climb up and out begins. The trail ends 0.2 mile later at a flat stopping point that allows you to look down Holbrook Canyon with views of the creek cascading down to the north and all the way downcanyon for a view of the Great Salt Lake, Antelope Island, and the city of Bountiful. Enjoy the view, and then return the way you came.

Note: The Forest Service requests that users are careful not to create extra side trails in the area.

Bountiful Trails Committee, Bountiful City, and the Forest Service are currently working on development of the Bountiful Shoreline Trail that will intersect with Holbrook Creek Trail in the near future.

Miles and Directions

0.0 Start at the Holbrook Canyon/Sessions Mountain trailhead.

0.4 The trail forks; follow the right fork.

0.45 The trail forks; either direction will get you to the trail on the other side of the stream.

2.0 Climb a steep root bank.

3.3 The trail crosses the gas pipeline thoroughfare.

4.5 Begin the climb out of Holbrook Canyon.

4.7 Arrive at the overlook. Return the way you came.

9.4 Arrive back at the trailhead.

Hike Information

There are a few alcoves along the trail with fire rings where you could backpack in and set up a primitive camp. There are no formal picnic tables or campsites.

11 Mueller Park to Elephant Rock

The Mueller Park Trail is the quintessential easy-access trail: From neighborhood to trailhead is only 500 feet. Beginning at a shaded bridge over Mill Creek, the trail climbs switchbacks beneath tall pine and fir and then winds deeper into the canyon through the hollows that crease the hillside. As the trail flanks the mountain it opens at times into scrubby Gambel oak and bigtooth maple. There are occasional viewpoints down into Bountiful and the Great Salt Lake below, but the trail is primarily embraced by foliage. Mueller Park is popular and used by mountain bikers, families, dog walkers, and trail runners as well as hikers. Elephant Rock has a bench perfectly situated for watching the sunset over the Great Salt Lake.

Start: Mueller Park picnic grounds and trailhead
Distance: 7.0 miles out and back
Hiking time: About 3 hours
Difficulty: Moderate
Elevation gain: 900 feet
Trail surface: Packed dirt and rock, bridge
Best season: Year-round; snowshoes often required in winter
Other trail users: Bikers, horses, motorbikes
Canine compatibility: Dogs permitted
Land status: Uinta-Wasatch-Cache National Forest

Nearest town: Bountiful
Fees and permits: No fees or permits required for hiking; day-use fee for the picnic area
Maps: USGS Fort Douglas
Trail contacts: Salt Lake Ranger District, 6944 South 3000 East, Salt Lake City 84121
Special considerations: This trail is popular with mountain bikers. Beware of bikers, and share the trail. The trail lies at a lower elevation than many Wasatch trails, so it is one of the first to clear of snow in the spring.

Finding the trailhead: From Salt Lake City head north on I-15. Take the Woods Cross exit (2600 South) and go east 0.9 mile. The road becomes Orchard Drive. Continue straight to 1800 South. Turn right onto 1800 South and follow the road east to its end at the mountain and Mueller Park picnic area and trailhead. The trailhead has parking for eight cars and additional parking down the side of the road. **GPS:** N40 51.83' / W111 50.205'

The Hike

The Mueller Park Trail begins at a shaded bridge that crosses Mill Creek as it runs out of the Sessions Mountains. The trail begins on the far side of the bridge (Trail 141) and begins with a set of switchbacks that climb beneath the shade of pine and fir on a packed-dirt trail. Most of the elevation gain is made in the first 1.0 mile of the trail

Hikers on Elephant Rock

as it climbs up the mountain face. The last 2.5 miles then head east as the trail hugs the curves of the mountain and heads deeper into the hills amidst scrubby Gambel oak and bigtooth maple interspersed with sections of evergreens.

Patches of shade and sun fluctuate along the trail. There is less elevation gain from here to the giant gray rock jutting out from the surrounding green of the forest— Elephant Rock.

At 1.7 miles the trail breaks through the taller trees and the view opens to the north side of the canyon where you can see a pipeline swath down the opposing mountain face. The "pipeline" is a wide treeless strip that looks like a ski run and is cleared to the top of the mountain. This swath is what remains of the placement of a 900-mile-long gas pipe that was built to carry natural gas from southwestern Wyoming to southern California.

The trail quickly heads back into the trees as it cruises deeper into the hills toward Elephant Rock. The occasional wooden bridge helps you cross any watery sections. Just before reaching Elephant Rock, you will hit a T in the trail. Look closely for this, as it appears to be a sharp right turn up the mountain. Take the left leg, which sweeps around the corner to a set of benches and Elephant Rock below. The right fork, which is a sharp turn to the south, continues on to Rudy's Flat and North Canyon if you wish to continue with either option.

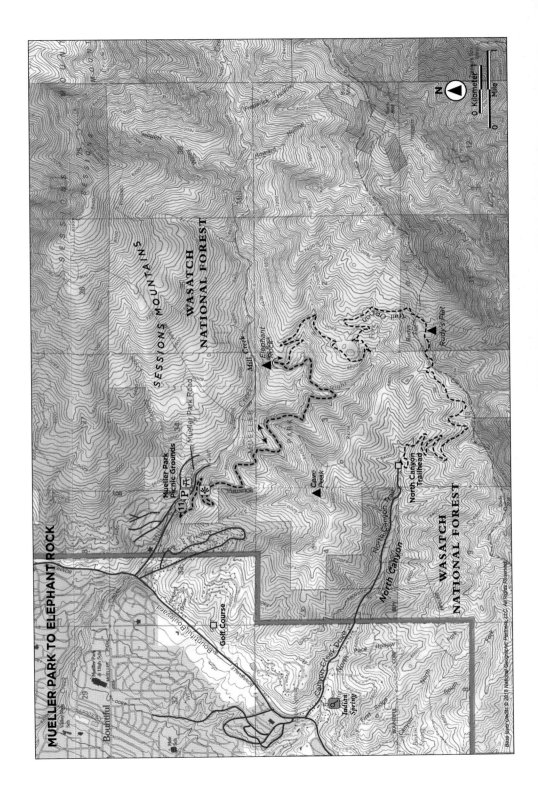

MUELLER PARK TO ELEPHANT ROCK

From the benches above Elephant Rock, Mueller Park stretches below, as do Bountiful, the foothills, the Great Salt Lake, Antelope Island, and everything between. A steep footpath leads down to Elephant Rock if you wish to climb onto the rock itself. Enjoy the view before returning the way you came.

Utah has five national parks and ten national monuments and recreation areas.

Miles and Directions

0.0 Start at Mueller Park picnic grounds and trailhead.

0.6 Come to the first scenic overlook.

1.0 After achieving most of its elevation gain, the trail begins a meandering eastern route into the mountains.

1.7 The trail opens for a scenic overlook to the north of the canyon. Elephant Rock is clearly visible from here.

3.5 Take the left fork to Elephant Rock. Return the way you came. (***Option:*** Rudy's Flat and North Canyon can be reached by turning right at the last fork before Elephant Rock.)

7.0 Arrive back at the trailhead.

Option

Mueller Park to North Canyon point-to-point hike: With a shuttle you can continue from Elephant Rock, past Rudy's Flat, and down North Canyon. This route will add 6.0 miles to the featured hike for a total one-way trek of 9.5 miles. North Canyon sits right at the top of a neighborhood—literally 50 feet from the nearest house—so access is easy but parking is limited.

To leave your shuttle vehicle at North Canyon, take I-15 to the 26th South exit 315 in Bountiful. Drive east to 1800 South and turn right (east). Follow 1800 South for 1.7 miles to Bountiful Boulevard and turn right (south). Follow Bountiful Boulevard for 1.6 miles to Canyon Creek Drive, which ends after 0.8 mile. This is the mouth of North Canyon. No parking is allowed in this circular turnaround. Parking for a couple cars is available a short way up the canyon road in a pullout. (Bountiful City has plans to build an established trailhead here.)

Hike Information

Local events and attractions: Mueller Park picnic grounds are open 7 a.m. to 10 p.m. There are ten single sites and two group sites that can accommodate up to one hundred people. Reservations are suggested, but there also are first-come, first-served sites. Reservations are required at least 5 days in advance and can be made at www.reserveamerica.com. There is a fee to enter the picnic grounds, and extra vehicle fees are charged. Dogs are allowed but must be on a leash at all times. Call (801) 292-2800 for more information.

Davis County

12 Farmington Creek Trail 11.1 (Sunset Trail)

A 30-foot waterfall near the top, open views of the canyon, tumbled and shot-up early-20th-century cars hidden in the trees, and the wonder of Farmington Creek are the interesting highlights of this easy-access trail located just up Farmington Canyon. The trail begins in a gravel parking lot at the point where the road up Farmington Canyon changes from paved to gravel. The trail cuts quietly up the canyon parallel-ing Farmington Creek up to Sunset Campground, a primitive Forest Service camp-ground. The views across the canyon, down to the creek, and out to the Great Salt Lake add to the flavor of the family-friendly trail.

Start: Gravel parking area off Farmington Canyon Road
Distance: 3.8 miles out and back
Hiking time: About 2.5 hours
Difficulty: Easy
Elevation gain: 1,110 feet
Trail surface: Dirt and rock path
Best season: Spring, fall, and winter. (The trail has complete southern exposure and gets very hot during the summer.)
Other trail users: Bikers, horses
Canine compatibility: Dogs permitted
Land status: Uinta-Wasatch-Cache National Forest

Nearest town: Farmington
Fees and permits: No fees or permits required
Maps: USGS Bountiful Peak, Peterson; A guidebook called *Guide to Farmington Trails* is available for purchase at 160 South Main St., Farmington, at the City Hall.
Trail contacts: Farmington Trails Committee; trail representative changes regularly. Farming-ton City can direct you to the current contact person, (801) 451-2383; Salt Lake Ranger District, US Forest Service, (801) 733-2660
Special considerations: No ATVs or other motorized vehicles allowed on the trail.

Finding the trailhead: From Salt Lake City head north on I-15 to exit 322. Follow the right fork off the exit ramp. At the first stop sign turn right onto State Street. Follow State Street for 2 blocks to 100 East and take a left. Follow 100 East for 2.3 miles into Farmington Canyon. The road up Farmington Canyon becomes a narrow one-lane road. Travel carefully as cars are allowed to go both directions.

The gravel parking lot is located up Farmington Canyon, on the right at the hairpin turn where the road changes from paved to gravel. Two trails leave the north side of the lot; both are the same trail. A small trail heads off the south side of the parking lot; this is just a user-made trail down to the stream. **GPS:** N41 00.026' / W111 59.978'

The Hike

There are big plans for the Farmington Creek Trail. The Farmington Trails Committee plans that this trail eventually will run from Sunset Campground down to the Great Salt Lake, but for now each section, both finished and planned, has a number. Section 11.1 is the top section of the trail that runs from Sunset Campground to the gravel parking area along Farmington Canyon Road. A new section of trail has been completed in the last few years and it begins just above Farmington Pond, but as of the completion of this book, this lower section of trail does not yet connect with 11.1 Sunset Trail.

Managed by the US Forest Service, this trail is not always pristine; people have been known to throw old tires and even cars off the canyon road above. The cars found below are early-20th-century models. Everyone can help keep the trail clean by carrying out a little more than you carry in.

Aside from the oddities of the trail, there are beautiful little waterfalls, open views across the canyon, a peaceful path, and a fun waterfall just before you reach the

Antique car that rolled down the mountain in the early 1900s

Left: First waterfall found along the trail
Right: Hiker and dog enjoying the trail

campground. This tributary canyon is a beautiful, peaceful route that climbs deeper into Farmington Canyon, away from motorized vehicles, allowing hikers to enjoy Farmington Creek and the side springs and creeks that tumble down the canyon.

The trail begins by climbing out of the gravel parking area on the north side. Two different trails have been worn into the dirt, but each hooks into the same trail. The trail travels above Farmington Creek, occasionally swooping near a tributary creek or spring. The trail runs high on the north side of the canyon, facing south with clear views across the canyon and down to the creek. Take plenty of water on hotter days, as the open south-facing component of the trail keeps it warm. The sound of the creek is refreshing as you hike, and if you bring a filter, you can purify water from the springs.

The California gull is Utah's state bird. It won this honor because huge flocks of the birds flew to the rescue of Mormon pioneers by eating a plague of crickets that attacked their crops shortly after they arrived in the Salt Lake Valley.

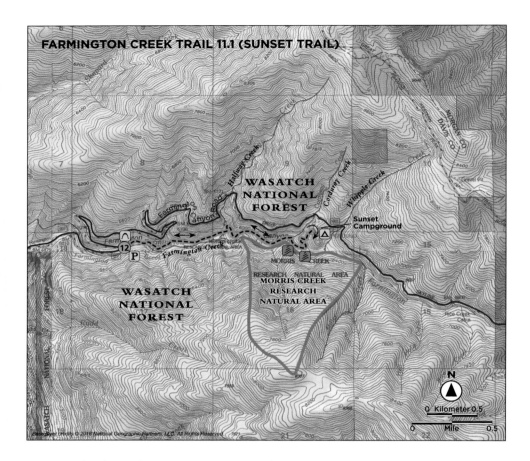

At 0.9 mile the trail enters aspen trees and passes next to a shaded alcove with boulders for sitting, right off the trail to the left. The first stream crossing is just past this area; a waterfall cascades down, feeding into the stream that hurries down the mountain into Farmington Creek below. The trail crosses and then climbs quickly away from the creek. During spring, when winter runoff is high, the sound of Farmington Creek can be heard all along the trail.

At 1.3 miles the old burned-out car sits off to the right (south) side of the trail. If you don't watch for it, you might walk right by it. A stream appears quickly at 1.5 miles for another easy crossing. Follow the trail to the right.

The largest waterfall is located just past this point, down off the trail to the right. There is a rock outcropping vantage point for viewing the falls, but some venture down the steep slope to examine the falls close up. Views downcanyon to the valley and Great Salt Lake are visible from here as well.

The trail continues east, and 250 feet later the trail forks. Head left to Sunset Campground, where the trail climbs 240 feet up to the west side of the campground. A wooden trail sign at the campground marks this end of the trail. If you did not leave a shuttle car at the campground, head back the way you came. You can also opt to leave a car at the parking area and hike this trail from the top down.

Miles and Directions

0.0 Start from the gravel parking lot in Farmington Canyon.

0.9 Come to your first stream crossing and waterfall.

1.3 Look for the burned-out car on the south side of the trail.

1.5 The trail crosses the stream and forks; head right.

1.6 Come to the waterfall down off the south side of the trail.

1.7 The trail forks to Sunset Campground.

1.9 Arrive at Sunset Campground. Return the way you came. (**Option:** Leave a shuttle car at Sunset Campground for a point-to-point hike. The campground is located 3.7 miles from the parking area, farther up Farmington Canyon on the dirt road.)

3.8 Arrive back at the parking area.

Hike Information

Camping: Sunset Campground, Skyline Drive Scenic Backway, Farmington 84025; sixteen sites available for tent and RV camping. Located on Farmington Canyon's scenic road, this campsite is nestled in the pines, which provide privacy. Vault toilets. No reservations required. Open June 1 through Sept 15. There is a fee to camp.

HOW MANY CALORIES CAN I BURN WHILE HIKING?

According to the Mayo Clinic, 3,500 calories equals about 1 pound of fat. If you want to lose weight, you must burn 3,500 calories more than you take in to burn off each pound. The US Department of Health and Human Services recommends at least 2 hours and 30 minutes a week of moderate aerobic activity (think hiking) or 1 hour and 15 minutes a week of vigorous aerobic activity (think running). Specific calorie burn varies with level of intensity and your individual situation, but according to the Mayo Clinic chart a 160-pound person would burn 188 calories an hour walking (at 2 miles per hour) and 511 calories an hour backpacking; hiking would fall in between. A 200-pound person would burn 228 calories an hour while walking and 637 calories backpacking.

13 Kays Creek Parkway

This Layton city park contains 2.5 miles of paved trails that run through 100 acres of sometimes-dense vegetation and more-open marshland. Although just minutes from large subdivisions and busy streets, the park is a quiet retreat in the bottom of Hobbs Hollow. Running through Kays Creek corridor, the east side of the trail runs next to Hobbs Reservoir and often next to Kays Creek. It's a quick retreat from the bustle of city life and a haven filled with a variety of wildlife and birds. Five trailheads provide a variety of access points, and the trails can be enjoyed in multiple directions. Pick one, or stroll them all.

Start: There are five trailheads: (1) Adam J. Welker trailhead, 2700 North 2125 East. This trailhead has twenty-five parking spaces and is considered the parkway's primary trailhead. (2) Canyon View trailhead, 2360 East Canyon View. No parking available. (3) Oak Forest trailhead, 2459 East 2750 North. No parking available. (4) Hidden Hollow, 2210 North 1450 East. Parking possible along the roadside. (5) Sunset Drive trailhead, 1851 E. Sunset Dr. No parking available.

Distance: 2.5 miles of trails

Hiking time: About 30 minutes to 2 hours

Difficulty: Easy

Elevation gain: Adam J. Welker trailhead to Oak Forest trailhead, 225 feet; Adam J. Welker to dead end at Kays Creek, 190 feet; Adam J. Welker to Canyon View trailhead, 168 feet; Adam J. Welker to Hidden Hollow trailhead, negligible

Trail surface: Paved and dirt

Best season: Year-round access

Other trail users: Bikers, skateboarders, people in wheelchairs and pushing strollers

Canine compatibility: Leashed dogs permitted

Land status: City park

Nearest town: Layton

Fees and permits: No fees or permits required

Schedule: Parkway open 1 hour before sunrise to 1 hour after sunset

Maps: Layton city and Kays Creek Parkway maps available online at www.laytoncity.org

Trail contacts: Layton City Offices, Parks and Recreation Department, 437 North Wasatch Dr., Layton 84041; (801) 336-3900

Special considerations: No motorized vehicles or fires allowed. No restrooms are available at any trailhead. No alcohol allowed.

Finding the trailhead: The Adam J. Welker trailhead is the only trailhead to provide parking, so it is the best trailhead for nonlocals. From Salt Lake City take I-15 north to the US 89 turnoff in front of Lagoon Amusement Park (exit 324). Follow US 89 for 8.7 miles to UT 193 (exit 404) and go toward Clearfield/Hill Air Force Base. Turn left off the exit ramp onto UT 193/Bernard Fisher Highway and travel 1.1 miles. Turn left onto 2000 East and then left onto Deere View Drive and continue 0.1 mile. Turn right onto 2125 East and follow the road 0.4 mile to where it dead-ends at the trailhead and parking area. **GPS:** N41 05.867' / W111 55.687'

The Hike

For his Eagle Scout project, in 2008 a local Scout put up information signs along the trail describing the flora and fauna of the area. The signs provide information on raccoons, porcupines, deer, cougars, red-tailed hawks, mourning doves, spotted towhees, red foxes, and magpies—all found at different times of the year in this patch of nature within the city. The trail is lined with Russian olive trees, so during spring the aroma is divine. A variety of trees and undergrowth provide a haven for birds and wildlife, while pulling us out of neighborhoods and into a peaceful, quiet stroll along Kays Creek, for which the parkway is named. Walking the trails affords you the sound of Kays Creek, birds, and crickets. Hobbs Hollow, the canyon the park is located in, sits well below the numerous neighborhoods that rim the area.

The five different trailheads allow access to Kays Creek Parkway from various neighborhoods around the east side of Layton, but only one provides parking—Adam J. Welker. This land was provided by the Welker family, which donated 20 acres to the park project.

The park covers an underground sewer line that services the surrounding neighborhoods. There are plans that someday the trail will continue west, expanding to Layton Commons Park.

Heading east for 0.3 mile from Adam J. Welker trailhead and parking lot, you will reach a fork in the trail. The right fork ascends 0.65 mile to Oak Forest trailhead,

Walking along the Kays Creek Parkway also affords beautiful views of the mountains.

Hobbs Reservoir is available for fishing and human-powered watercrafts.

which sits in a neighborhood. The left fork takes you to the Canyon View access and farther into the hollow and to a Kays Creek bridge and crossing. There is a picnic table at the bridge crossing, and the trail continues for another 0.25 mile until it dead-ends at a grove of trees. It is 1.6 miles from Adam J. Welker trailhead to the dead end past Canyon View trailhead. Hobbs Reservoir, used for irrigation, is well fenced off on this east side of the parkway. Walk-in only access is allowed to the reservoir from Canyon View Drive trailhead and Oak Forest trailhead. There is also access from the east side of the reservoir on a dirt trail, but it is difficult to find. Fishing is allowed and nonmotorized watercraft can be used, but swimming is prohibited. Built in 1919 the reservoir is of earthen construction with a capacity of 1,580 acre-feet and drains an area of 2 square miles.

If you head west from Adam J. Welker trailhead toward the Hidden Hollow and Sunset Drive trailheads, the vegetation is more marshland than forest. In 0.35 mile the trail forks; both forks head in the same direction and loop back together in 0.2 mile. It is 0.7 mile to the Hidden Hollow trailhead and 0.5 mile to the Sunset Drive trailhead.

Garbage cans and doggie potty bags are available at all trailheads. Enjoy any section of the trail or all for as long as you like, and then return to your car.

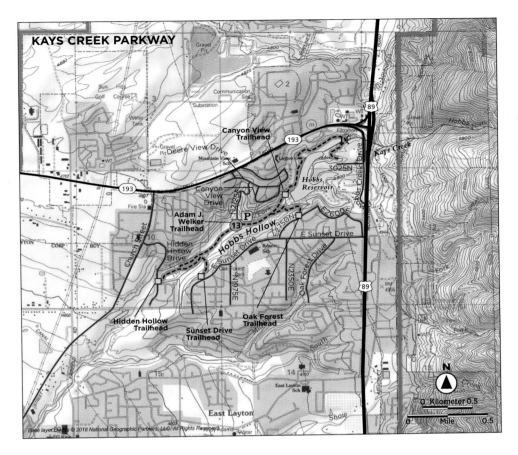

Miles and Directions

0.0 Start at the Adam J. Welker trailhead. There are 2.5 miles of possible trails within the parkway.

14 Farmington Bay Waterfowl Walk

The Great Salt Lake Nature Center at Farmington Bay Waterfowl Management Area is a great place to observe four different types of habitat: upland, emergent marsh, big open water, and riparian. Different birds and animals frequent each type of habitat, including a range of raptors and hundreds of other species. These marshy wetlands are a waterfowl sanctuary, and in 2010 a nature trail was created that circles through sections of these habitats to take birding to the next level. Famous for the numerous bald eagles that winter here, the nature center also sees international visitors, especially during February, the height of the season, when the on-site bald eagle count ranges from 100 to 400. This easy, pleasant trail provides bridges over marshy areas and observation decks with benches for sitting, waiting, and enjoying the birding experience. It is a peaceful foray perfect for families and is wheelchair accessible. A new nature center, the Robert N. Hasenyager Great Salt Lake Nature Center, will be installed in mid-2018 and will provide maps and information on the birds and surrounding area.

Start: Northeast of the nature center off the main road
Distance: 1.3-mile horseshoe; 1.5 miles if you take trail spurs to observation blinds on Big Pond
Hiking time: About 1 hour
Difficulty: Easy
Elevation gain: Negligible
Trail surface: Gravel and boardwalk
Best season: Year-round; snowshoes potentially required in winter; Feb for bald eagles
Other trail users: Bikers, people in wheelchairs
Canine compatibility: Dogs permitted on leash during the off-nesting season (Sept 16 through Feb 29). Leashes protect the wildlife from upset and protect your dog from interaction with traps, raccoons, and other wildlife.

Land status: Waterfowl management area
Nearest town: Farmington
Fees and permits: No fees or permits required
Schedule: Open during daylight hours. Nature center open 5 to 7 days a week during daylight hours.
Maps: Great Salt Lake Nature Center trail map, available at the nature center/trailhead
Trail contacts: Robert N. Hasenyager Great Salt Lake Nature Center, c/o DWR–Northern Regional Office, 515 East 5300 South, Ogden 84405; and Utah Division of Wildlife Resources at dwrcomment@utah.gov
Special considerations: Take binoculars and your birding book. Mar through Sept is nesting season for bald eagles, so be sure to stay on the trail.

Finding the trailhead: From Salt Lake City head north to Farmington on I-15. Take exit 322 (UT 227) and go right at the fork. Turn right onto the frontage road for 0.6 mile and then right onto Glovers Lane/925 South. Head straight west on Glovers Lane for 1.9 miles to the second turnoff into the waterfowl management area. Turn left (south) and follow the road to the nature center and parking area. If the gates are closed you can park outside the gates and enter by foot. The trails take off from the parking area. There are two gravel trails; start at the one farthest north. The south trail is the exit. **GPS:** N40 57.745' / W111 56.662'

The Hike

In 1935 the National Park Service, Utah Fish and Game Department, and the Civilian Conservation Corps joined forces to work on the eastern shores of the Great Salt Lake and the improvement of 3,800 acres of avian habitat. From that early start the Farmington Bay Waterfowl Management Area had grown to 18,000 acres as of 2007.

There seems to be a hundred-year cycle where the Great Salt Lake rises substantially, and as a terminal basin with no outflow, these rising lake levels cause a large disruption by flooding the surrounding area. As the climate shifts and the Great Salt Lake recedes, the mudflats are exposed for wildlife. These marshy wetlands are used as a waterfowl sanctuary. A small nature center was erected in 2007 to educate the public on this ecosystem and the wonderful refuge it provides along the migratory routes of millions of birds. A new and modern nature center was erected in 2018 to expand the services and education available at the refuge. Biologists have documented 200 species of birds at the bay and as many as 400 bald eagles during the winter months. More than five million birds are estimated to visit the bay each year.

Notice the great blue heron breeding nests in the background of the bay.

Welcome to the Farmington Bay Waterfowl Management Area and Nature Center.

The trail was built through four different habitats to give walkers and birders a chance to see a variety of birds. Of special note are a great blue heron rookery on Glover Pond and viewing decks on Big Pond. Maps available at the nature center further explain the various habitats.

The trail begins a few hundred feet back down the road, northeast of the nature center. There are two gravel trails with entry to the road—each one end of the trail. Start at the one farthest north, which immediately brings you to East Pond, a pond fed by Farmington Creek. The Emergent Marsh is next. The marsh is wet year-round and is filled with tall cattails and bulrushes. You pass two observation blinds on the right side of the trail in the next 0.25 mile.

FARMINGTON BAY WATERFOWL WALK

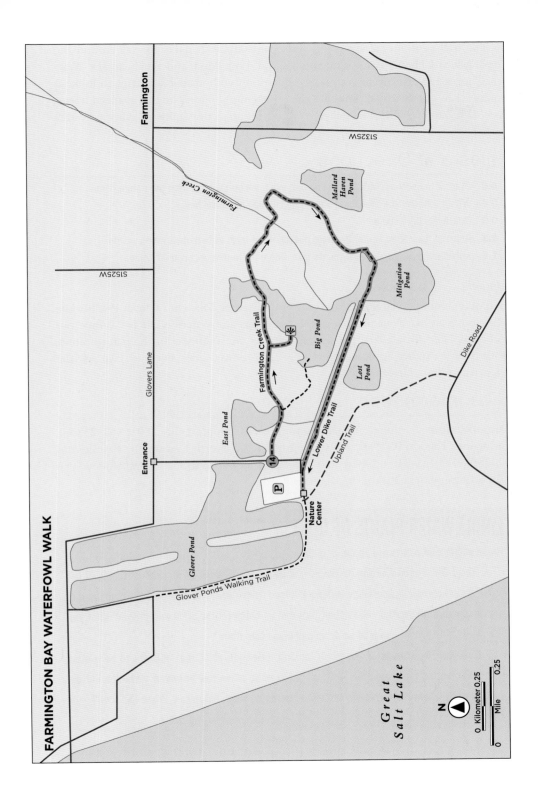

Farmington

S1325W

S1325W

Glovers Lane

Entrance

Farmington Creek

Farmington Creek Trail

East Pond

Big Pond

Mallard
Haven
Pond

Mitigation
Pond

Lost
Pond

Lower Dike Trail

Upland Trail

Dike Road

14

P

Nature
Center

Glover Pond

Glover Ponds Walking Trail

G r e a t
S a l t   L a k e

N

0   Kilometer 0.25   0.25
0   Mile

The trail continues along gravel and boardwalk as it makes its way around Big Pond, Mallard Haven Pond, Mitigation Pond, Lost Pond, and finally to the Western Chorus Frog Area. The trail is 1.3 miles long without the side trips to lookout points—1.5 miles with the forays to the observation blinds. The trail makes a horseshoe as it explores the area and exits along the road just south of where the trail started.

Miles and Directions

0.0 Start at the second, wide gravel trail that sits back up the road from the nature center.

0.04 Within 200 feet the East Pond and Emergent Marsh habitat begin.

0.5 Reach the Big Pond area.

1.3 Arrive at the nature center if you do not take side trails to bird observation points.

1.5 Arrive at the nature center if you do take side trails to bird observation points.

Options

Two other, unimproved trails start at the nature center. One rims Glover Pond to the west and is an excellent place to view shorebirds and waterfowl. It is 1.0 mile out and back. The Upland Trail (1.0 mile) wraps to the southwest of the nature center. Both trails are indicated by nothing more than mowed grass, but they give you the opportunity for a pleasant walk.

Hike Information

Organizations: Farmington Trails Committee, Farmington City; (801) 451–2383
Camping: Lagoon RV Park and Campground, 375 North Lagoon Dr., Farmington 84025; (801) 451–8100. Open May through Oct; reservations recommended. The Lagoon Amusement Park is the largest in Utah.

EDIBLE WATER PLANTS OF UTAH

These edible wild plants are common in areas with rivers, lakes, streams, and creeks:

Water lily: Found floating on ponds and lakes; the flowers, seeds, and rhizomes of the water lily are all edible. According to Terry Ellefsen from eHow, one can "peel the corky rind of the rhizome to uncover an edible plant that can be eaten raw or dried and ground into flour. The seeds of the plant can also be dried and made into flour."

Cattails: Many parts of the funny-looking waterside plant that appears to be a stem with a hot dog on top are edible. Young shoots can be eaten raw or boiled, while the bottom section of the stem is reported to taste like cucumber when eaten raw. When the seed heads are young and green, they can be boiled and eaten like corn on the cob.

Salt Lake City

S alt Lake City borders directly on the surrounding foothills and provides hikes that are easy to get to and enjoy. These hikes are two of the local favorites and both trailheads sit right within the bordering neighborhoods. Loved for their phenomenal views of the city and the sunset, each hike has its own personality and they differ significantly in the things they offer.

15 The Living Room

After a nice hike, what's better than kicking back in the living room and propping the old feet up with a cool drink? On this hike you get this opportunity even before you hike back down the trail. Just make sure your water bottle has ice in it, and you'll be set. The Living Room affords a view across the valley to the west, so hikes to watch the sunset are a favorite. This view can be enjoyed while sitting on chairs and couches built of slabs of stone and resting your feet on stone ottomans. The high-definition view of the valley below is better than anything you'll get at home. With an easy-access trailhead in the foothills behind the University of Utah, this popular trail sees a lot of traffic. Not too long, and kid appropriate, the whole family can enjoy the fun of this trail. It has also become a favorite of trail runners.

Start: Second trailhead along the east side of Colorow Way
Distance: 2.6 miles out and back
Hiking time: About 2 hours
Difficulty: Moderate
Elevation gain: 1,000 feet
Trail surface: Rock, gravel, dirt
Best season: Late spring through fall
Other trail users: None
Canine compatibility: Leashed dogs permitted
Land status: Uinta-Wasatch-Cache National Forest
Nearest town: Salt Lake City
Fees and permits: No fees or permits required

Schedule: The trail is often used at night to enjoy the views of the sunset and lights of the city.
Maps: USGS Fort Douglas
Trail contacts: Salt Lake Ranger District, 6944 South 3000 East, Salt Lake City 84121; Uinta-Wasatch-Cache National Forest, 8236 Federal Building, 125 South State St., Salt Lake City 84138
Special considerations: The trail officially climbs up George's Hollow, and you'll notice a maze of trails in the area. There is more than one way to the top, but to make sure you don't miss The Living Room, follow the suggested route until you are familiar with the area and location.

Finding the trailhead: From Salt Lake City take I-80 east to exit 129 (Foothill Drive). Continue north on Foothill Drive for 3.1 miles to Wakara Way (670 South). Head east 0.7 mile to Colorow Way (2310 East) and turn right onto Colorow Way just before the entrance to Red Butte Gardens. Continue on Colorow Way to the second trailhead on the left.

Alternate route: Take the 400 South Exit from I-15 in Salt Lake City. Head east on 400 South for 4 miles to Wakara Way. Turn east/left on Wakara Way 0.7 mile to Colorow Way (2310 East) and turn right onto Colorow Way just before the entrance to Red Butte Gardens. Continue on Colorow Way to the second trailhead on the left. No markers name the trail but it is generically signed, and bags are provided to clean up after Fido. **GPS:** N40 45.560' / W111 49.277'

The Hike

The Living Room sits above the University of Utah and Fort Douglas. The easy-access trailhead makes it a favorite with college students, trail runners, and people who work in the research park below. It can be a quick workout or a romantic place to watch the sunset, but either way the trail is well traveled. The trail cuts off from the Bonneville Shoreline Trail (BST) into George's Hollow directly behind the research park.

The trail begins under a canopy of trees and forks within a few hundred feet. Both forks cross over a very small stream and connect again to one another.

At 0.2 mile you hit the Bonneville Shoreline Trail (wider gravel path leading north and south). Although the dirt hiking trail you are on appears to head straight up the mountain, instead head to the right along the BST for 50 feet or so to another dirt trail that heads up the mountain. This trail will take you to George's Hollow. In 0.1 mile the trail intersects with a wider gravel trail and turns left toward the canyon. Head left and stay on this main trail as it heads up George's Hollow, skipping the two side trails that enter from the left.

From The Living Room you can enjoy the view of the Southern Wasatch Front.

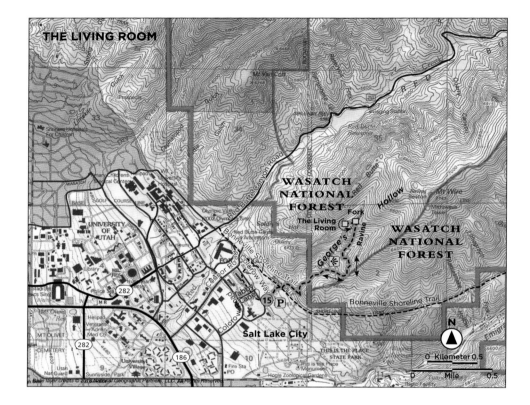

The trail forks again at 0.4 mile. Take the right fork and continue east up into the canyon. The wider, better established trail has old railroad ties for footing. Gambel oak and bigtooth maple snuggle up to the trail.

At 0.54 mile the trail curves into a ravine and climbs up for a view across the Wasatch Front. This vantage point provides a pleasant view and rest stop. From here go right, up the steep incline following the well-established trail. At 1.2 miles, the trail forks one last time just before you get to The Living Room. Take the left fork and follow the trail around to the front side of the mountain, where you will find the seating arrangements waiting and the view impressive.

The view looks out to the Oquirrh Range to the west and down onto the University of Utah, the research park, and Salt Lake Valley below. Slabs have been stacked to make this Flintstones sitting area. Chances are you will not be the only one kicking back.

> **The Oquirrh Range is 30 miles long and makes up the western border of the Salt Lake Valley. The name Oquirrh was taken from a Goshute word meaning "wooded mountain."**

Miles and Directions

0.0   Start at the Colorow Way trailhead.

375 feet   Reach the first fork; head right or left.

  0.2   Hit the Bonneville Shoreline Trail.

  0.25 Turn off Bonneville Shoreline Trail and head up mountain.

  0.3   Turn left on gravel trail heading toward George's Hollow.

  0.4   Trail forks head right.

  0.8   Climb up the ravine.

  1.0   The trail opens to an overlook view to the west.

  1.2   Reach final fork; head left around to the front of the mountain.

  1.3   Arrive at The Living Room. Return the way you came.

  2.6   Arrive back at the trailhead.

Hike Information

Local events and attractions: Red Butte Botanical Garden and Red Butte Canyon are northern neighbors to this trail. Red Butte itself is a steep foothill that rises more than 1,500 feet in just over a mile. Red Butte Gardens offers a summer concert series, and a hike around the beautiful gardens can be peaceful. For more information call (801) 585-0556 or visit www.redbuttegarden.org.

Hikers enjoying the view from The Living Room

16 Ensign Peak

The historic Ensign Peak Trail climbs to an overlook used by Brigham Young and other Latter-Day Saint church leaders upon settling the valley. The viewpoint from the historical obelisk atop the peak provides a view of the Salt Lake Valley as it sits cradled between the Wasatch Mountains on the east and the Oquirrh Range on the west. This short hike up a barren, grass-lined trail takes you to the point where you can view it all—both mountain ranges, the valley between, the Great Salt Lake, the heart of downtown Salt Lake City, and everything in between. This hike is all about the view and the history.

Start: Ensign Peak Nature Park
Distance: 1.0 mile out and back
Hiking time: About 30 minutes
Difficulty: Moderate due to steepness of trail
Elevation gain: 398 feet
Trail surface: Dirt path with a paved section
Best season: Year-round
Other trail users: None
Canine compatibility: Leashed dogs permitted
Land status: Salt Lake City park, managed by the city and the Ensign Peak Foundation
Nearest town: Salt Lake City

Fees and permits: No fees or permits required
Schedule: Open daily sunrise to sunset
Maps: USGS Salt Lake City North; Ensign Downs Park
Trail contacts: Salt Lake City Parks and Public Lands; (801) 972-7800
Special considerations: Stay on the designated trail to protect the native grasses and flowers.
Other: No water or restrooms are available at the trailhead. Carry out your own trash. No campfires or camping permitted.

Finding the trailhead: From the State Capitol building in Salt Lake City, take East Capitol Boulevard (135 East), the road found on the east side of the Capitol building, north for 0.5 mile to Edgecombe Drive (800 North). Turn left onto Edgecombe Drive, which becomes Ensign Vista Drive, and continue for 0.2 mile to the Ensign Peak Nature Park trailhead and entry plaza on the left.
GPS: N40 47.518' / W111 53.291'

The Hike

On July 26, 1847, 2 days after Mormon prophet Brigham Young declared Salt Lake Valley the place where his followers were to set up their new community, he and a party of prominent church leaders climbed this hill as a vantage point to survey the valley and decide how they would lay out their future city. It was suggested that this peak was a fitting place to set up an ensign, and it was named Ensign Peak. On July 26, 1934, an obelisk was erected atop the peak. Today the hike to overlook the entire valley is defined by a dirt path lined with information markers describing the history, geology, flora, and fauna of the area.

As you head up the trail you immediately come to the Vista Mound offshoot trail to your left. This side trail is a nice lookout point from which you can see the Oquirrh

View of Salt Lake City and the Capitol Building from Ensign Peak

Mountains to the west; Kennecott Copper Mine to the southwest; and downtown Salt Lake City, the Capitol Building, Temple Square, the University of Utah, and the Wasatch Mountains to the east. The first path to Vista Mound is a short steep paved trail. The second is found 400 feet up the trail and is a dirt path that leads out to Vista Mound.

The trail is lined with grasses, thistle, and Gambel oak, but no shade. The well-marked trail provides places to sit if you tire on the steady climb to the top.

On the way up there are two additional overlooks. The first, at 0.33 mile, is called Valley View and it is marked by stone seats and an informational marker about the valley. You can sit, read, and take in the view. The second is called the Great Salt Lake overlook. It is found at 0.38 mile where the trail splits. The right fork goes to the Great Salt Lake Overlook and you can look down on the industrial area at the northern point of the mountain moving into Davis County. You can also see the Great Salt Lake, Antelope Island, and the north corner of the Oquirrh Mountains. The left fork takes you straight to Ensign Peak. Both connect with each other.

The Great Salt Lake is 80 miles long and 30 miles wide, with an average depth of 13 feet. The shoreline changes dramatically with any change in depth.

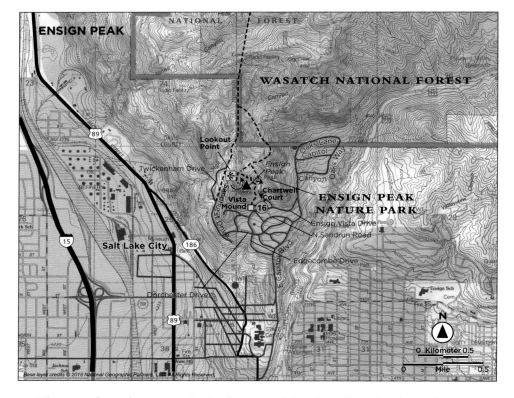

The view from the top overlooks the entire Salt Lake Valley. The obelisk holds a historic plaque, and railings line the walking deck.

On July 26, 1996, president of the Church of Jesus Christ of Latter-Day Saints, Gordon B. Hinckley, dedicated Ensign Peak Nature Park, which included Ensign Peak and an additional 66 acres surrounding it. President Hinckley dedicated it that it may "be a place of pondering, a place of remembrance, a place of thoughtful gratitude, and a place of purposeful resolution." The effort was headed by the Ensign Peak Foundation, later known as the Mormon Historic Sites Foundation, which worked closely with the Salt Lake City Corporation. The Church of Jesus Christ of

Brigham Young laid out Salt Lake City with wide streets and 10-acre blocks. The temple block was to be the heart of the city. When the temple was finished in 1893, the population of Salt Lake City was 45,000. Today the population of the Wasatch Front is estimated to be more than two million strong. Finding your way around the Salt Lake area is easy in the areas that are on this acre-block grid system. Addresses are plotted on an east–west and north–south grid moving out from Main Street running north and south and Center Street running east and west.

Latter-Day Saints also constructed a memorial garden near the base of the peak that tells of its significance and the early pioneers who built up Salt Lake Valley.

After enjoying the vast vista, return to the trailhead the same way you came up.

Miles and Directions

0.0 Start at the trailhead in Ensign Peak Nature Park.

100 feet Trail forks. Vista Mound trail to the left. Ensign Peak to the right.

400 feet Second trail split for Vista Mound.

0.33 Valley View viewpoint.

0.38 Reach the overlook with a westerly view to the Great Salt Lake and north to the industrial area below.

0.5 Arrive at Ensign Peak summit. Return the way you came.

1.0 Arrive back at the trailhead.

Hike Information

Local Sightseeing: Salt Lake City Convention and Visitors Bureau, www.visitsalt lake.com; for guided city and historic tours. Temple Square also has free tours for the public.

East of Salt Lake City

The gorgeous, majestic mountains of the Wasatch Range make up the eastern border of the Salt Lake Valley. Four major canyons of the range dump into the valley. The four most developed canyons include Mill Creek, Big Cottonwood, Little Cottonwood, and Parley's Canyons. All four canyons contain developed roads, but Parley's Canyon is the only through canyon. I-80 runs through Parley's Canyon and is the connecting route between the Salt Lake Valley and the Park City area. The Cottonwood Canyons received their names from the streams originating there. UT 190 runs 14 miles up Big Cottonwood Canyon, providing access to those trails, while UT 210 extends up Little Cottonwood Canyon to provide access there. A county road climbs up Mill Creek Canyon, providing access all the way to the Big Water trailhead at the top of the canyon. Sections of all four canyons are in the Wasatch Front watershed area that feeds Salt Lake County below.

Mill Creek Canyon

17 Pipeline Trail

The Pipeline Trail does not climb to a peak or access a hidden waterfall deep within a canyon. Rather the trail runs horizontal, hugging the curves of the gullies and contours of the south-facing canyon wall of Mill Creek Canyon. The trail is popular because it is nearly level, running around 6,200 to 6,800 feet. An easy traverse that fluctuates between canopies of trees and views down Mill Creek Canyon, this is a trail with options. To get to the Pipeline Trail there are four possible trailheads. Each of these entry and exit points climbs from the floor of Mill Creek Canyon from various points along the highway to hook into the Pipeline Trail, where you can then hike in either direction according to how long you'd like to make the hike and where you want to exit. The Pipeline Trail can be a "Build Your Own" hike. The four possible trailheads—one at each end and two in the middle—give you many options to play with. You can create a shuttle or hike out and back. This classic, easy trail also extends to a Salt Lake City overlook on the far west side as it follows what was once a hydroelectric power generation venture in the early 1900s.

Start: Elbow Fork trailhead
Distance: Elbow Fork to Burch Hollow trailhead, 2.7 miles point to point; Elbow Fork to Church Fork picnic grounds, 4.6 miles point to point; Elbow Fork to Rattlesnake Gulch trailhead, 7.0 miles point to point; Elbow Fork to Salt Lake Overlook and out to Rattlesnake Gulch trailhead, 8.7 miles point to point
Hiking time: Varies according to the trail you choose
Difficulty: Easy to moderate
Elevation gain: The Pipeline Trail runs between 6,200 and 6,800 feet as it traverses the canyon. The steepest climb is from Rattlesnake Gulch trailhead to the Pipeline Trail: 600 feet.
Trail surface: Dirt and rock singletrack
Best season: July 1 to Nov 1. The winter gate located halfway up Mill Creek Canyon is closed until July 1. Elbow Fork trailhead sits past this gate. All other trailheads are open and provide pleasant hiking mid-May through Nov 1. You can enjoy the trail on snowshoes in winter.

Other trail users: Mountain bikers, horses
Canine compatibility: Dogs permitted. Must be leashed on even-numbered days; may be off-leash on odd-numbered days but must be in sight of handler. Dogs must be leashed at all times in campgrounds, roadways, and trailheads. Be sure to clean up after your dog.
Land status: Uinta-Wasatch Cache National Forest, Boy Scouts of America land
Nearest town: Salt Lake City
Fees and permits: Fee to enter Mill Creek Canyon
Schedule: 8:00 a.m. to 10:00 p.m.
Maps: USGS Mount Aire; Mill Creek Canyon Salt Lake Ranger District handout
Trail contacts: Salt Lake County Parks and Recreation, (385) 468-1800; Salt Lake Ranger District, 6944 South 3000 East, Salt Lake City 84121
Special considerations: You'll need to arrange for a shuttle car unless you decide to hike out and back.

Finding the trailhead: From Salt Lake City take I-15 south. Merge onto I-80 east via exit 304 for 5 miles. Merge onto I-215 south via exit 128 and follow for 2.6 miles. Take the 3900 South exit/exit 4.

Turn left onto 3900 South and then immediately onto Wasatch Boulevard. Take your first right onto 3800 South, which becomes East Mill Creek Canyon Road. Follow the road east into the canyon where you will find the fee station at the mouth of the canyon. There are four possible trailheads, or entry/exit points, to the Pipeline Trail:

- Rattlesnake Gulch trailhead is 0.7 mile up Mill Creek Canyon from the fee station. **GPS:** N40 41.490' / W111 46.137'
- Church Fork picnic grounds is 2.3 miles up Mill Creek Canyon from the fee station. **GPS:** N40 42.029' / W111 44.580'
- Burch Hollow trailhead is 3.5 miles up Mill Creek Canyon from the fee station. **GPS:** N40 41.967' / W111 43.275'
- Elbow Fork trailhead is 6.3 miles up Mill Creek Canyon from the fee station. **GPS:** N40 42.397' / W111 41.428'

The Hike

The Pipeline Trail once served as the bed of a pipeline (built in the early 1900s) that carried water for a hydropower generation venture that operated in the canyon for 65 years. After the two Mill Creek power plants were decommissioned, the right-of-way for their pipelines became a favorite hiking trail. When the pipeline was no longer needed, many sections were removed, but remnants of wire hoops and steel elbows occasionally show up in and along the trail.

Elbow Fork is the point at which the Pipeline Trail directly intersects the road up Mill Creek Canyon. The name Elbow Fork was derived from the sharp, 90-degree turn the road makes at this point. This is the uppermost trailhead for the Pipeline Trail. The other trailheads set you on a connector trail that will hook you into the Pipeline Trail, but Elbow Fork trailhead enters the Pipeline directly from the road. The Pipeline Trail begins directly from the road 100 feet or so down the road from the Mount Aire trailhead. A restroom and garbage cans are available. Parking is on the south side of the road.

From Elbow Fork you find yourself hiking under an arching 15-to-20-foot-high canopy of Gambel oak and bigtooth maple. Geraniums and bluebells can be seen at the right time of year, but the defining factor of the trail is the relaxed, somewhat-level traverse as it runs parallel with the road on its way down the canyon—though much higher up the mountain. Views cross-canyon and down into the Salt Lake Valley provide mountain sightseeing. The trail provides pleasant strolling amidst broad viewpoints and tree canopies. Because this trail is unrelentingly south facing, exposed sections receive constant sun and can be very hot on a sunny day, especially the

> Rattlesnake Gulch was originally named Rattlesnake Hollow in 1891, when early pioneer miners W. H. Stout and H. K. North located the Rattlesnake Lode there.

The Pipeline Trail

western section of the trail toward Rattlesnake Gulch and the Overlook. Be sure to carry plenty of water. On a cool day you'll enjoy the southern exposure.

The Pipeline Trail intersects the Burch Hollow connector 2.5 miles from Elbow Fork. The exit to Burch Hollow is not marked. If you exit here, it is only 0.2 mile down this connector to the Burch Hollow trailhead, which has parking for eight to ten cars. There are garbage cans, signs, and doggie waste bags at all the trailheads.

Continue west along the Pipeline to reach the Church Fork trailhead intersection, which is another 1.6 miles down the Pipeline. The exit down to Church Fork is marked. This is also the intersection for the hike to Grandeur Peak. If you exit here,

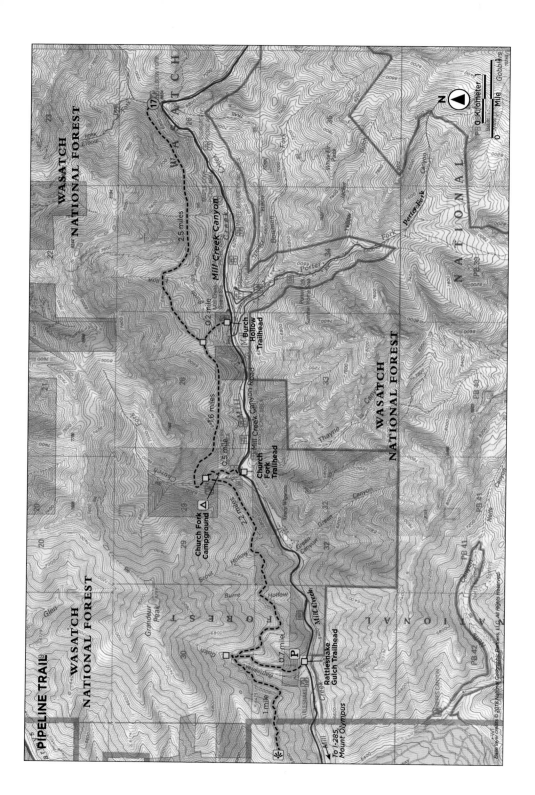

PIPELINE TRAIL

WASATCH
NATIONAL FOREST

WASATCH NATIONAL FOREST

WASATCH
NATIONAL FOREST

WASATCH
NATIONAL FOREST

NATIONAL FOREST

NATIONAL FOREST

Mill Creek Canyon

2.5 miles

0.2 mile

1.6 miles

0.5 mile

2.2 miles

0.7 mile

1 mile

Burch
Hollow
Trailhead

Church Fork
Campground

Church Fork
Trailhead

Mill Creek Canyon Road

Rattlesnake
Gulch Trailhead

To I-285
Mount Olympus

Base layer credit: © 2016 National Geographic Partners, LLC. All Rights Reserved.

N

0   Kilometer 1

0   Mile   1

According to Charles L. Keller in his book *The Lady in the Ore Bucket,* the Boy Scouts of America gained their massive land holdings in Mill Creek Canyon—a total of 1,320 acres—from the sole surviving director of the Salt Lake Southern Railway Company, who had originally acquired the land through claims in the early 1900s. In 1923 Russel L. Tracy, a Salt Lake City banker, gifted the Scouts with the construction of a two-story lodge. The lodge was a memorial to his two sons, who had died, and stood for 60 years before it had to be replaced. The camp went through a handful of names before becoming known as Camp Tracy. Today the Boy Scout camp extends over 1.5 miles up the Mill Creek Canyon road. Over the years the Boy Scouts of America have established multiple Cub Scout day camps that continue to host hundreds of Scout troops from across the Wasatch.

it is 0.5 mile from the Pipeline Trail, through the picnic area and down to the road where most hikers park. Parking is allowed either along the highway or at the top of the picnic ground next to the Grandeur Peak trailhead. As the trail cuts through the Church Fork picnic area, you will be enchanted by a stream and a waterfall or two.

From the Pipeline Trail you can continue west, straight through the intersection for Grandeur Peak and Church Fork picnic grounds and on to Rattlesnake Gulch. From here it is 2.2 miles to the Rattlesnake Gulch intersection.

The 0.7-mile descent down Rattlesnake Gulch to the trailhead is steep with a spattering of rocks. This is the last exit point on the trail. From the Rattlesnake Gulch intersection with the Pipeline Trail, it is only 1.0 mile out to the overlook. The overlook is beautiful at sunset and affords gorgeous views of Mount Olympus and Olympus Cove. This section of the trail is exposed to the sun and would be most enjoyed in the early morning or later evening. The hike to the overlook is out and back. Rattlesnake Gulch trailhead is the nearest entry and exit and has plenty of parking, signage, garbage cans, and a map.

Miles and Directions

See the accompanying map for mileage.

Hike Information

To reserve any of the picnic sites available in Mill Creek Canyon you can visit Salt Lake County Park Operations in person at 3383 South 300 E. Salt Lake City, Utah; or reserve on-line at www.slco.org/parks

18 Wasatch Crest Trail

The Wasatch Crest Trail is a daylong adventure filled with five-star scenery and unparalleled vantage points. As its name indicates, the trail climbs to the crest of the Wasatch Range between Big Cottonwood Canyon to the south and Summit County to the northeast. From this one ridge you can see into both canyons and beyond. During July and into August wildflowers add color to the alpine trailside, and the path into Mill Creek Canyon provides a beautiful, green, packed trail through the trees.

Start: Guardsman Pass trailhead in Big Cottonwood Canyon
Distance: 12.5 miles point to point
Hiking time: About 6 hours
Difficulty: Strenuous due to length
Elevation gain: 660 feet
Trail surface: Packed dirt and rock; doubletrack dirt road and singletrack trail
Best season: Summer and fall
Other trail users: Mountain bikers on even-numbered days
Canine compatibility: Dogs prohibited. (Big Cottonwood Canyon is a watershed.)
Land status: Watershed; Uinta-Wasatch-Cache National Forest. The Salt Lake City Water and Utilities Departments and several mining companies own land along this trail, which is part of the Great Western Trail.
Nearest town: Brighton

Fees and permits: Fee to enter Mill Creek Canyon
Maps: USGS Brighton, Mount Aire, and Park West
Trail contacts: Salt Lake County Parks and Recreation, (385) 468-1800
Special considerations: This route is one of Utah's most popular mountain biking trails, but bikes are allowed only on the Mill Creek side of the trail on even-numbered days. If you wish to hike on a day without bikes, pick an odd-numbered day.
Other: More than 60 percent of the drinking water used by the residents of the Salt Lake Valley comes from the Wasatch Mountains. For this reason Big Cottonwood and Little Cottonwood Canyons have strict watershed restrictions. No domestic animals are allowed in the canyons, and hikers are asked to pack it in, pack it out.

Finding the trailhead: From Salt Lake City take I-15 south. Merge onto I-215 east via exit 298. Follow I-215 for 5.5 miles to UT 190/6200 South to exit 6 toward the ski areas. Head east off the exit and follow the road for just under 2 miles to the mouth of Big Cottonwood Canyon Road/ UT 190. From the mouth of Big Cottonwood Canyon travel 14.2 miles upcanyon to the Guardsman Pass turnoff—a very sharp hairpin turn to the north. A sign on the south side of the road indicates the turn, but the road is not easily seen, so watch for it. Travel up this road 2 miles. The Guardsman Pass trailhead is located on the left-hand (north) side of the road. It is a small dirt road that heads north and hosts a restroom and trail kiosk 100 feet off the main road. **GPS:** N40 36.824' / W111 34.259'

The Hike

The Wasatch Crest Trail can be hiked from either end, but I recommend starting at Guardsman Pass, which decreases the uphill climbing required and ends with a pleasant stroll through enclosed forest. You will need to leave a shuttle car at Big Water trailhead in Mill Creek Canyon.

The well-defined Guardsman Pass trailhead has a restroom and kiosk, but the trail quickly runs into a large metal gate. The trail bypasses the gate on the left (north) side. The old jeep trail climbs to Scott's Pass and the intersection with Park City ski resort in the first 1.0 mile. The road continues up the mountain to the cell towers as it climbs to the Wasatch Crest for which it is named. Once you reach the towers, the old access road turns into a single forested track as it crosses the Wasatch Ridge. Most of the elevation gain is achieved in the first 2.5 miles. At the Wasatch Crest the views open into grand vistas that make the hike worth every step. At the right time of year the beautiful wildflowers on both sides of the trail accentuate its magic.

Wildflowers blooming along the Wasatch Crest trail

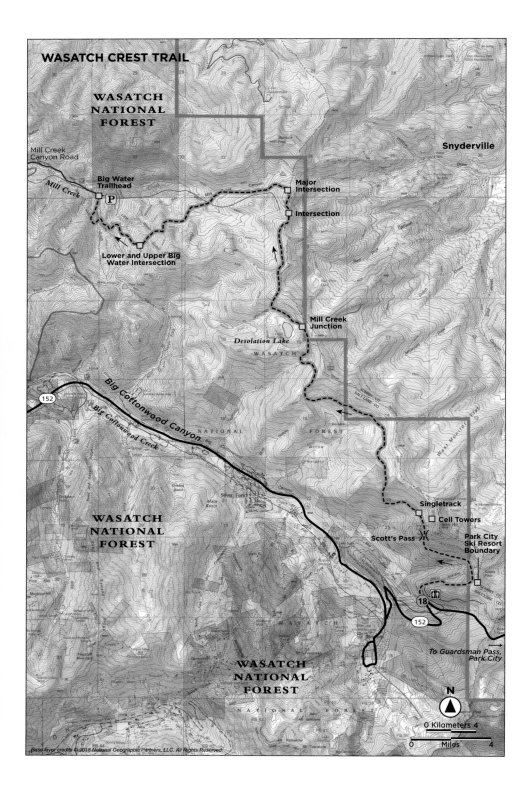

WASATCH CREST TRAIL

WASATCH NATIONAL FOREST

Snyderville

Mill Creek Canyon Road

Mill Creek

Big Water Trailhead

Major Intersection

Intersection

Lower and Upper Big Water Intersection

Mill Creek Junction

Desolation Lake

WASATCH

152

Big Cottonwood Canyon

Big Cottonwood Creek

WASATCH NATIONAL FOREST

FOREST

Singletrack

Cell Towers

Scott's Pass

Park City Ski Resort Boundary

18

152

WASATCH NATIONAL FOREST

To Guardsman Pass, Park City

N

0 Kilometers 4

0 Miles 4

From the crest of the Wasatch, the trail continues to head north and makes its way across the mountain, where it will eventually drop you down into the canyon on the north side. At 2.74 miles you enter the Wasatch National Forest and continue cross-country, where you will find Desolation Lake. The lake is a destination all its own, but from this trail you look down on it to your left.

The last half of the hike down into Mill Creek Canyon sweeps along a singletrack path that is often well shaded and meanders through the trees. This trail is part of the Great Western Trail, and the entire trail is well used and maintained. I suggest using trekking poles to help negotiate some of the rocky downhill sections you'll travel on your way across and into Mill Creek Canyon.

The final 4.0 miles drop you into Mill Creek Canyon, where watershed restrictions are lifted and dogs are allowed. About 1.0 mile from the exit trailhead, signed intersections direct you to the Lower Big Water and Upper Big Water trailheads. Either trailhead is fine. These sister trailheads sit right next to each other on the Mill Creek Canyon road, and it takes only minutes to walk from one to the next. There is parking at both trailheads.

Miles and Directions

0.0   Start at the Guardsman Pass trailhead.

1.0   Reach the first intersection with four potential offshoot trails. Stay on the main road that curves up and around to the northwest, ignoring the smaller, singletrack trail that heads in the same direction. This intersection is the boundary for the Park City ski resort to the east.

1.3   The views to the south open to the Brighton and Solitude ski resorts.

1.5   Crest the ridge and be treated to open, clear views south down Big Cottonwood Canyon and north into Summit County and The Canyons ski resort. You're on the Wasatch Crest.

1.9   The trail starts to curve to the north, still on a rocky, dirt doubletrack trail.

2.3   Arrive just below the cell phone towers; the doubletrack changes to singletrack.

2.7   Cross into the Wasatch National Forest.

4.7   The singletrack winds north again around the mountain. There is a small trail that leads to a rocky outcropping, but stay on the main trail.

5.3   Desolation Lake comes into view on your left.

5.7   Reach a fork in the road; take the right fork to get to Mill Creek Canyon.

6.0   Drop into Mill Creek Canyon.

6.8   The trail rounds to the east side and opens again to views of Summit County and The Canyons ski resort.

7.4   A singletrack trail leads off to the right toward The Canyons ski resort. Stay on the main trail.

8.0   Hit a major spaghetti-bowl intersection for Summit County/Big Cottonwood Canyon/Mill Creek Canyon. This three-way intersection is unmarked, but the trails head east to Summit County, southwest to Big Cottonwood Canyon, and northwest into Mill Creek Canyon. Take the northwest trail and head into Mill Creek Canyon.

10.7	Reach a well-marked intersection. Turning down the mountain takes you to the trailhead on a steeper route; left takes you to Dog Lake. Continue straight for a more-meandering route.
10.9	Reach another intersection; head right toward Big Water trailhead.
12.0	Come to one last fork in the trail. The left takes you to Lower Big Water trailhead, which is only 100 yards or so down the road from the Upper Big Water trailhead on the right.
12.5	Reach Upper Big Water trailhead and pick up your shuttle car.

Option

Start the trail from the other side at Big Water trailhead, 9 miles up Mill Creek Canyon at the end of the road. This direction gives you more uphill. Mill Creek Canyon is located on the far east side of 3800 South in Salt Lake City. From Salt Lake City take I-15 south. Merge onto I-80 east via exit 304 for 5 miles. Merge onto I-215 south via exit 128 and follow for 2.6 miles. Take the 3900 South exit, exit 4. Turn left onto 3900 South and then immediately onto Wasatch Boulevard. Take your first right onto 3800 South, which becomes East Mill Creek Canyon Road. Follow the road east into the canyon where you will find the fee station at the mouth of the canyon. From here it is 9 miles to Big Water trailhead at the top of Mill Creek Canyon. **GPS:** N40 41.081' / W111 38.902'

Hike Information

Local events and attractions: Wildflower Festival in mid-July; www.wildflower festival.org

Camping: Camping is available in Big Cottonwood Canyon (UT 190) at the Spruces Campground, Redman Campground, and Jordan Pines. Camping at Jordan Pines is by reservation only. Spruces Campground, 9.7 miles up Big Cottonwood Canyon, is the largest campground in the Salt Lake Ranger District. Redman Campground is located 13 miles up Big Cottonwood Canyon. For reservations contact www.reserveamerica.com.

GREEN TIP
Hiking and snowshoeing are great carbon-free activities.

Mill Creek Canyon

19 Dog Lake from Mill Creek

Dog Lake is a centerpiece in the maze of trails that run between Mill Creek and Big Cottonwood Canyons. Sitting below higher peaks, it is often passed by on the way to other destinations, but well-worn trails from both canyons leading to the aspen-lined respite nestled into the mountain attest to its destination-worthy status. The wide, packed trail from Mill Creek is easy to follow and climbs amidst a lush alpine environment. Well-traveled by dog walkers, bikers, and hikers, the trail is a Mill Creek favorite.

Start: Big Water trailhead at the top of Mill Creek Canyon
Distance: 5.0-mile loop
Hiking time: About 2 hours
Difficulty: Easy
Elevation gain: 974 feet
Trail surface: Packed dirt path and bridges
Best season: Late spring through fall
Other trail users: Bikers, horses
Canine compatibility: Dogs permitted. Must be leashed on even-numbered days; may be off-leash on odd-numbered days but must be in sight of handler. Dogs must be leashed at all times in campgrounds, on roadways, and at trailheads. Be sure to clean up after your dog.

Land status: Mount Olympus Wilderness Area; Uinta-Wasatch-Cache-National Forest
Nearest town: Salt Lake City
Fees and permits: Fee to enter Mill Creek Canyon. The fee station is at the bottom of the canyon; payment is requested upon exit.
Maps: USGS Mount Aire
Trail contacts: Salt Lake County Parks and Recreation, (385) 468-1800
Special considerations: Dog Lake sits right on the border of the watershed boundary between Mill Creek and Big Cottonwood Canyons. For this reason dog owners don't hesitate to bring Fido up from the Mill Creek side, but no dogs can approach Dog Lake from the trailheads in Big Cottonwood Canyon.

Finding the trailhead: Mill Creek Canyon is located on the far east side of 3800 South in Salt Lake City. Follow 3800 South, which leads directly into Mill Creek Canyon. Big Water trailhead sits at the top of Mill Creek Canyon. The road dead-ends at the parking and trailhead, which is the starting point for three trails. The trail to Dog Lake begins at the south side of the parking area.
GPS: N40 41.065' / W111 38.820'

The Hike

This route to Dog Lake begins at the Big Water trailhead and ends at the Little Water trailhead, both of which are located in the Big Water parking area. Both Big Water and Little Water are gulches that drain into Mill Creek from the top of the canyon. The gulches were named by pioneer settlers, and water still flows in both. The route begins by heading south out of the parking lot on a lovely, wide, packed-dirt trail that

Left: The trail to Dog Lake
Right: Hiker and dog enjoying the trail to Dog Lake

is marked with the Great Western Trail sign marker. As you start out you immediately cross a stream on a small bridge and the trail curves southeast, bypassing a small fork that leads down to the Lower Big Water parking area.

The trail is well shaded by tall trees, which makes for comfortable hiking even at midday. You quickly hit a trail junction. The trail to Dog Lake continues straight.

The trail crosses a stream every so often along the way, so if Fido is on the trail with you he will enjoy a drink and a cool splash and the occasional bridge crossing. At the first bridge there are small trails that lead off to the south of the bridge, but continue on the main trail as it curves to the north.

At 1.4 miles there is another trail intersection. These intersections serve as cross-roads for various trails in the area. Most are well marked, including this one. Continue straight for another 1.2 miles to the next major intersection. This intersection has trails going in every direction. Two directional markers point you to Dog Lake. Either direction works, but I suggest taking the hairpin turn, as we'll come down the other trail on the return trip.

At 2.9 miles the trail to Dog Lake that we didn't take at the last intersection merges back with the trail. From here you descend down the old jeep road straight to the lake. Fall is a wonderful time to enjoy this hike. The colors sweep the landscape, and quaking aspen leaves float like gold coins on the lake's surface. Enjoy the lake and the view before heading back.

On the return trip take a more direct course back to the trailhead via the Little Water route. This route is steeper and rockier, but it allows you to see more of the mountainside. If you prefer, you can simply return the way you came or, when you get back to the top of the jeep road, veer right down the trail that merged with the main road. You will quickly end up back at the last intersection you passed on the way up. Continue straight down the Little Water route. There are nice wildflowers along this route late in summer, and the trail runs parallel to the stream much of the time.

At 4.7 miles the trail forks. Cross the bridge and head west. The trail intersects Old Red Pine Road Trail, which is part of the Great Western Trail. The trail back to the trailhead continues straight, but the area near the Old Red Pine Bridge provides a nice wading pool and hangout area. From here you can see the Little Water trailhead and the parking area.

Miles and Directions

- **0.0** Start at the Big Water parking area and trailhead.
- **0.3** Reach a trail junction; continue straight.
- **0.9** Come to a bridge crossing; continue north.
- **1.4** Reach a trail junction; continue straight.

Dog Lake

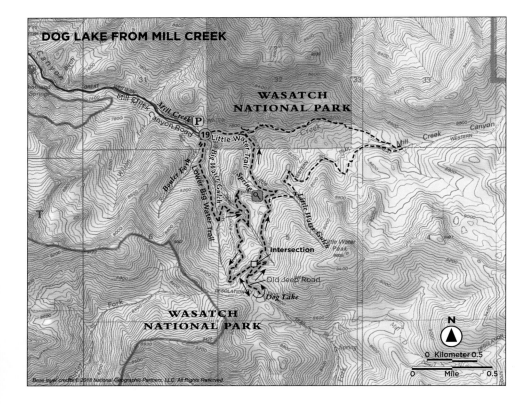

DOG LAKE FROM MILL CREEK

2.6 Reach another trail junction; take the hairpin turn, following the sign to Dog Lake.

2.9 Hit the old jeep road.

3.0 Reach Dog Lake. (***Option:*** Return the way you came for a 6.0-mile out-and-back hike.)

4.7 Reach a trail junction; head left over the bridge.

4.9 Meet the intersection with Old Red Pine Road Trail.

5.0 Arrive at Little Water trailhead and the Big Water parking area.

Hike Information

Local events and attractions: Mill Creek Canyon is dotted with picnic sites, all accessible from the main road up the canyon. Picnic sites include Church Fork, Box Elder, Terraces, Maple Grove, White Bridge, Maple Cove, Evergreen, Fir Crest, and Clover Springs.

Camping: Overnight camping is not available in Mill Creek Canyon. For more detailed information go to www.parks.slco.org/Mill CreekCanyon/index.html. For reservations at campgrounds in other areas, contact Salt Lake City Parks and Recreation at (801) 483-5473.

Mill Creek Canyon

20 Little Water–Great Western Trail Loop

The Little Water trailhead is less well known and sits quietly on the northeast side of the Upper Big Water parking area and trailhead. This well-defined, packed trail twists beneath tall aspen and evergreens, often traveling next to Mill Creek, and explores the east end of Mill Creek Canyon. At the eastern terminus the trail intersects a section of the Great Western Trail and then eventually loops back to the Little Water Trail. The golden aspen, tall evergreens, and lush vegetation make tackling this trail pleasant and cool in summer and colorful in the fall.

Start: Little Water trailhead, northeast side of Upper Big Water trailhead parking area
Distance: 4.1-mile lollipop
Hiking time: About 1.5 hours
Difficulty: Easy
Elevation gain: 850 feet
Trail surface: Dirt path and bridges
Best season: Summer through winter
Other trail users: Bikers allowed on even-numbered days
Canine compatibility: Dogs permitted. Must be leashed on even-numbered days; may be off-leash on odd-numbered days but must be in sight of handler. Dogs must be leashed at

all times in campgrounds, on roadways, and at trailheads. Be sure to clean up after your dog.
Land status: Uinta-Wasatch-Cache National Forest
Nearest town: Salt Lake City
Fees and permits: Fee to use Mill Creek Canyon. The fee station is at the bottom of the canyon; payment is requested upon exit.
Maps: USGS Mount Aire
Trail contacts: Salt Lake County Parks and Recreation, (385) 468-1800; Salt Lake Ranger District, 6944 South 3000 East, Salt Lake City 84121

Finding the trailhead: Mill Creek Canyon sits on the far east side of 3800 South in Salt Lake City. Follow 3800 South, which leads directly into Mill Creek Canyon. Upper Big Water trailhead is at the top of Mill Creek Canyon where the road dead-ends at the parking area. The Little Water Trail leaves from the northeast corner of the parking lot. **GPS:** N40 41.070' / W111 38.800'

The Hike

The Little Water Trail begins as a doubletrack forested trail that heads east, deeper into Mill Creek Canyon. A Little Water Trail sign marks the trailhead. The trail immediately dives into aspen and evergreens—a lush and pleasant alpine environment. Within only 300 feet the trail forks. Continue straight up the right fork. At 0.25 mile you hit the first critical intersection after crossing a bridge. The more used trail curves to the right and continues toward Dog Lake. The trail marker is a wooden arrow that

Left: Trail junction where Little Water Trail splits off of Old Red Pine Road Trail
Right: One of the Mill Creek crossings along the Little Water Trail SHERRY HOLMES

points you in this direction. Do not follow the arrow; instead take the left fork and continue straight ahead.

The beautiful, shaded forest trail follows Mill Creek along its south shore on a packed-dirt singletrack. At just under 1.0 mile the trail appears to climb up the mountain to your right. Instead cross the stream here and follow the trail on the north side of Mill Creek. As the trail continues up the canyon, the incline increases, as do the size of the rocks and boulders in the trail. Keep climbing up to the intersection with the Great Western Trail. This easy-to-find junction is marked with wooden trail markers. Head right, down the trail.

The Great Western Trail is a unique corridor in the western United States comprising braided and paralleling trails that traverse 4,455 miles through Arizona, Utah, Idaho, Wyoming, and Montana. The trail cuts through desert and canyon landscapes, plateaus, woodlands, dense forests, and alpine meadows while linking eighteen national forests and tribal, state, and Bureau of Land Management (BLM) administered lands. The Great Western Trail intersects many popular Utah trails, including this loop.

The most serious contributor to heat-related illness is dehydration. Bring plenty to drink, and sip even when you don't feel thirsty. Drink early, during your hike, and after you've stopped for the day. You won't "feel" thirsty until your body is already 2 to 5 percent dehydrated; your thirst will disappear when only two-thirds of the fluid deficit has been replaced.

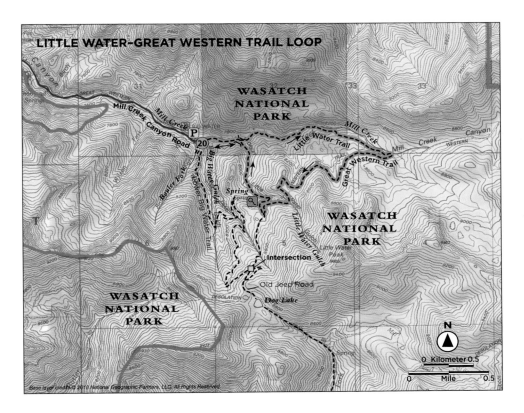

LITTLE WATER–GREAT WESTERN TRAIL LOOP

This section of the Great Western Trail cuts through thick aspen groves and crosses another bridge before coming to a major four-way intersection where the Great Western Trail continues forward, Dog Lake Trail heads straight up the mountain, and Little Water Trail turns down the mountain for a 1.0-mile descent back to the trailhead. Along the descent the trail hooks back into the original trail to complete the loop and then crosses back over the bridge and heads west back to the trailhead.

Miles and Directions

0.0 Start at the Little Water trailhead.

300 feet Come to a fork in the trail; continue straight.

0.25 Cross a bridge to an intersection; continue straight past the arrow sign that points right.

0.9 The trail forks. Cross the stream to the left and follow the trail on the north side of Mill Creek.

1.0 The trail incline increases.

1.6 The trail joins the Great Western Trail.

3.2 Reach a major four-way trail intersection; head right (north) down the mountain.

3.9 The trail hooks back into the original trail and completes the loop. Cross the bridge and head left (west) back to the trailhead.

4.1 Arrive back at the trailhead.

View from the Little Water Trail in the fall SHERRY HOLMES

Hike Information

Local events and attractions: Mill Creek Canyon is dotted with picnic sites, all accessible from the main road up the canyon. Picnic sites include Church Fork, Box Elder, Terraces, Maple Grove, White Bridge, Maple Cove, Evergreen, Fir Crest, and Clover Springs.

Camping: Overnight camping is not available in Mill Creek Canyon. For more detailed information go to www.parks.slco.org/Mill CreekCanyon/index.html. For reservations at campgrounds in other areas, contact Salt Lake City Parks and Recreation at (801) 483-5473.

21 Grandeur Peak

Church Fork picnic grounds welcome you with the sounds of a cascading waterfall—one of the nicest approaches to a trailhead. The popular and busy Grandeur Peak Trail takes you to overlooks of the Wasatch Front and surrounding canyons and valleys. The waterfall and stream flow generously in spring, making the trail especially pleasant. Fall brings gorgeous color, and all seasons bring great views across Mill Creek and the Wasatch Front. The hike climbs up Church Fork to the Mill Creek Ridge and then up to Grandeur Peak for the final 360-degree view. The first mile is nicely shaded; the rest of the trail is exposed and open, which results in great views, but you may want to hike this trail in the early morning or evening to avoid full sun exposure during midday.

Start: Grandeur Peak trailhead at the top of Church Fork picnic grounds

Distance: 6.4 miles out and back

Hiking time: About 4 hours

Difficulty: Moderate

Elevation gain: 2,451 feet

Trail surface: Asphalt, dirt and rock path

Best season: Spring through fall

Other trail users: None

Canine compatibility: Dogs permitted. Dogs must be leashed on even-numbered days; may be off-leash on odd-numbered days but must be in sight of handler. Dogs must be leashed at all times in campgrounds, on roadways, and at trailheads. Be sure to clean up after your dog.

Land status: Uinta-Wasatch-Cache National Forest; Boy Scouts of America land

Nearest town: Salt Lake City

Fees and permits: Fee to use Mill Creek Canyon. The fee station is at the bottom of the canyon; payment is requested upon exit.

Schedule: Gates to Church Fork picnic ground are closed from 10 p.m. to 8 a.m.

Maps: USGS Mount Aire, Sugar House; Trails Illustrated Wasatch Front (709)

Trail contacts: Salt Lake County Parks and Recreation, (385) 468-1800; Salt Lake Ranger District, 6944 South 3000 East, Salt Lake City 84121

Finding the trailhead: The Church Fork picnic area lies 2.3 miles past the fee station in Mill Creek Canyon, at the top of 3800 South off Wasatch Boulevard in Salt Lake City. Church Fork sits on the north side of the road. Hikers must park on the highway by the picnic area or at the top of the picnic area at the Grandeur Peak trailhead parking. Parking is not allowed in other picnic area sites. It is 0.35 mile from Church Fork, through the picnic area, to the Grandeur Peak trailhead. **GPS:** N40 42.043' / W111 44.546'

The Hike

Church Fork gained its name in 1854 when Abraham O. Smoot, assigned the task of building a structure to house sugar-making machines, petitioned the court for control of

Left: Dogs are allowed in Mill Creek Canyon, one of the few non-watershed canyons.
Right: View from the top PHOTOS BY SHERRY HOLMES

the timber in this fork. Since his work was at the bidding of the LDS Church, the fork became known as Church Fork. In the early 1900s the land became part of a mining claim that was later deeded to the Boy Scouts of America, with public access allowed.

Today the lower end of Church Fork holds a picnic ground through which you must walk along a paved road 0.35 mile to get to the Grandeur Peak trailhead on the far north end of the grounds. The walk is a pleasant jaunt past waterfalls and the stream that runs down Church Fork.

Grandeur Peak trailhead is marked with a kiosk, garbage cans, and doggie-waste bags. The trail transitions from pavement to dirt here. A few feet up the trail you'll find a map; cross a bridge and continue 0.2 mile to the intersection with the Pipeline Trail, which runs perpendicular and downcanyon. Cross the Pipeline Trail and head north farther up Church Fork.

The climb up Church Fork is consistently steep and travels next to the stream. The trail turns west 1.0 mile up; the dirt becomes red and the trail heads out of Church Fork, away from the stream to the Mill Creek Ridge. Here the view opens and you leave the shade of taller trees and enter the open exposure of low-lying scrub. Mill Creek Canyon and the surrounding mountains come into view. The trail quickly makes a hairpin turn. Take the turn and stay on the larger, more defined trail. At 1.8 miles the trail surface changes to chunky, orange-and-brown scree.

At 2.4 miles the trail comes to the first saddle at 7,600 feet. To the right in a few hundred feet is a no-name peak that makes a nice place to stop and take in the view. Views of Parley's Canyon to the north and Mount Olympus to the south are additional eye candy from this grand ridge. Continue up the ridge to the left (southwest) to get to Grandeur Peak. At 2.6 miles you reach the second saddle view. Continue climbing east to the peak. The last 0.5 mile is a steep climb to the top. Return the way you came.

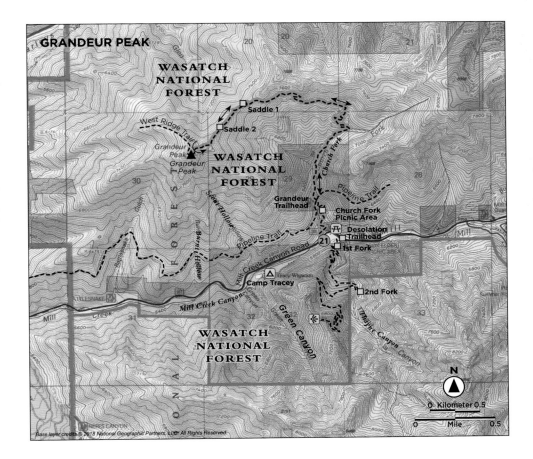

Miles and Directions

0.0 Start at the Grandeur Peak trailhead.

0.2 The trail intersects the Pipeline Trail.

1.0 The trail exits Church Fork.

2.4 Come to the first saddle.

2.6 Reach the second saddle.

3.1 Reach Grandeur Peak. Return the way you came.

6.4 Arrive back at the trailhead.

Hike Information

Local events and attractions: Picnic tables, pit toilets, and drinking water are available at the Church Fork picnic grounds. Reservations can be made at (801) 483-5473 for June 1 through Sept 30. Reservations must be made at least 5 days in advance. Two group sites seat up to fifty people each.

22 Desolation Trail to Salt Lake Overlook

Long, winding, and shaded, the Desolation Trail makes its way up to an overlook complete with rocks for sitting back to enjoy the view of the Salt Lake Valley or to take in the sunset and have a picnic on an evening foray. The trail sits just minutes from Salt Lake City, and though it seems to wind on indefinitely, the shallow climb (due to long switchbacks) makes it easy for children to tackle the trail. Mostly shady, the trail cuts through a forested mountainside as it winds up and out the top of Thayne's Canyon. Make it a romantic evening hike or a midday trail run; this hike is great for both.

Start: Desolation Trail 019, South Box Elder picnic ground
Distance: 5.2 miles out and back
Hiking time: About 3 hours
Difficulty: Easy
Elevation gain: 1,150 feet
Trail surface: Loose rock and dirt path
Best season: Summer and fall
Other trail users: None
Canine compatibility: Dogs permitted. Dogs must be leashed on even-numbered days; may be off-leash on odd-numbered days but must be in sight of handler. Dogs must be leashed at all times in campgrounds, on roadways, and at trailheads. Be sure to clean up after your dog.

Land status: Uinta-Wasatch-Cache National Forest; Boy Scouts of America land
Nearest town: Salt Lake City
Fees and permits: Fee to use Mill Creek Canyon. The fee station is at the bottom of the canyon; payment is requested upon exit.
Schedule: Toll booth at the mouth of the canyon is active from 8:00 a.m. to 10:00 p.m.
Maps: USGS Mount Aire; Trails Illustrated Wasatch Front (709)
Trail contacts: Salt Lake County Parks and Recreation, (385) 468-1800; Salt Lake Ranger District, 6944 South 3000 East, Salt Lake City 84121

Finding the trailhead: Mill Creek Canyon sits at the top of 3800 South off Wasatch Boulevard in Salt Lake City. South Box Elder picnic area and the Desolation trailhead are located 3 miles past the Mill Creek Canyon fee station. The trail begins on the west side of the restrooms. **GPS:** N40 41.854' / W111 44.395'

The Hike

This trail explores the west side of Thayne's Canyon. Originally used for milling, and repeatedly named for those who owned the mills, Thayne's Canyon gets its name from John Thayn [sic] who ran the mill for many years. Thayne Flat, or the South Box Elder picnic area at the base of the canyon, has two main trails that can take you to various spots and extend into Big Cottonwood and Neff Canyons. As you begin the trail, a trail sign a couple hundred feet from the restrooms indicates the many trails

Trail to Salt Lake overlook

that can be accessed from this point. A few feet later the trail enters a forested, covered area and forks. These two main trails are the access point. The trail to the right climbs to the Salt Lake Overlook on the west ridge of Thayne's Canyon. Built by the US Forest Service in 1967, the trail can be followed as far as Desolation Lake in Big Cottonwood Canyon (17 miles), but the long, winding switchbacks usually satiate hikers by the time they hit the overlook.

When hiking downhill, your feet slip around inside your boots. Before you begin a long downhill stretch, tighten your bootlaces and put moleskin on any "hot spots" you can feel.

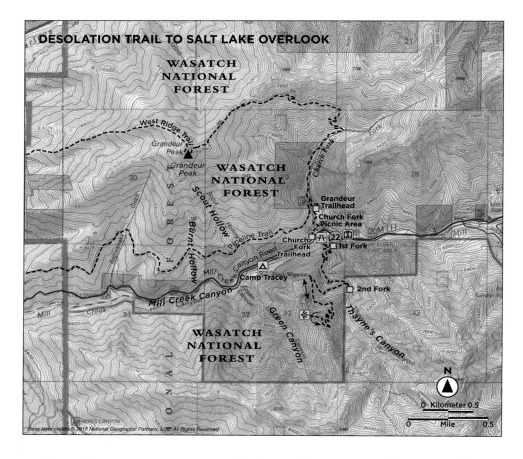

The trail becomes a nicely groomed singletrack. The protection of the trees makes this a good trail for warm summer days. At 1.0 mile the trail comes to a three-way intersection. Follow the trail up and around to the right over rocks and tree roots, continuing to the west. At 1.4 miles the trees open for a moment and views of Mill Creek Canyon open to the north side of the canyon. From here you can see the Pipeline Trail running along the north canyon face as it makes its way down Mill Creek Canyon.

The trail is easy to follow and eventually winds to the overlook. The view includes Mill Creek Canyon, across the Salt Lake Valley, and over to the Oquirrh Mountains. Take some time to enjoy the view, and then return the way you came.

Miles and Directions

0.0 Start at the Desolation trailhead on the west side of the restrooms.

1.0 Come to a three-way intersection; follow the trail right and to the west.

1.4 The trail opens to views.

Tall trees along the trail create shaded areas—nice on hot summer days.

2.6 Reach the Salt Lake Overlook. Return the way you came.

5.2 Arrive back at the trailhead.

Hike Information

Local events and attractions: South Box Elder picnic grounds has six single sites that can be used at no charge. One group site that can accommodate up to twenty-five people is available for $35 a day. Reservations can be made for the group site only June 1 through Sept 30 by calling (801) 483-5473.

Big Cottonwood Canyon

23 Brighton Lakes Tour

The Brighton Lakes Trail passes three lakes: Lakes Mary, Martha, and Catherine. Before you come to the first lake, there is also a spur to Dog Lake, which sits only 500 feet off the main trail. Known for its lush summer wildflowers, this area is the home of the Wasatch Wildflower Festival, and during late July and early August wildflowers typically line the path. This is a popular, family-friendly hike, and you will find people of all ages making the trek to these scenic alpine lakes. This hike often makes the list of Most Family Friendly Hikes near Salt Lake City.

Start: Lake Mary/Catherine Pass trailhead, south of the Brighton Center
Distance: 4.4 miles out and back
Hiking time: About 2.5 hours
Difficulty: Moderate
Elevation gain: 1,100 feet
Trail surface: Gravel and dirt path
Best season: Summer and fall
Other trail users: Mountain bikes allowed but not recommended
Canine compatibility: Dogs prohibited (Big Cottonwood Canyon is a watershed.)
Land status: Uinta-Wasatch-Cache National Forest; Brighton ski resort
Nearest town: Brighton
Fees and permits: No fees or permits required
Maps: USGS Brighton Quad

Trail contacts: Salt Lake County Parks and Recreation, (385) 468-1800; Salt Lake Ranger District, 6944 South 3000 East, Salt Lake City 84121; Uinta-Wasatch-Cache National Forest, 8236 Federal Building, 125 South State St., Salt Lake City 84138
Special considerations: Watch out for moose around the lakes; never approach wild animals. Remember your insect repellent—mosquitoes breed near bodies of water.
Other: Big Cottonwood Canyon is a protected watershed area for Salt Lake City and the Wasatch Front. No swimming or wading is permitted in any lake, no domestic animals are allowed in the canyon, and no camping is permitted within 200 feet of any lake or stream.

Finding the trailhead: The Lake Mary/Catherine Pass trailhead sits at the very top of Big Cottonwood Canyon at the base of Brighton ski resort. Travel 15 miles up Big Cottonwood Canyon to a one-way loop; just continue driving and the loop will bring you to Brighton ski resort. Park in the big parking area next to Brighton Center Lodge. The clearly marked trailhead is to the south of the lodge. **GPS:** N40 35.897' / W111 35.053'

The Hike

The Brighton Lakes tour takes you into a high alpine environment complete with a stream, lakes, flowers, the occasional moose sighting, and wonderful views. Because it is popular, as it has been since early pioneer days, you will almost always find others on the trail with you. The trail is not too steep, and the lakes are fun destinations. Lake Mary was originally much smaller, but it was dammed in 1915 and Lake Mary and Lake Phoebe were combined. The dam, just over 1.0 mile up the trail, helps regulate the water flow of the watershed area. Lake Martha lies only 0.5 mile later but is very different from Lake Mary's granite cliff border and granite island. Lake Martha is surrounded by forest and open meadow. Lake Catherine, just 0.7 mile after Lake Martha, is the highest lake in the basin.

The trail begins with 200 feet of rocky gravel placed between railroad ties and then curves to the right and heads up the mountain. Follow the signs to Lake Mary. The trail climbs beneath the ski lift and between fields of flowers during July and August. Asters, Coville's columbines, fireweed, speckled rockets, lupines, geraniums, giant coreopsis, tie-dye roses, Indian paintbrush, Jacob's ladder—they are all here, and the trail is rich with color.

At the fork for Dog Lake (left) at 0.8 mile, you can also break to the right for your first overlook down over Brighton and into Big Cottonwood Canyon below and to the right. Enjoy both.

Shortly after this point the trail climbs next to a stream draining from Lake Mary. Climb a stone staircase to the lake while enjoying the pleasant gurgle of the stream. From here you get your first sightings of the dam. The trail climbs up and around the south side of the dam to Lake Mary.

Continue along the path that follows the east side of Lake Mary as it heads up the mountain. Lake Mary is nestled at the base of the cirque amidst granite mounds, walls, and crumbling chunks of the rugged mountains surrounding it.

At 1.4 miles you come to a fork in the trail. The right fork takes you to the other side of Lake Mary. Take the left fork to continue another 0.1 mile to Lake Martha.

From Lake Martha you will climb onward to Lake Catherine. Along the trail you will quickly be able to look down to your left and see Dog Lake below. This gives a whole new perspective to where you are and where you've been.

A half mile later (2.1 miles) another fork splits the trail. The right fork will take you to Catherine Pass; take the left to reach Lake Catherine at 2.2 miles.

Blast those blisters: Carry moleskin, adhesive bandages, or gauze and tape. Cut a circle of moleskin and remove the center to relieve pressure on the blister.

Lake Mary

In 1871 William Brighton and Catherine Bow brought their family to the top of Big Cottonwood Canyon. Loving the alpine scenery and the fishing, they built a summer cabin. Within a couple years they built a single-story hotel, for the miners who traveled between Alta and Park City. Catherine was known as an expert fisherwoman, and she fed her guests well. Lake Catherine and Catherine Pass are named for her.

According to the Big Cottonwood Stream Survey Report, Big Cottonwood Creek is home to rainbow, brook, and brown trout and the native Bonneville cutthroat trout. The Utah Division of Wildlife Resources stocks the creek with rainbow trout annually near Silver Lake next to Brighton. The water from Brighton Lakes flows into Big Cottonwood Creek.

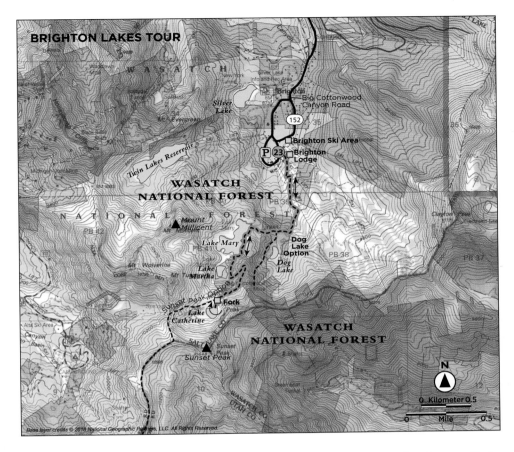

Enjoy Lake Catherine and then return the way you came, or head up to Catherine Pass for a longer foray.

Miles and Directions

0.0 Start at Lake Mary/Catherine Pass trailhead.

0.8 Reach the fork to Dog Lake. Dog Lake Spur (left) is a short 500-foot trek off the main trail. Dog is a small lake that sits in its own little canyon. The quick, easy side trip allows you to take in all four area lakes in one hike.

1.1 Reach Lake Mary.

1.4 Come to the fork in the trail that will take you around Lake Mary; take the left fork to continue to Lake Martha.

1.5 Reach Lake Martha.

2.1 Reach a fork in the trail; bear left and continue toward Lake Catherine.

2.2 Reach Lake Catherine. Return the way you came.

4.4 Arrive back at the trailhead.

Options

Catherine Pass is the mountain saddle located to the west of Lake Catherine. To reach the pass, head right rather than left at the last fork in the featured trail (2.1 miles) before Lake Catherine. The trail will take you to the pass, which connects Brighton and Alta. The trail to Catherine Pass is just over 2.5 miles one way.

From Catherine Pass you can continue on to Sunset Peak, on the southeast corner of Lake Catherine. To reach it, continue up the southeast ridge from Catherine Pass to the peak. This option adds some wonderful views to the beautiful lake hike. See the Catherine Pass and Sunset Peak hike.

Hike Information

Local events and attractions: Wasatch Wildflower Festival; www.wasatch wildflowerfestival.org; usually held the end of July and celebrated primarily at the four main ski resorts in both Big and Little Cottonwood Canyons—near the top of both canyons. A collaboration between the nonprofits Alta Community Enrichment, The Cottonwood Canyons Foundation, and The Snowbird Renaissance Center, the festival is also supported through the efforts of Alta Ski Area, Snowbird Ski and Summer Resort, Solitude Ski Area, Brighton Ski Area, and the US Forest Service.

Camping: The Salt Lake Ranger District manages three campgrounds up Big Cottonwood Canyon (UT 190): Jordan Pines, Spruces, and Redman. Jordan Pines is located 8.8 miles up Big Cottonwood Canyon. To reach the campground turn right onto Cardiff Fork Road across from the Mill D trailhead. The entrance is 0.25 mile from UT 190. Camping at Jordan Pines is by reservation only, and the campground is well suited for groups. Spruces Campground, the largest campground in the Salt Lake Ranger District, is 9.7 miles up Big Cottonwood Canyon. It has ninety-seven campsites with tables, grills, and fire circles. Redman Campground is 13 miles up Big Cottonwood Canyon and has forty-three campsites. There are no RV hookups, and most sites are first-come, first-served.

Camping is permitted in designated campgrounds only. For reservations call the National Recreation Reservation Service at (877) 444-6777 or go to www.reserve usa.com.

Big Cottonwood Canyon

24 Lake Blanche

This is not the road less traveled. Though the climb is strenuous, the trailhead is easily accessible, the trail straightforward, and the destination a scenic glacial tarn at the base of Sundial Peak, which lords over the cirque below. One of the area's more popular hikes, it provides a climb through shaded forest, up canyon meadows, and over glacially cut quartzite to three lakes at the top of the canyon: Lake Blanche and her sister lakes, Lillian and Florence, to the west. Slabs of quartzite and the surrounding forests allow space and time for reflection and exploration once you reach the lakes at the top.

Start: East side of the Mill B South trailhead
Distance: 7.0 miles out and back
Hiking time: About 4.5 hours
Difficulty: Strenuous
Elevation gain: 2,720 feet
Trail surface: Sidewalk, packed-dirt path, rock, boulders, and talus
Best season: Late spring through early fall; avalanche hazard during winter months
Other trail users: None
Canine compatibility: Dogs prohibited
Land status: Twin Peaks Wilderness Area of the Uinta-Wasatch-Cache National Forest
Nearest town: Cottonwood Heights

Fees and permits: No fees or permits required
Maps: USGS Mount Aire
Trail contacts: Salt Lake County Parks and Recreation, (385) 468-1800; Salt Lake Ranger District, 6944 South 3000 East, Salt Lake City 84121; Uinta-Wasatch-Cache National Forest, 8236 Federal Building, 125 South State St., Salt Lake City 84138
Special considerations: Due to the wilderness area and watershed status, no campfires, dogs, horses, or bicycles are allowed. All backcountry camping must be at least 200 feet away from trails, lakes, or streams. There is a limit of ten campers per group.

Finding the trailhead: In Salt Lake City take I-215 south to 6200 South (exit 6). Turn east off the exit and continue along 6200 South as it changes to Wasatch Boulevard for 1.7 miles to the mouth of Big Cottonwood Canyon (UT 190). Turn left (east) at the signal and head 4.2 miles up the canyon to the Mill B South trailhead. The trailhead sits just before the S curves in the road on the right (south) side of the road. If the good-size parking lot is filled, hikers park out along the canyon road. **GPS:** N40 37.994' / W111 43.420'

The Hike

Lake Blanche lies in the upper section of Mill B South Fork. This area has been popular with hikers since the late 1800s when the lakes were named for the daughters of artists Henry L. A. Culmer and Alfred Lambourne. Lake Blanche was named for Blanche Cutler by a friend of Culmer and Lambourne. The names were publicized in their writings and thus stuck. Lambourne was also responsible for the naming of Sundial

Peak. The lakes were called the Three Sisters, and the drainage in which they lay was called Hidden Valley. Lambourne was so taken by Hidden Valley that he once spent a summer there, recording his experience in a notebook for others who came after. Today the three lakes have been dammed and are larger than they were in Lambourne's day.

The trail to Lake Blanche begins near the restroom on the east side of the trailhead. The walkway starts out paved and after 0.25 mile takes off to the right on a trail of dirt and boulders. A sign marker indicates the trail intersection.

Soon after entering the trail, it forks (0.3 mile). Take the left fork and stay on the main trail over the bridge in front of a memorial bench. From here the trail crosses to the north side of the creek and begins its climb up into the canyon. At 0.5 mile the trail enters the Twin Peaks Wilderness area of the Uinta–Wasatch–Cache National Forest. A stream accompanies the trail for this first section as you steadily climb east into the canyon. The trail is well defined and easy to follow.

At 3.0 miles the trail changes from its eastern route and begins to switchback up the south-facing mountain to reach the upper cirque. When the trail runs into a quartzite boulder slide, make a small, sharp U-turn and proceed off the slide boulders to the east, where the trail continues. Within a few hundred feet other large quartzite

Sundial Peak and reflection in Lake Blanche ROBERT BUNKHALL

formations become visible. Make your way across these interesting, glacially carved rocks to stay on the trail. Quartzite is prominent the rest of the way to Lake Blanche. Notice the striations on the quartzite that are still visible from the glacial carving that took place during the canyon's creation.

You cannot see Lake Blanche until you're right upon it. An old dam wall shows past lake boundaries. Follow the wall to crest the rock and look down upon the lake. Head west to the broken dam you can see on the other side of Lake Blanche, from which vantage point you can see Lake Florence and Lake Lillian. The old dams were built in the 1930s to contain much larger lakes. Lake Blanche's western dam broke in 1983. Footpaths are visible around all three lakes.

Sundial Peak is the majestic mountain that overlooks Lake Blanche from the east. It is as much an attraction as Lake Blanche itself. Take time to enjoy the scenery and peaceful lakeside ambiance before returning the way you came.

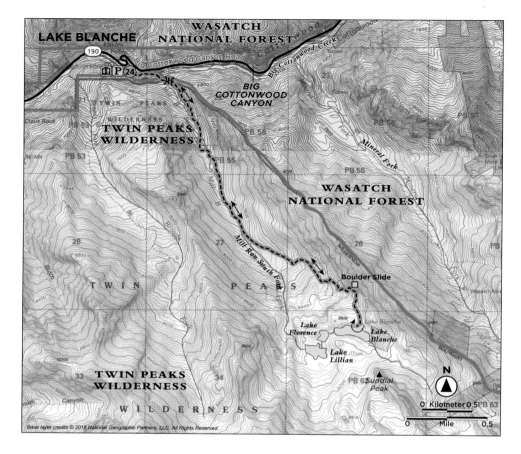

Miles and Directions

0.0 Start at Mill B South trailhead.

0.25 Exit the paved path onto a dirt trail.

0.3 Come to your first fork; head left on the main trail, crossing the bridge.

0.5 Enter Twin Peaks Wilderness Area.

3.0 The trail starts switchbacking up the south-facing mountain to climb to the cirque.

3.1 Come to the quartzite boulder slide.

3.5 Arrive at Lake Blanche. Return the way you came.

7.0 Arrive back at the trailhead.

Hike Information

Camping: The Salt Lake Ranger District manages three campgrounds up Big Cottonwood Canyon (UT 190): Jordan Pines, Spruces, and Redman. Jordan Pines is located 8.8 miles up Big Cottonwood Canyon. To reach the campground turn right

Lake Florence and Lake Lillian

onto Cardiff Fork Road across from the Mill D trailhead. The entrance is 0.25 mile from UT 190. Camping at Jordan Pines is by reservation only, and the campground is well suited for groups. Spruces Campground, the largest campground in the Salt Lake Ranger District, is 9.7 miles up Big Cottonwood Canyon. It has ninety-seven campsites with tables, grills, and fire circles. Redman Campground is 13 miles up Big Cottonwood Canyon and has forty-three campsites. There are no RV hookups, and most sites are first-come, first-served.

Camping is permitted in designated campgrounds only. For reservations call the National Recreation Reservation Service at (877) 444-6777 or go to www.reserveusa.com.

Quartzite boulder section of the trail

25 Willow Heights Trail

The trail to Willow Heights Pond provides a quick, pleasant outing when you want a short route, a quick climb, a picnic in a place of solitude, or a day with the kids. The trail runs through beautiful aspen groves, which makes fall an especially colorful time to hit the trail, and in summer the trees shade the route nicely. Don't be fooled by the shortness of the route; it's still a workout, gaining 600 feet of elevation in 0.75 mile. Enjoy the protected status of the conservation area, and keep an eye out for wildlife.

Start: Willow Heights Conservation Area trailhead
Distance: 1.6 miles out and back
Hiking time: About 1 hour
Difficulty: Moderate due to elevation gain
Elevation gain: 600 feet
Trail surface: Rock and dirt path
Best season: Year-round; snowshoes advised in winter
Other trail users: None
Canine compatibility: Dogs prohibited
Land status: Conservation area; watershed
Nearest town: Brighton
Fees and permits: No fees or permits required
Maps: USGS Park City West

Trail contacts: Utah Open Lands Conservation Association, Inc., 2188 South Highland Dr., Ste. 203, Salt Lake City 84106, (801) 463-6156; Save Our Canyons, 68 South Main St., Ste. 400, Salt Lake City 84010, (801) 363-7283; Salt Lake Ranger District, 6944 South 3000 East, Salt Lake City 84121, (801) 733-2660
Special considerations: The ducks that frequent the pond are so comfortable with hikers that they will nibble your feet. Remember not to feed wildlife—it causes the animals to become dependent on human handouts, endangers them by reducing their fear factor, and plays havoc with their natural diet.

Finding the trailhead: From Salt Lake City take I-215 south to 6200 South (exit 6). Turn east off the exit and continue along 6200 South (it changes to Wasatch Boulevard) for 1.7 miles to the mouth of Big Cottonwood Canyon (UT 190). Turn left (east) at the signal. The Willow Heights Conservation Area trailhead sits directly off the road 11 miles up Big Cottonwood Canyon. The trailhead sign is not visible until you get 50 feet up the trail, so use your odometer to find the correct location. There is a yellow "CURVES AHEAD" sign on the right side of the road right at the trailhead. Park along UT 190. The trail takes off from the north side of the road. **GPS:** N40 37.822' / W111 36.276'

The Hike

In 2000–01 Save Our Canyons helped rally such groups as Utah Open Lands and Utah Growth Commission, in an effort to protect 155 acres of open space up Big Cottonwood Canyon that was being threatened by development. After lengthy

Willow Heights Pond WILLIAM BARBA

negotiations the Willow Heights drainage was purchased from Park City Mines for $2 million. Utah Open Lands oversees the conservation easement for the Willow Heights drainage, which will now be forever preserved. Willow Heights Pond, the surrounding aspen groves, the wildlife that live there, and the watershed are protected under this conservation area. We now get to enjoy the beaver ponds, aspen meadows, and the short but steep climb to the pond.

Willow Heights Conservation Area trailhead is marked with a stone trail marker, engraved to tell passersby that they are entering a conservation area. No vehicles, fires, or dogs are allowed in the area. Because the trail to the lake climbs 500 feet in the first 0.5 mile, the first section is a steady climb through beautiful aspen groves. When it opens up you can look south to Solitude ski resort and see the runs cutting down the mountain on the other side of the road.

After the initial climb, the trail evens out to a nice winding path and quickly breaks out of the quaking aspen (0.7 mile) to cut across an open meadow. The cement floor and foundation of an old barn used by the pioneer Bagley family can be seen off to the right of the trail. The trail leads up to the berm on the other side of the meadow; the pond lies just beyond the berm. At the top of the berm, follow the trail to the left (west) to the edge of the pond at 0.8 mile. The pond area is boggy if you head around it to the right, but the trail to the left circles to the northeast edge of the pond on drier ground. This is premier moose habitat, and birds of prey frequent the area.

Top: The trail to Willow Heights Pond cutting through a beautiful grove of aspen trees
Bottom: Willow Heights Trail as it crosses the meadow PHOTOS BY WILLIAM BARBA

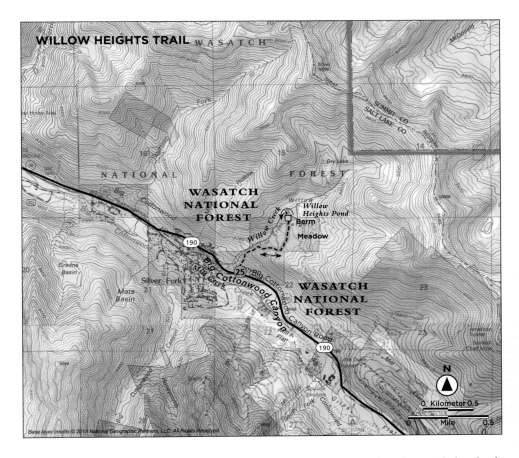

WILLOW HEIGHTS TRAIL

Be sure to follow the same path down on your return. Another trail that leads from the top of the berm and slightly west will dump you downcanyon in a development below Silver Fork Lodge.

Miles and Directions

0.0 Start at the Willow Heights Conservation Area trailhead and begin a steady climb.
0.5 The climb levels out.
0.7 The trail breaks out of the quaking aspen into the meadow.
0.8 Arrive at Willow Heights Pond. Return the way you came.
1.6 Arrive back at the trailhead.

Hike Information

Camping: The Salt Lake Ranger District manages three campgrounds up Big Cottonwood Canyon (UT 190): Jordan Pines, Spruces, and Redman. Jordan Pines is located 8.8 miles up Big Cottonwood Canyon. To reach the campground turn right

Aspen groves in the Willow Heights area WILLIAM BARBA

onto Cardiff Fork Road across from the Mill D trailhead. The entrance is 0.25 mile from Big Cottonwood Road (UT 190). Camping at Jordan Pines is by reservation only, and the campground is well suited for groups. Spruces Campground, the largest campground in the Salt Lake Ranger District, is 9.7 miles up Big Cottonwood Canyon. It has ninety-seven campsites with tables, grills, and fire circles. Redman Campground is 13 miles up Big Cottonwood Canyon and has forty-three campsites. There are no RV hookups, and most sites are first-come, first-served.

Camping is permitted in designated campgrounds only. For reservations call the National Recreation Reservation Service at (877) 444-6777 or go to www.reserve usa.com.

Because of the abundance of fish and wildlife, the Ute, Fremont, and Shoshone Indians all lived in the valleys of northern Utah. The first non-Indian trappers and explorers, such as Jim Bridger, Kit Carson, and Jedediah Smith, made their way to these canyons and mountains in the 1820s. The first group of permanent settlers arrived in 1847 when Mormon leader Brigham Young said, "This is the place." After a cross-country trek to flee religious persecution, the Mormons made the Salt Lake Valley their home.

26 Butler Fork to Mount Raymond

The hike to Mount Raymond via Butler Fork provides a rich selection of eye candy and experiences: lush aspen forests, open views up Big Cottonwood Canyon, fun rock scrambling, 360-degree summit views, and the challenge of a vertical climb combined with strolling through an aspen grove. It's a winning combination that takes you to a 10,241-foot peak. In fall the aspens spread gold across the canyon, and during summer's wildflower season Mount Raymond is dotted with color.

Start: Butler Fork trailhead
Distance: 7.8 miles out and back
Hiking time: About 4.5 hours
Difficulty: Strenuous
Elevation gain: 3,100 feet
Trail surface: Dirt and rock path
Best season: Summer and fall
Other trail users: None
Canine compatibility: Dogs prohibited
Land status: Uinta-Wasatch-Cache National Forest; Walter F. Mueggler–Butler Fork Natural

Research Area; Mount Olympus Wilderness Area
Nearest town: Brighton
Fees and permits: No fees or permits required
Maps: USGS Mount Aire
Trail contacts: Salt Lake County Parks and Recreation, (385) 468-1800; Salt Lake Ranger District, 6944 South 3000 East, Salt Lake City 84121; Uinta-Wasatch-Cache National Forest, 8236 Federal Building, 125 South State St., Salt Lake City 84138

Finding the trailhead: From Salt Lake City take I-215 south to 6200 South (exit 6). Turn left (east) off the exit and continue for 1.7 miles (6200 South becomes Wasatch Boulevard) to the mouth of Big Cottonwood Canyon (UT 190). Turn left at the signal onto UT 190 and drive 8.2 miles up Big Cottonwood Canyon to the small parking area and trailhead on the left side of the road. **GPS:** N40 38.963' / W111 39.707'

The Hike

Mount Raymond is one of the most prominent peaks on the north side of Big Cottonwood Canyon. The well-defined trail runs through a protected area called the Walter Mueggler–Butler Fork Natural Research Area. The area serves as a high-quality control area for the study of natural ecological processes. It was established here in the Butler Fork drainage because although most of Utah's aspen stands have experienced moderate to heavy impacts from mining, logging, and cattle, this drainage has been excluded from such invasions for more than one hundred years. The aspen communities in this 1,270-acre natural research area are as pristine as can be

Left: Butler Fork trailhead
Right: Rocky Ridge leading to the summit

found in this region. Butler Fork was named for the Butler brothers, who established a steam sawmill in the fork in 1877.

The trail begins next to a stream as it heads up the Butler Fork drainage, and as you cross the stream on wooden bridges and low water areas, the stream moves from the right to the left side of the trail. Nice tall evergreens and a spattering of the quaking aspens you will see farther up the trail shade some sections, while other sections of the trail open up to the sun.

The trail enters the Mount Olympus Wilderness Area at 0.4 mile and you reach the first signed intersection at 0.5 mile. Head toward Mill A Basin whenever the trail signs give you the option. The stream continues for the first 0.75 mile of the trail, and at 1.3 miles you break out of the trees and gain a view down Butler Fork and Big Cottonwood Canyon.

At 1.7 miles you get your first good look to the west at the big rocky slab face of Mount Raymond. You also get your first look at some of Big Cottonwood's tallest peaks across the canyon on the south side. Twin Peaks (11,302 feet) sits to the west; Sundial Peak (10,282 feet) sits to the south. This is a nice vantage point for locating and identifying the peaks and drainages that surround you.

At 1.9 miles you enter the aspen groves that stretch across Mill A Basin, and the climb slows to a stroll through the beautiful, colorful aspen. A few hundred feet later a trail junction points you left toward Mill A Basin or right to Dog Lake. Head toward Mill A Basin.

Mount Raymond

At 2.2 miles the view opens to the south. The two peaks on the far west are Twin Peaks, the peak east of this is Dromedary, the next peak is Sunrise, and the peak that is covered with trees and sitting in the forefront is Mount Kessler. From here the trail continues to scoot through the aspen. At 3.0 miles you come to the first unmarked trail junction. The left fork heads down past the foot of Mount Raymond into Mill A Basin; the right fork goes up to the Baker Pass saddle between Mount Raymond and Gobblers Knob. Take the right fork and climb out of the trees to the saddle. Here, above the tree line, the trail heads along the ridge to the southwest and the trail becomes a stairway of crumbly limestone and quartzite. The trail follows steeply along the ridge and winds down to the west side a bit as it makes its way up to the summit. From the saddle to the top you have expansive views the entire 0.7 mile.

As you get closer to the summit, the rock piles become larger and the trail becomes less defined. You can see the summit, so you know the direction you are heading, but the last 0.2 mile is all rock scrambling to make it to the summit. At 3.8 miles you'll have to climb up a sheer striated rock slab to continue. The thin trail picks up again as it weaves through the rock piles to the top.

The Mount Raymond summit is a pile of rocks from which you have 360-degree views west over the Salt Lake Valley, Kennecott Copper mine, and the Great Salt Lake. To the north lies Mill Creek Canyon. For those familiar with the stark steepness of Little Cottonwood Canyon, this vantage point accentuates the difference between the two canyons as you note the rolling nature of Big Cottonwood Canyon to the east. A USGS marker marks the summit. Return the way you came.

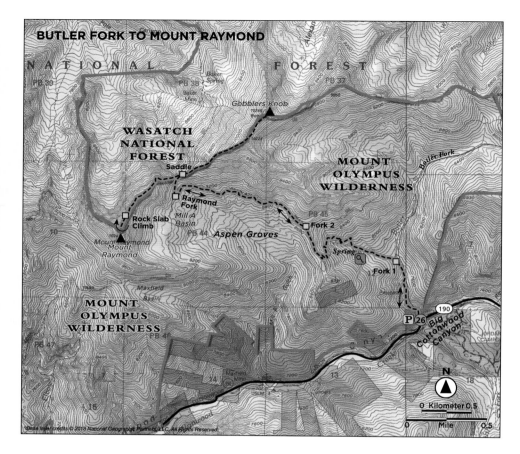

Miles and Directions

0.0 Start at the Butler Fork trailhead.

400 feet Come to a bridge crossing.

0.4 Enter Mount Olympus Wilderness Area.

0.5 Reach the first trail intersection; continue toward Mill A Basin.

1.3 The trail breaks from the trees for views down Butler Fork.

1.7 Enjoy your first sighting of Mount Raymond.

1.9 Enter the aspen groves.

1.95 Come to the second trail intersection; head left toward Mill A Basin.

2.2 The view to the south opens for a ridgeline view of the south side of Big Cottonwood Canyon.

3.0 Come to an unmarked trail intersection; head right to climb to the saddle.

3.2 Arrive at the saddle of Baker Pass.

3.8 Come to a rock slab that must be climbed.

3.9 Arrive at the summit of Mount Raymond. Retrace your steps to the trailhead.

7.8 Arrive back at the trailhead.

Option

From the saddle at Baker Pass you can head northeast and take in the hike to Gobblers Knob, which is only 5 feet higher than Mount Raymond. This route climbs 900 feet in 0.8 mile for a total out-and-back hike of 8 miles. Many hikers will hit both peaks in 1 day.

Hike Information

Camping: The Salt Lake Ranger District manages three campgrounds up Big Cottonwood Canyon (UT 190): Jordan Pines, Spruces, and Redman. Jordan Pines is located 8.8 miles up Big Cottonwood Canyon. To reach the campground turn right onto Cardiff Fork Road across from the Mill D trailhead. The entrance is 0.25 mile from Big Cottonwood Road (UT 190). Camping at Jordan Pines is by reservation only, and the campground is well suited for groups. Spruces Campground, the largest campground in the Salt Lake Ranger District, is 9.7 miles up Big Cottonwood Canyon. It has ninety-seven campsites with tables, grills, and fire circles. Redman Campground is 13 miles up Big Cottonwood Canyon and has forty-three campsites. There are no RV hookups, and most sites are first-come, first-served.

Camping is permitted in designated campgrounds only. For reservations call the National Recreation Reservation Service at (877) 444-6777 or go to www.reserve usa.com.

EDIBLE WILD PLANTS OF UTAH

Have you ever wondered what you might do if you were lost in the woods, you forgot the GORP, and an emergency situation arose? Fortunately Utah is full of edible plants. You must be careful to understand which wild plants can be eaten, as many are poisonous, but here are a few easy-to-identify plants that are safe for consumption:

Wild raspberry: Found in sunny places near lakes, streams, and often roads, the plant looks like a regular raspberry bush and the fruit is easy to recognize. Not only can you eat the fruit but the young stems also can be peeled and eaten.

Dandelion: An infamous weed seen in many a lawn, the dandelion can be found throughout Utah's mountains as well. The good news is that the entire plant is edible: Leaves can be eaten raw or boiled, and the roots can be boiled or roasted. The seeds of the plant are also edible and can even be ground into flour.

Clover: You're in luck—clovers are actually edible. And they're found just about everywhere there's an open grassy area. You can spot them by their distinctive trefoil leaflets. You can eat clovers raw or boil it.

Big Cottonwood Canyon

27 Donut Falls

Donut Falls is a popular, fun, family-friendly hike. With a destination involving the unusual phenomenon of a waterfall cascading through a round hole in the rock surface, it's bound to draw the crowds it does. The trail is under 1.0 mile and easy to follow, but once you arrive there is the challenge of carefully making your way up the stack of boulders that make up the mountain below the falls. An original destination, a little challenge—and all on a trail that can be enjoyed in an hour.

Start: Mill D South Fork Upper/Donut Falls trailhead
Distance: 1.8 miles out and back
Hiking time: About 1 hour
Difficulty: Moderate due to rock scramble to reach the falls
Elevation gain: 320 feet
Trail surface: Dirt and rock; boulder climbing at the falls
Best season: Late spring through fall; snow-shoes advised in winter
Other trail users: None
Canine compatibility: Dogs prohibited
Land status: Uinta-Wasatch-Cache National Forest
Nearest town: Brighton

Fees and permits: No fees or permits required
Schedule: Open daily 7 a.m. to 10 p.m.
Maps: USGS Mount Aire
Trail contacts: Salt Lake County Parks and Recreation, (385) 468-1800; Salt Lake Ranger District, 6944 South 3000 East, Salt Lake City 84121, (801) 733-2660; Uinta-Wasatch-Cache National Forest, 8236 Federal Building, 125 South State St., Salt Lake City 84138
Other: Suggested footwear is a water sandal with a good traction sole. This trail is so popular that often the parking lot fills and cars are forced to park down the sides of the road and hike to the trailhead. This is more the rule than the exception. Plan accordingly as it can tack on another 0.25-mile hike at times.

Finding the trailhead: From Salt Lake City take I-215 south to 6200 South (exit 6). Turn east off the exit and continue along 6200 South (changes to Wasatch Boulevard) for 1.7 miles to the mouth of Big Cottonwood Canyon (UT 190). Turn left (east) at the signal and travel 9 miles up the canyon to the Mill D trailhead. Across the road from Mill D, on the south side of the canyon, is another road (Mill D South) that heads to Jordan Pines Campground. Follow this road for 0.7 mile to the Mill D South Fork Upper/Donut Falls trailhead. The trailhead has parking for fifteen cars; extra vehicles can park along the roadside. Restrooms are available at the trailhead. **GPS:** N40 38.369' / W111 39.077'

Three major physiographic provinces are found within the state of Utah: the Rocky Mountain Province, the Great Basin Province, and the Colorado Plateau.

The Hike

Donut Falls was named for the hole in the rock through which water cascades into an alcove reached by climbing up the rocky mountain face below the falls and ducking under an arch into a grotto. The splash of the water is cool and refreshing, and the site is certainly different from the usual open waterfall.

Closed to public access between 2004 and 2006, the Donut Falls was purchased by Salt Lake County in 2007 and reopened to the public. The trail begins on the south side of the parking lot to the west of the restrooms along a well-worn dirt doubletrack that climbs past spruce, fir, aspen, and pine. The trail is easy to follow and well marked with small sign markers along the route.

At 0.5 mile you come to a nice grove of trees and a bridge crossing the stream. Directly on the other side of the bridge, the trail intersects an old gravel jeep road. Turn left onto this road and follow it south. You'll quickly see a small trail that heads to the right, but stay on the main gravel trail. A short distance farther you will reach a small rock face that must be climbed down to reach the creek. Children and less-agile hikers may need help making their way down this section.

Left: Donut Falls
Right: View of the stream while crossing the bridge toward the falls

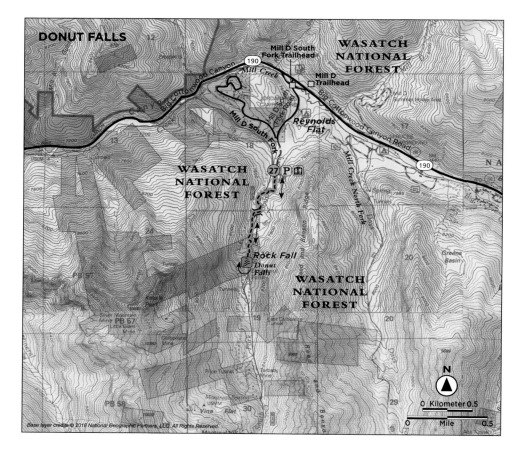

After the descent the trail follows the stream to the base of the rocky mountain face the water flows down. To view the falls, these rocks must be navigated to the top. Exercise extreme caution while climbing these rocks. Water flow is heavier during spring runoff or right after a storm. Return following the same route.

Miles and Directions

0.0 Start at the Mill D South Fork Upper/Donut Falls trailhead.

0.5 Come to a bridge crossing; turn left onto an open gravel jeep road.

0.6 The trail forks; bear left.

0.7 Come to the short rock face you must scale down to get creekside.

0.8 Arrive at the base of the rock mountain below the falls. Scramble across the stream and up the rocks to Donut Falls.

0.9 Arrive at the waterfall crashing through the hole in the rock. Return the way you came.

1.8 Arrive back at the trailhead.

Hike Information

Camping: The Salt Lake Ranger District manages three campgrounds up Big Cottonwood Canyon (UT 190): Jordan Pines, Spruces, and Redman. Jordan Pines is located 8.8 miles up Big Cottonwood Canyon. To reach the campground turn right onto Cardiff Fork Road across from the Mill D trailhead. The entrance is 0.25 mile from Big Cottonwood Road (UT 190). Camping at Jordan Pines is by reservation only, and the campground is well suited for groups. Spruces Campground, the largest campground in the Salt Lake Ranger District, is 9.7 miles up Big Cottonwood Canyon. It has ninety-seven campsites with tables, grills, and fire circles. Redman Campground is 13 miles up Big Cottonwood Canyon and has forty-three campsites. There are no RV hookups, and most sites are first-come, first-served.

Camping is permitted in designated campgrounds only. For reservations call the National Recreation Reservation Service at (877) 444-6777 or go to www.reserve usa.com.

Big and Little Cottonwood Canyons were named for the giant cottonwood trees that grow by the creek bottoms.

28 Mill D to Dog Lake

Whether it's summer, fall, or winter, the trail to Dog Lake from Mill D trailhead is filled with beautiful scenery. Views cross-canyon are a treat on the first section of the trail, while the destination is a small mountain lake where dogs frolic and hikers and bikers relax after making their way in from either Mill Creek Canyon (the only way you can bring dogs in) or Big Cottonwood Canyon. Surrounded by aspen trees and evergreens, fall is a colorful time at the lake.

Start: Mill D Trailhead
Distance: 5.2 miles out and back
Hiking time: About 2.5 hours
Elevation gain: 1,500 feet
Trail surface: Dirt and rock
Best season: Summer and fall
Other trail users: Bikers
Canine compatibility: Not allowed
Land status: US Forest Service
Nearest town: Brighton
Fees and permits: No fees or permits required
Maps: USGS 7.5' Mount Aire

Trail contacts: For more information contact Salt Lake County Parks and Recreation, (385) 468-1800
Special considerations: Wading, boating, horses, and dogs are all prohibited in watershed area. While dogs are allowed at Dog Lake, they can only be brought in through Mill Creek Canyon. No dogs or domestic animals are allowed in Big Cottonwood Canyon. Toilets are not available at Mill D, but you can find a restroom across the road on Cardiff Canyon Road.

Finding the trailhead: From Salt Lake City take I-215 south to 6200 South (exit 6). Turn east off the exit and continue along 6200 South (changes to Wasatch Boulevard) for 1.7 miles to the mouth of Big Cottonwood Canyon (UT 190). Turn left (east) at the signal and travel 9 miles up the canyon to the Mill D trailhead. Mill D is on the north side of the canyon; the turnoff for Donut Falls is on the south side across the road.

There is a large park-and-ride at the mouth of Big Cottonwood Canyon. During peak times it will be best to carpool to the trailhead as it is popular and often crowded.

The Hike

Mill D trailhead is one of the largest and most recognized trailheads in Big Cotton Canyon. Sitting right off the side of the main thoroughfare up the canyon, a prominent trailhead sign and parking on the north side of the road make the trailhead hard to miss. The trail is easy to follow as it is a favorite and well-worn path that leads to two destinations: Dog Lake and Desolation Lake. The first section of the trail is open to the sun because of the southern exposure; then it rounds the bend of the mountain and heads north deeper into the range.

Left: Dog Lake
Right: Hiker enjoying the fall colors on the way to Dog Lake

From the trailhead the trail heads into the mountains and curves to the right heading upcanyon. The southern exposure provides phenomenal views cross-canyon to the beautiful mountains on the other side of the road. At 0.3 mile the trail enters a *Lord of the Rings*–esque clearing with rocks, moss, and tall thick trees. This sheltered and beautiful space houses the trail for 0.2 mile. At 0.5 mile the trail rounds the corner of the mountain and the view opens again as it heads north. Take time to enjoy the view upcanyon to the east. At 1.4 miles a small stream sidles up to the trail. The trail parallels the creek off-and-on as it heads north. At 2 miles the trail forks for Desolation and Dog Lake. Signage shows that Dog Lake hikers must head to the left. From here the trail is a steady climb of 0.6 mile up to the lake. At the top of the climb you will find Dog Lake. Other trails lead around the lake on both sides. You can see the wide trail on the northwest corner of the lake that comes in from Mill Creek Canyon. When you are finished enjoying your time at the lake, return the way you came.

Miles and Directions

0.0 Mill D Trailhead.

0.3 *Lord of the Rings*-esque clearing.

0.5 Trail rounds corner.

1.4 Trail parallels stream.

2.0 Trail forks for Desolation and Dog Lake—head left.

2.6 Reach Dog Lake; return the way you came.

5.2 Arrive back at the trailhead.

Big Cottonwood Canyon and Little Cottonwood Canyon contain significant biodiversity and are home to a number of rare plant species. The Wasatch shooting star is one example.

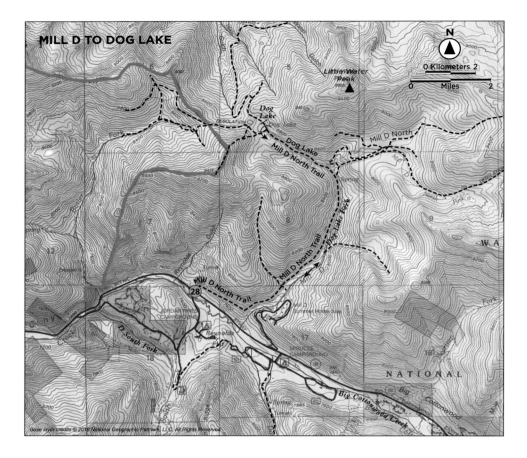

Hike Information

Camping: The Salt Lake Ranger District manages three campgrounds up Big Cottonwood Canyon (UT 190): Jordan Pines, Spruces, and Redman. Jordan Pines is located 8.8 miles up Big Cottonwood Canyon. To reach the campground turn right onto Cardiff Fork Road across from the Mill D trailhead. The entrance is 0.25 mile from Big Cottonwood Road (UT 190). Camping at Jordan Pines is by reservation only, and the campground is well suited for groups. Spruces Campground, the largest campground in the Salt Lake Ranger District, is 9.7 miles up Big Cottonwood Canyon. It has ninety-seven campsites with tables, grills, and fire circles. Redman Campground is 13 miles up Big Cottonwood Canyon and has forty-three campsites. There are no RV hookups, and most sites are first-come, first-served.

Camping is permitted in designated campgrounds only. For reservations call the National Recreation Reservation Service at (877) 444-6777 or go to www.reserve usa.com.

Big Cottonwood Canyon

29 Silver Lake, Lake Solitude, and Twin Lakes

Silver Lake has been the heart of the upper Big Cottonwood area since early pioneer days. Originally called "Plesant [sic] Lake" by a pioneer scout, it has gone through several names, including Fish Lake when pioneers discovered the abundant fishing. This hike begins at what is now the Silver Lake Interpretive Trail—a 1.0-mile-long boardwalk that circles Silver Lake and provides informational signs describing the surrounding ecosystem. This is a favorite family spot, and weekends are generally crowded. From here the route climbs to Lake Solitude, which provides just the opposite of Silver Lake—most likely no more company than a few ducks floating on the pond. To round out the adventure the trail then climbs to Twin Lakes, a large, beautiful blue lake sitting in one of the many granite cirques of these high mountains. Mountain lakes are a refuge for people and animals alike, and though you will find fewer folks here than at Silver Lake, chances are good that a group or two will be enjoying the dazzling show of sun on water. The trail offers the wonders of quaking aspen, wildflowers, mountain lakes, and peaceful evergreen stands.

Start: Silver Lake Interpretive trailhead
Distance: 5.4 miles out and back
Hiking time: About 3 hours
Difficulty: Moderate due to some climbing
Elevation gain: 710 feet
Trail surface: Boardwalk, dirt and rock path
Best season: Summer and fall
Other trail users: Mountain bikers on Solitude ski resort
Canine compatibility: Dogs prohibited (Big Cottonwood Canyon is a watershed.)
Land status: National forest, federal land, Solitude ski resort easement, private mining claims, Salt Lake City land
Nearest town: Brighton
Fees and permits: No fees or permits required
Schedule: Silver Lake Nature Center: The hours change each season according to employee availability. Trail is always open.

Maps: USGS Brighton
Trail contacts: Uinta-Wasatch-Cache National Forest, 3285 East 3300 South, Salt Lake City 84109; Silver Lake Nature Center/Solitude Nordic Center, (801) 536-5774
Special considerations: No wading, swimming, or dogs are permitted in Big Cottonwood Canyon due to its watershed status. Overnight camping is not allowed in the Silver Lake area. Backcountry camping must be at least 200 feet from any water source. Picnic tables can be found around the Silver Lake Nature Center for lunch at the lake. Moose are often sighted around the Silver Lake area. Remember to respect wildlife and keep your distance.
Other: The nature center also serves as the Solitude Nordic Center in winter.

Finding the trailhead: From Salt Lake City take I-15 south. Merge onto I-215 east via exit 298. Follow I-215 for 5.5 miles to UT 190/6200 South exit 6 toward the ski areas. Head east off the exit and follow the road for just under 2 miles to the mouth of Big Cottonwood Canyon Road/UT 190. Follow UT 190 for 15 miles up the canyon to Brighton ski resort. The Silver Lake Recreation Area and parking are on your right as you first enter the Brighton Loop. The trail begins behind the visitor center on the northwest side of the building. **GPS:** N40 36.203' / W111 35.074'

The Hike

Mount Evergreen towers over Silver Lake and the boardwalk below. The trail begins on the Silver Lake Interpretive Trail boardwalk heading to the northwest corner of Silver Lake. Willow, wild rose, and other plants line the pathway. Anglers enjoy casting a line along the boardwalk, and families enjoy exploring the wetland without getting wet.

At the northwest corner of Silver Lake, a large trail sign indicates where the trail exits the boardwalk (0.3 mile) to get to Lake Solitude and Twin Lakes. The path is an easy dirt trail that heads into large groves of aspen.

Silver Lake

The next fork in the trail (0.4 mile) divides the routes to Solitude and Twin Lakes. The right fork, or path forward, leads toward Solitude Lake, the left, uphill, toward Twin Lakes. Take the right fork. If you choose the loop return option, you will be descending down this left fork.

The trail climbs through a thick cover of aspen and fir into the Solitude ski resort. The ski resort offers lift-assisted mountain biking on summer and fall weekends, so be prepared to share the trail with the occasional mountain biker. The trail meanders through the forest and offers plenty of shade, fresh fragrance, and eye candy. At 0.8 mile a number of trails converge on the path. Cut straight across and continue on the middle trail across the mountain. The path crosses beneath Solitude's Sunrise ski lift. Follow the signs to Solitude Lake. The trail is well marked for the mountain bikers and will take you directly to Lake Solitude.

Moose resting at Twin Lake

Lake Solitude is aptly named. The shallow lake lies secluded among willows, pines, granite, and mine tailings. The lake is more of a swampy pond that attracts ducks and other waterfowl, unless it's a high water year. It fluctuates with the runoff. Lake Solitude is at the head of Mill F South Fork and was originally called Lizard Lake by pioneers because salamanders were found in many Wasatch lakes. On the far south side of the lake, an old mine shaft—the Solitude Tunnel—has been filled in with rock. You can't enter the shaft, but if you stand next to it you can feel the cold air rushing out of the earth. Some affectionately call this spot the "air conditioner." To find it, go to the far southwest corner of the lake and look right against the cliff wall (**GPS:** N40 36.207' / W111 36.107').

The trail continues on the dirt road on the other side of the lake as it climbs up the mountain to Twin Lakes overlook. At 2.5 miles, an overlook juts out to the right, providing a wonderful view of Twin Lakes sitting serenely in Wolverine Cirque. Descend to Twin Lakes by taking the trail to the east and enjoy your time on the shore. Twin Lakes sit at 9,472 feet elevation. The site originally held two lakes. They were combined in 1915 when Twin Lakes reservoir and dam was built.

Miles and Directions

0.0 Start at the trailhead for the Silver Lake Interpretive Trail.

0.3 Exit the Silver Lake Interpretive Trail onto a packed-dirt trail heading west into the forest. This is also the trailhead for Lake Solitude and Twin Lakes.

0.4 Come to the trail junction for Twin Lakes and Lake Solitude; take the right fork.

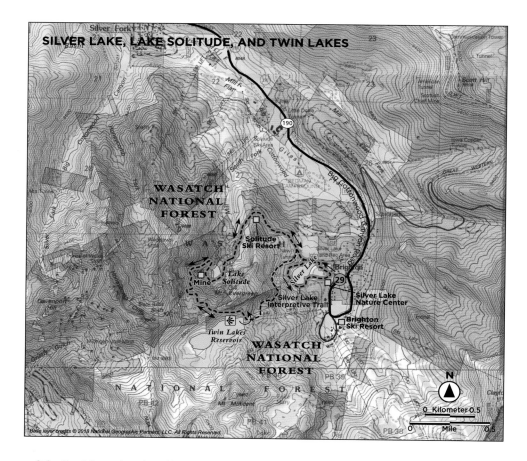

SILVER LAKE, LAKE SOLITUDE, AND TWIN LAKES

0.8 Head forward on the middle trail.

1.7 Reach Lake Solitude.

2.5 Come to an overlook with a view of Twin Lakes.

2.7 Reach Twin Lakes. Return the way you came or take the loop option and head back to Silver Lake (4-mile loop).

5.4 Arrive back at the Silver Lake Nature Center.

Option

To make this a loop hike, rather than turning around at Twin Lakes, head down below the dam on the east side of the lake. The Twin Lakes Trail enters from the northeast (**GPS:** N40 35.932' / W111 35.714'). Follow the trail marked "Easy Out." From here to Silver Lake is 1.3 miles. When you return to Silver Lake, take a right and continue around the rest of the boardwalk to enjoy the full Silver Lake palette.

Wasatch **is a Ute word meaning "low place in high mountains."**

Hike Information

Camping: The Salt Lake Ranger District manages three campgrounds up Big Cottonwood Canyon (UT 190): Jordan Pines, Spruces, and Redman. Jordan Pines is located 8.8 miles up Big Cottonwood Canyon. To reach the campground turn right onto Cardiff Fork Road across from the Mill D trailhead. The entrance is 0.25 mile from Big Cottonwood Road (UT 190). Camping at Jordan Pines is by reservation only, and the campground is well suited for groups. Spruces Campground, the largest campground in the Salt Lake Ranger District, is 9.7 miles up Big Cottonwood Canyon. It has ninety-seven campsites with tables, grills, and fire circles. Redman Campground is 13 miles up Big Cottonwood Canyon and has forty-three campsites. There are no RV hookups, and most sites are first-come, first-served.

Camping is permitted in designated campgrounds only. For reservations call the National Recreation Reservation Service at (877) 444-6777 or go to www.reserve usa.com.

Hiker looking over Twin Lake

30 White Pine Lake

White Pine Lake sits at almost 10,000 feet at the top of White Pine Canyon surrounded by crumbling granite cliffs. The canyon is a glacial trough carved out during the last ice age. Mountain goats trip their way across the granite boulders that surround the lake, and in summer the clear waters draw hikers to the cool recess of the higher elevations and alpine lake (though swimming is not allowed). The trail follows an old jeep road as it winds carefully up the canyon, climbing then, just before the lake, descending 140 feet to the shores of beautiful White Pine Lake.

Start: White Pine trailhead
Distance: 10.4 miles out and back
Hiking time: About 6 hours
Difficulty: Moderate
Elevation gain: 2,425 feet
Trail surface: Dirt, rock, bridges
Best season: Summer and fall; trail usually snow covered until mid-June (use snowshoes in winter)
Other trail users: None
Canine compatibility: Dogs prohibited
Land status: Uinta-Wasatch-Cache National Forest; watershed

Nearest town: Sandy
Fees and permits: No fees or permits required
Maps: USGS Dromedary Peak
Trail contacts: Salt Lake County Parks and Recreation, (385) 468-1800; Salt Lake Ranger District, 6944 South 3000 East, Salt Lake City 84121, (801) 733-2660; Uinta-Wasatch-Cache National Forest, 8236 Federal Building, 125 South State St., Salt Lake City 84138
Special considerations: This trail is one of three trails (Red Pine Lake and Maybird Lakes Trails are the others) that start at this same trailhead.

Finding the trailhead: From Salt Lake City drive south on I-215 to 6200 South (exit 6). Turn left and follow 6200 South past Big Cottonwood Canyon, where the road becomes Wasatch Boulevard. Little Cottonwood Canyon is located 4 miles past the mouth of Big Cottonwood Canyon. Continue straight until you reach the park-and-ride lot at the base of the canyon. From here the White Pine trailhead is 5.6 miles upcanyon, just past Tanner's Campground. White Pine trailhead is a large, busy trailhead with restrooms and parking for forty-plus cars. If the lot is full, cars can be parked along the road. **GPS:** N40 34.530' / W111 40.843'

The Hike

The White Pine Trail climbs White Pine Fork. The name, originally given by miners, came from the logging slide located there in the late 1800s—the White Pine Slide. Today the White Pine trailhead is the most popular and well-developed trailhead in Little Cottonwood Canyon.

Views in all directions are beautiful from the White Pine Lake Trail. This is a view from the trail backward up Little Cottonwood Canyon.

The trail to White Pine Lake leaves the trailhead on the south side and quickly descends a paved path to a bridge across Little Cottonwood Creek. The trail crosses the bridge then heads west and then south as it settles into the canyon. The old Forest Service signs indicate it is only 4 miles to White Pine Lake, but my GPS indicates it is 5.2 miles. The first 1.0 mile winds into White Pine Canyon and comes to the signed White Pine/Red Pine junction with a gain of only 450 feet. Red Pine Canyon hikers will diverge from the trail at this junction. A stream passes at the west side of the junction; many stop for a snack in this area.

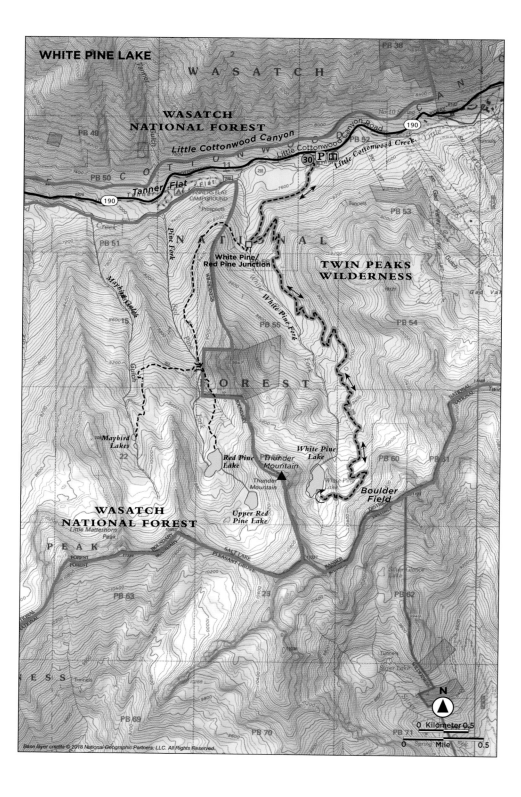

WHITE PINE LAKE

W   A   S   A   T   C   H

WASATCH
NATIONAL FOREST

Little Cottonwood Canyon

190

Little Cottonwood Canyon Road

Little Cottonwood Creek

PB 52

PB 53

Tanner Flat

190

PB 50

TANNERS FLAT
CAMPGROUND

PB 51

White Pine/
Red Pine Junction

TWIN PEAKS
WILDERNESS

N   A   T   I   O   N   A   L

White Pine Fork

PB 54

PB 55

FOREST

Maybird Lakes

Maybird
Lakes
22

Red Pine
Lake

Thunder
Mountain

White Pine
Lake

Boulder
Field

PB 60

PB 61

WASATCH
NATIONAL FOREST

Little Matterhorn
Peak

Upper Red
Pine Lake

PEAK

PB 63

23

PB 62

NESS

N

PB 69

PB 70

PB 71

0   Kilometer   0.5

0   Mile   0.5

Base layer credits © 2018 National Geographic Partners, LLC. All Rights Reserved

The trail to White Pine Lake heads east on an old jeep road that was built during the early 20th century to access mines in the area. The original boundaries of Lone Peak Wilderness Area, drawn up in 1977, were meant to include White Pine Lake, but lobbyists for Snowbird ski resort to the east succeeded in having White Pine Canyon excluded. Though this is not a designated wilderness area, the Forest Service no longer allows motor vehicles along the trail, so the old jeep road is unused and in many places barely definable as a road. Closer to the top of the canyon, the rockfall, streams, and vegetation disguise this winding route to the lake.

The trail follows the jeep road the entire route to the lake. Amidst tall evergreens, trees downed by avalanches, plenty of rocks and rockslides, groves of quaking aspen, and the wonders of a deep alpine environment, hikers climb to the top of White Pine Canyon, crossing several small streams and enjoying a view of some of the Wasatch Range's tallest peaks.

At 4.4 miles you have climbed to the upper reaches of the canyon and entered into the massive rockslides and debris that have collapsed into the canyon from the peaks above. The trail winds through these slides and piles as it climbs the last 0.8 mile to the lake. From here the trail is more jumbled, but the lake lies west over the ridge in front of you. The jeep road makes long switchbacks at the top of the canyon, mellowing the steepness of the path.

At the top of the canyon the road drops down to the shores of White Pine Lake. The lake sits in a large open cirque basin with the crumbling granitoid rock masses and sedimentary formations that make up the area. Originally carved by glaciation, erosion is now the main cause of change, and the area appears to be in a constant state of destruction with large crumbling boulder fields that begin from the peaks and make their way down to the cirque. Return the way you came.

Miles and Directions

0.0 Start at the White Pine trailhead.

1.0 Arrive at the White Pine/Red Pine junction; head left (east), continuing on the White Pine Trail.

4.4 The trail enters the crumbling rockslides of the upper canyon.

5.0 The trail hits the crest before dropping down to the lake.

5.2 Arrive at White Pine Lake. Return the way you came.

10.4 Arrive back at the trailhead.

Hike Information

Local events and attractions: The Wasatch Wildflower Festival (http://cotton woodcanyons.org/events/wasatch-wildflower-festival/) is usually held the end of July and celebrated primarily at the four main ski resorts in both Big and Little Cottonwood Canyons—near the top of both canyons. A collaboration between the nonprofits Alta Community Enrichment, The Cottonwood Canyons Foundation,

Left: Bridge crossing at the White Pine trailhead
Right: The first mile of the White Pine Lake Trail is shared with the trails to Red Pine Lake and Maybird Lakes.

and The Snowbird Renaissance Center, it is also supported through the efforts of Alta Ski Area, Snowbird Ski and Summer Resort, Solitude Ski Area, Brighton Ski Area, and the US Forest Service.

Camping: There are two campgrounds located in Little Cottonwood Canyon: Tanner's Flat and Albion Basin. Tanner's Flat lies at an elevation of 7,200 feet; there are thirty-six sites available. Albion Basin sits at the top of Little Cottonwood Canyon at an elevation of 9,500 feet. There are twenty-four sites, and they fill quickly. The campground is along the dirt road past Alta ski resort, and the basin hosts profuse wildflower displays in season.

Backcountry camping is allowed in the White Pine area; camps should be at least 200 feet away from water sources. Campfires are allowed in the White Pine area.

Remember to take extra batteries for your GPS. If you are unsure of your destination, make sure you have a compass and map along—just in case.

31 Red Pine Lake

A consistent climb up Red Pine Fork brings you to one of Utah's popular high-mountain lakes. Red Pine Lake sits in the Lone Peak Wilderness Area, which boasts of wildflowers in summer and an array of birds to watch throughout the seasons. Red Pine Fork contains two high-mountain lakes: Upper and Lower Red Pine Lakes. This trail leads to the lower lake, but you can add on the upper lake as well. Red Pine Dam was built in 1920 and still sits along the west side of the lake. Lake levels vary with runoff, which varies by season, but the area is always an alpine retreat. Popular with day hikers and often a destination for overnighters, this is one of Little Cottonwood Canyon's most beloved hikes.

Start: White Pine trailhead
Distance: 6.8 miles out and back
Hiking time: About 3.5 hours
Difficulty: Strenuous
Elevation gain: 1,940 feet
Trail surface: Dirt path with rocks and roots
Best season: Summer and fall; snow in the upper elevations until mid-June
Other trail users: None
Canine compatibility: Dogs prohibited
Land status: Lone Peak Wilderness Area; Uinta-Wasatch-Cache National Forest; watershed
Nearest town: Sandy

Fees and permits: No fees or permits required
Maps: USGS Dromedary Peak
Trail contacts: Salt Lake County Parks and Recreation, (385) 468-1800; Salt Lake Ranger District, 6944 South 3000 East, Salt Lake City 84121, (801) 733-2660; Uinta-Wasatch-Cache National Forest, 8236 Federal Building, 125 South State St., Salt Lake City 84138
Special considerations: All backcountry camps must be set up at least 200 feet from the trail, the lake, and all other water sources. Little Cottonwood Canyon is a watershed area, and no swimming or wading is permitted. No campfires are allowed in the Red Pine area.

Finding the trailhead: From Salt Lake City drive south on I-215 to 6200 South (exit 6). Turn left off the ramp and follow 6200 South past Big Cottonwood Canyon, where the road becomes Wasatch Boulevard. Little Cottonwood Canyon is located 4 miles past the mouth of Big Cottonwood Canyon. Continue straight until you reach the park-and-ride lot at the base of the canyon. From here the White Pine trailhead is 5.6 miles upcanyon, just past Tanner's Campground. White Pine trailhead is a large, busy trailhead with restrooms and room for forty-plus cars. If the lot is full, cars can be parked along the road. **GPS:** N40 34.530' / W111 40.843'

The Hike

Red Pine Fork is a drainage on the south side of Little Cottonwood Canyon. Originally called Upper Slide Canyon because of the logging slide once used to bring

Hiker on the trail near Red Pine Lake

lumber down to the Wooley Sawmill farther down Little Cottonwood Canyon, it was quickly given the name of Red Pine Mountain when Mr. Wooley began calling it that. Today the area is known as Red Pine Fork and Red Pine Lake.

The hike to Red Pine Lake begins at White Pine trailhead. The trail descends from the parking area next to the restrooms and follows a paved path down to a bridge that crosses Little Cottonwood Creek. The first 1.0 mile of the trail follows White Pine Canyon through beautiful alpine environs to the White Pine/Red Pine fork, where the trails to White Pine and Red Pine Lakes diverge. Take the trail that cuts behind the trail sign on a singletrack trail. You'll reach the Red Pine Bridge 400 feet past this junction. Cross the bridge and head west over the roots, rocks, and wooden bridges that lead you into Red Pine Canyon.

At 1.4 miles you enter the Lone Peak Wilderness Area. At 1.5 miles the view down Little Cottonwood Canyon opens to the Salt Lake Valley and then quickly, after a few hundred feet, drops back into the trees. This midsection of the trail provides

The Lone Peak Wilderness is a 30,088-acre wilderness area located within the Uinta and the Uinta-Wasatch-Cache National Forests. It was established in 1978 as part of the Endangered American Wilderness Act.

River at the Red Pine/White Pine trail junction

the most challenge as it climbs steadily to the top of Red Pine Canyon. At 2.7 miles you pass the bridge to Maybird Gulch. A trail sign indicates that you must go straight up the side of the streambed to continue up Red Pine Canyon. This section of the trail makes its way across water running downcanyon; the area is swampy for a short while before the trail becomes a boulder-strewn path that isn't always defined. Just make your way up the canyon over the talus and rock jumbles and the trail reverts to a defined singletrack path.

When you reach Lower Red Pine Lake at 3.4 miles, there are plenty of rocks to sit on and enjoy lunch. The dam to the west can be crossed on foot to reach the other side of the lake. Return the way you came.

Miles and Directions

0.0   Start hiking at the White Pine trailhead.

1.0   Arrive at the White Pine/Red Pine junction; follow the singletrack trail that cuts behind the trail sign. Cross a bridge in 400 feet and head west.

1.4   Enter Lone Peak Wilderness Area.

1.5   The view down Little Cottonwood Canyon opens to the north.

2.7   Pass the bridge to Maybird Gulch.

3.4   Arrive at Lower Red Pine Lake. Return the way you came.

6.8   Arrive back at the trailhead.

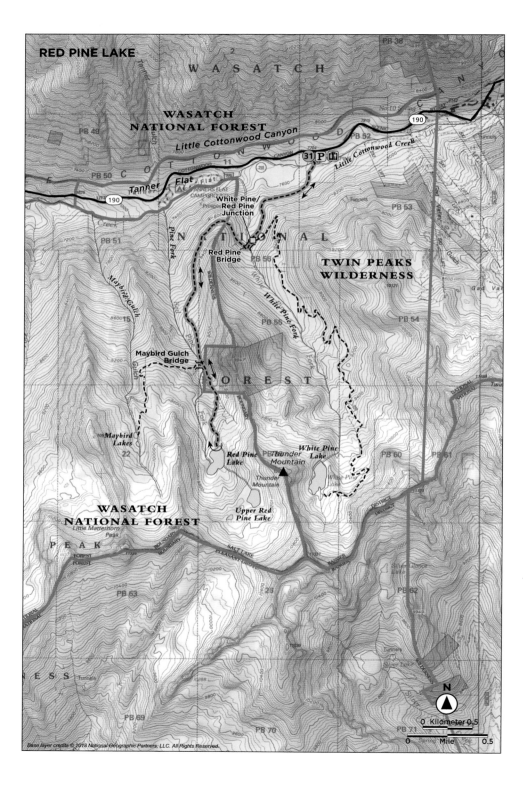

Option

Upper Red Pine Lake sits 400 feet above and 0.4 mile distant from Lower Red Pine Lake. The upper lake is not visible from below. A focused scramble upcanyon to the southeast will take you to the upper lake for more solitude and beauty.

Hike Information

Local events and attractions: The Wasatch Wildflower Festival (http://cotton woodcanyons.org/events/wasatch-wildflower-festival/) is usually held the end of July and celebrated primarily at the four main ski resorts in both Big and Little Cottonwood Canyons—near the top of both canyons. A collaboration between the nonprofits Alta Community Enrichment, The Cottonwood Canyons Foundation, and The Snowbird Renaissance Center, it is also supported through the efforts of Alta Ski Area, Snowbird Ski and Summer Resort, Solitude Ski Area, Brighton Ski Area, and the US Forest Service.

Camping: There are two campgrounds located in Little Cottonwood Canyon: Tanner's Flat and Albion Basin. Tanner's Flat lies at an elevation of 7,200 feet; there are thirty-six sites available. Albion Basin sits at the top of Little Cottonwood Canyon at an elevation of 9,500 feet. There are twenty-four sites, and they fill quickly. The campground is located along the dirt road past Alta ski resort. Reservations must be made at least 3 days in advance at www.reserveamerica.com.

Backcountry camping is popular in this area, but campfires are prohibited. Backcountry campsites should be set up at least 200 feet from any water sources.

GREEN TIP
Carry a reusable water container that you fill up at the tap. Bottled water is expensive, lots of petroleum is used to make the plastic bottles, and they're a disposal nightmare.

32 Maybird Lakes

Maybird Lakes (there are three) sit at the top of Maybird Gulch at the base of the Pfeifferhorn, which towers 11,326 feet above. More like ponds, unless it's a heavy snow year, these lakes nestle in a beautiful area. Granite boulders of all sizes have crumbled from the mountains above and surround the lakeshores. This leg off the Red Pine Lake Trail affords more solitude and is less used but is no less beautiful and a bit more dramatic. The trail takes you to the middle lake, where you can enjoy the surrounding effects of a steep gulch and a high-mountain lake.

Start: White Pine trailhead
Distance: 8.6 miles out and back
Hiking time: About 5 hours
Difficulty: Moderate
Elevation gain: 2,000 feet
Trail surface: Dirt path with rocks and roots, bridges
Best season: Summer and fall; snow in these upper elevations until mid-June
Other trail users: None
Canine compatibility: Dogs prohibited

Land status: Uinta-Wasatch-Cache National Forest; watershed; Lone Peak Wilderness Area
Nearest town: Sandy
Fees and permits: No fees or permits required
Maps: USGS Dromedary Peak
Trail contacts: Salt Lake Ranger District, 6944 South 3000 East, Salt Lake City 84121, (801) 733-2660; Uinta-Wasatch-Cache National Forest, 8236 Federal Building, 125 South State St., Salt Lake City 84138

Finding the trailhead: From Salt Lake City drive south on I-215 to 6200 South (exit 6). Turn left off the ramp and follow 6200 South past Big Cottonwood Canyon, where the road becomes Wasatch Boulevard. Little Cottonwood Canyon is located 4 miles past the mouth of Big Cottonwood Canyon. Continue straight until you reach the park-and-ride lot at the base of the canyon. From here the White Pine trailhead is 5.6 miles upcanyon, just past Tanner's Campground. White Pine trailhead is a large, busy trailhead with restrooms and room for forty-plus cars. If the lot is full, cars can be parked along the road. **GPS:** N40 34.530' / W111 40.843'

The Hike

This trail is one of three trails (White Pine and Red Pine Trails are the other two) that start at this same trailhead.

The Maybird Gold, Silver and Lead Mining Company claim was filed in June 1874. Like most of the other names in Little Cottonwood Canyon, the name of this gulch was derived from its history in mining.

Top: Bridge crossing from the Red Pine to the Maybird Trail
Bottom: Maybird Lake with Pfeifferhorn in the background

The trail begins on the south side of the parking area next to the restrooms and fol–lows a small paved path down to the bridge and official White Pine trailhead. The trail crosses the bridge over Little Cottonwood Creek and then cuts west and south as it makes its way into the steep side canyons that dump into Little Cottonwood Canyon.

Maybird Lake

The trail is easy to follow, and the first 1.0 mile is a pleasant alpine jaunt up White Pine Canyon to the White Pine/Red Pine junction, where the trails to White Pine and Red Pine Lakes diverge. Maybird Gulch is an offshoot from the Red Pine Lake Trail, so from the junction follow the trail that winds behind the kiosk trail sign and heads into Red Pine Canyon. A couple hundred feet up the trail you hit the Red Pine bridge and cross the stream. The trail into Red Pine Canyon begins heading west over roots, wooden bridges, and a rock-strewn trail before it begins the consistent climb into Red Pine Canyon. At 1.4 miles you enter the Lone Peak Wilderness Area, where the aspen and evergreens shade and cool. At 1.5 miles the view down Little Cottonwood Canyon opens into the Salt Lake Valley below.

The most difficult aspect of this trail is the consistent climb up Red Pine Canyon to the lakes at the top. At 2.9 miles and an elevation of 8,950 feet, the Maybird Gulch Bridge exits the Red Pine Trail. Cross this bridge and follow the singletrack trail as it heads west. Once the trail climbs out of Red Pine Canyon, the hike becomes a level, pleasant stroll through the trees as you head into Maybird Gulch. As you travel west you can see across Little Cottonwood Canyon to the steep cliff walls that make up the other side of the canyon.

At 3.3 miles (0.4 mile from the bridge), the trail winds into Maybird Gulch and begins to climb up boulders and roots. Because this trail is used less, there are small sections that are less clear. Stay aware so you don't end up on a side jaunt. As the trail crests the top of the hill, big chunks of granite that define the upper canyon take over

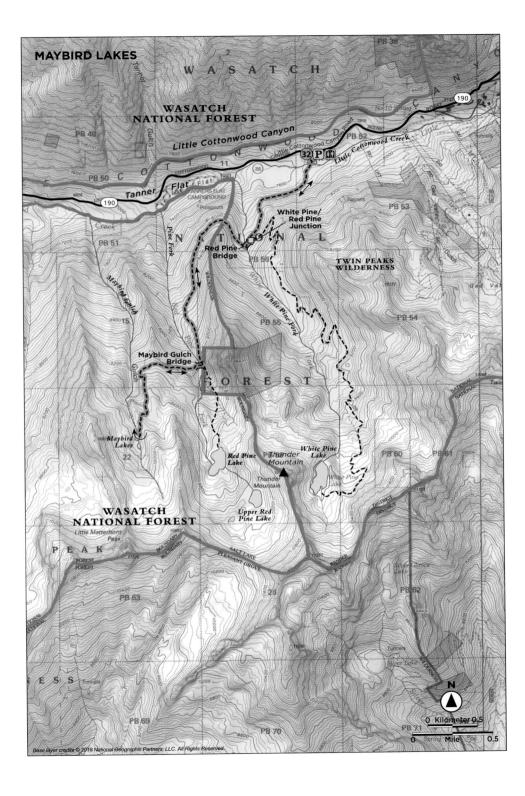

MAYBIRD LAKES

During winter this area is prone to long and violent avalanches. As you hike, see if you can find the debris from past avalanche paths.

the landscape. The trail makes a small dip into the trees below. Maybird's middle lake sits 1.6 miles from the Maybird bridge, or 4.3 miles from the White Pine trailhead.

The trail exits the trees and enters what can only be called the massive destruction of granite cliffs and mountains, as piles of granite boulders take over the landscape. Maybird Lakes are the accumulation of snow runoff that settles in the low spots in these boulder fields. The cliffs and surrounding mountains seem to be crumbling into a state of deconstruction. The chunks of granite cover the mountains' sides, the gulch, and surround the lakes. There is no wading or swimming in these watershed lakes, but you can enjoy the dramatic scenery before returning the way you came.

Miles and Directions

0.0 Start at the White Pine trailhead.

1.0 Arrive at the White Pine/Red Pine junction; follow the trail that winds behind the kiosk trail sign.

1.4 Enter Lone Peak Wilderness Area.

1.5 Views down Little Cottonwood Canyon open up.

2.9 Arrive at the Maybird bridge; cross here and exit the Red Pine Trail.

3.3 The trail rounds into Maybird Gulch.

4.3 Arrive at Maybird Lakes. Return the way you came.

8.6 Arrive back at the trailhead.

Hike Information

Local events and attractions: The Wasatch Wildflower Festival (http://cotton woodcanyons.org/events/wasatch-wildflower-festival/) is usually held the end of July and celebrated primarily at the four main ski resorts in both Big and Little Cottonwood Canyons—near the top of both canyons. A collaboration between the non-profits Alta Community Enrichment, The Cottonwood Canyons Foundation, and The Snowbird Renaissance Center, it is also supported through the efforts of Alta Ski Area, Snowbird Ski and Summer Resort, Solitude Ski Area, Brighton Ski Area, and the US Forest Service.

Camping: Tanner's Flat Campground is located a mile before White Pine trailhead in Little Cottonwood Canyon. Shaded with pine and aspen, Little Cottonwood Creek runs through the campground; fishing is allowed in the stream. Some of the fifty-seven sites are available on a first-come, first-served basis. Reservations for other sites must be made at least 3 days in advance at www.reserveamerica.com.

Backcountry camping is popular in this area, but campfires are not allowed and camps should be set up at least 200 feet from any water source.

Little Cottonwood Canyon

33 Cecret Lake from Albion Basin

The hike to Cecret Lake is a quick, family-friendly trek that is popular for those very reasons. Sitting in Albion Basin, the lake is surrounded by some of the most prolific wildflower displays in the Wasatch. Because the trailhead is located at the Albion Basin Campground, there is plenty of traffic on this short, but wonderful trail. The signs at the trailhead give inaccurate hike distance, but the interpretive signs along the trail impart interesting details about the flora and fauna that enrich the experience. The lake sits in a rock-rimmed cirque below Devil's Castle and Sugarloaf Peak.

Start: Cecret Lake trailhead in Albion Basin Campground
Distance: 1.6 miles out and back
Hiking time: About 45 minutes
Difficulty: Easy
Elevation gain: 598 feet
Trail surface: Dirt and rock path
Best season: Summer and fall
Other trail users: None
Canine compatibility: Dogs prohibited

Land status: Uinta-Wasatch-Cache National Forest, Alta ski resort
Nearest town: Alta
Fees and permits: No fees or permits required
Maps: USGS Brighton
Trail contacts: Salt Lake County Parks and Recreation, (385) 468-1800; Salt Lake Ranger District, 6944 South 3000 East, Salt Lake City 84121, (801) 733-2660; Uinta-Wasatch-Cache National Forest, 8236 Federal Building, 125 South State St., Salt Lake City 84138

Finding the trailhead: Cecret Lake sits in Albion Basin, which is a part of Alta ski resort. From Salt Lake City take I-15 south. Merge onto I-215 east via exit 298. Follow I-215 for 5.5 miles to UT 190/6200 South to exit 6 toward the ski areas. Head east off the exit and follow the road past Big Cottonwood Canyon where it will lead you straight onto UT 210 and into Little Cottonwood Canyon. Follow UT 210 up Little Cottonwood Canyon for 10 miles to the very top of the canyon. Pass all the Alta parking areas and drive past the information booth heading southeast on the dirt road (Albion Basin Road) for 2.4 miles. Drive under the Sunnyside lift and past the Catherine Pass trailhead, and continue down the hill to the Cecret Lake parking lot at the mouth of Albion Basin Campground. Because parking is limited the information booth at the beginning of the dirt road will let you know if the parking lot is full. If it is, there is an Albion Basin Shuttle on weekends and holidays. The shuttle runs every 20 minutes between the parking lot at the top of Alta, the Albion Basin Campground, and the Catherine Pass trailhead. This is a busy area and parking along the road is not allowed. The trailhead is located just inside Albion Basin Campground to the west.
GPS: N40 34.641' / W111 36.802'

The Hike

The name of "Cecret" Lake and the obvious misspelling has caused many a hiker to wonder at its origin. Like most of the names given to the lakes, mountains, and gullies of Little Cottonwood Canyon, Cecret Lake, located high in Albion Basin, derived its name from mining claims. There is no doubt that the claim was supposed to be "secret," as the Secret Mining and Milling Company was hired to work the claim, but many miners and prospectors were marginally literate and spelled words phonetically. The name of the claim was always used as it appeared in the mining recorder's book, and thus "Cecret" Lake was preserved.

Cecret Lake Trail is managed by the Forest Service, and more than 20,000 people visit the basin each summer. More than 50 feet of snow falls here each winter, and the wildflowers of the basin pop their heads out as soon as the snow melts. Over 150 species of wildflowers grow in Albion Basin, and hikers come from all over during July and August to enjoy them.

Cecret Lake

Alta was the first mining community in Little Cottonwood Canyon. The name "Alta" comes from the Latin *altus,* meaning high. What started as a mining camp grew into a small city. Tramways, built for hauling ore down from the mines, were key to the area. The gravity-powered tramways used the weight in the descending buckets to push the ascending buckets up the hill.

In his book *Lady in the Ore Bucket,* Charles L. Keller recounts: "An adventurous young lady, at first identified only as 'Miss S,' on being challenged by her male companion, climbed into one of the tramway's ore buckets and soared high above Alta's north slopes for nearly nine minutes before reaching the upper terminal. When the *Salt Lake Herald* reported this event, a number of ladies in the city made enquiries into who this woman might be, but the editors chose not to reveal her name, only saying she had 'Scaled on foot the highest peaks of the Cottonwoods and explored the cavernous recesses of the deepest mines.'" Miss S, whoever she was, can be counted as one of the first female hikers of the Cottonwood Canyons.

The trail begins just inside the Albion Basin Campground, where a sign indicates the beginning of the trail. Vault toilets are located off to the side of the trailhead. The trail travels next to the Albion Basin Campground until it reaches a T junction with an old jeep road. Head right on the jeep road and quickly pass the first interpretive sign. The trail is easy to follow, and though little side trails occasionally veer in, stick to the main trail.

A few hundred feet after the trail passes beneath the Supreme ski lift, you can look to the south to see Devil's Castle. The jumble of rocks you see scattered across the basin are the result of glacial carving and boulders breaking off from Devil's Castle above. At 0.3 mile the road forks; take the left fork. The right fork goes to privately owned cabins in the area. At 0.4 mile you cross a small trickle of water and continue straight west. The first 0.5 mile of the trail is a nice wandering climb amidst evergreens and seasonal wildflowers. At 0.5 mile the trail crosses a rock slab and the trail begins to gain elevation as it climbs up the hillside to Cecret Lake at the top.

The last section of the trail is a steep climb up scattered rocky switchbacks to the lake above, which does not become visible until you are upon it. Utah is the second-driest state in the nation, and Albion Basin supplies 15 percent of the Salt Lake Valley's drinking water. Cecret Lake is part of that watershed, so wading and swimming are prohibited.

Some interesting mountains surround Albion Basin. Patsy Marley, the peak to the north, was named for a miner and rebel rouser who mined that mountain. Moving from north to southwest the peaks following are Wolverine and Tuscarora; Catherine Pass dips down before Supreme, East Castle, Devil's Castle, and then Sugarloaf to the southwest form the semicircle of the basin. After enjoying the surrounding scenery, return the way you came.

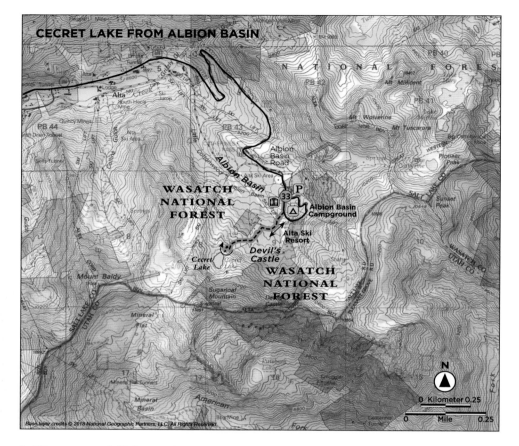

CECRET LAKE FROM ALBION BASIN

Miles and Directions

0.0 Start at the Cecret Lake trailhead in Albion Basin Campground.

0.1 Come to the old jeep road and turn right.

0.2 Pass under the Supreme ski lift, with a view of Devil's Castle to the south.

0.3 Come to a fork in the road; take the left fork.

0.5 The trail crosses a rock slab and begins to climb.

0.8 Arrive at Cecret Lake. Return the way you came.

1.6 Arrive back at the trailhead.

Hike Information

Local events and attractions: The Wasatch Wildflower Festival (http://cotton woodcanyons.org/events/wasatch-wildflower-festival/) is usually held the end of July and celebrated primarily at the four main ski resorts in both Big and Little Cottonwood Canyons—near the top of both canyons. A collaboration between the nonprofits Alta Community Enrichment, The Cottonwood Canyons Foundation, and

The Snowbird Renaissance Center, it is also supported through the efforts of Alta Ski Area, Snowbird Ski and Summer Resort, Solitude Ski Area, Brighton Ski Area, and the US Forest Service.

Camping: The Cecret Lake trailhead is located within Albion Basin Campground. Picnic and camping sites are available for a fee. Sitting at 9,500 feet of elevation, the campground does not open until mid-July and closes in September. Reservations for the twenty-six campsites can be made at www.reserveamerica.com and should be made early as the campground fills early for the year. Please note that no domestic animals are allowed in a watershed area. Fines are levied for bringing animals into Little Cottonwood Canyon.

> **Each wildflower color attracts different birds and insects to pollinate the flowers. Flies and beetles prefer green and brown, hummingbirds are drawn to red, and bees like them all.**

Left: Cecret Lake wildflowers
Right: Wildflowers along the trail

34 Catherine Pass and Sunset Peak

Little Cottonwood Canyon is a steep canyon that holds fewer hiking trails than Big Cottonwood because of its steepness. But when you head to the top of Little Cottonwood Canyon, into the Albion Basin area where the Alta ski resort is located, you find unique geology, hidden lakes, springs and streams, colorful blankets of wildflowers, and a couple incredible trails with unrivaled views. The hike to Catherine Pass and Sunset Peak is one of these. Moose are often seen in the area, as are deer and mountain goats on occasion. A small stream runs through the basin giving life and the sound of running water. The hike to Catherine Pass travels a weaving trail as it climbs the mountain, wanders through meadows, and travels next to the stream on its way up through this alpine paradise. From Catherine Pass you can see the beautiful Catherine Lake, and as you ascent to Sunset Peak you will soon find the other Brighton Lakes—Mary and Martha. From this very peak you will also be able to see Silver Lake over near Solitude ski resort as well. The hike is a beautiful mix of flowers and incredible views down multiple canyons, including Big Cottonwood Canyon, Little Cottonwood Canyon, and even the canyons to the south. Its incredible beauty and moderate nature make it one of the most beloved and popular hikes in the Wasatch.

Start: Catherine Pass Trailhead, Little Cottonwood Canyon

Distance: 4.4 miles out and back

Hiking time: About 3 hours

Difficulty: Moderate

Best season: Late summer to early fall: Snow often does not melt out of the area until July. The gate to Albion Basin usually opens July–Nov.

Other trail users: Bikers

Canine compatibility: Dogs not allowed; Little Cottonwood Canyon is a watershed area and bringing domestic animals into the canyon can result in a fine.

Land status: Uinta-Wasatch-Cache National Forest

Fees and permits: Donations are optional at the Alta Information Booth.

Maps: USGS Brighton

Trail contacts: A temporary summer information booth is set up where the summer road begins at the top of the canyon. They can provide information and maps. Salt Lake Ranger District (801) 733-2660.

Schedule: The gate to Albion Basin generally opens July–Nov; shuttles run on weekends and holidays during busy summer days to accommodate hikers.

Other: Swimming is not allowed in the lakes due to the watershed designation. Others may be accessing Catherine Pass and Sunset Peak from the Big Cottonwood Canyon side. See the Brighton Lakes Tour hike for more on this option.

Finding the trailhead: From I-215 East, take the 6200 South exit and travel a mile east to Wasatch Boulevard. Continue straight on Wasatch Boulevard 3 miles south to the junction with Little Cottonwood Canyon/Highway 210. Take a left at the Y and travel up Little Cottonwood Canyon to the very top. At 7.6 miles you hit the city of Alta. At 8.5 miles you hit a summer checkpoint welcoming the users of Albion Basin. Pass this checkpoint and the road splits; you can descend into Alta or continue left onto the summer road that goes farther up the canyon and Albion Basin. Take this road to Albion Basin. The dirt road winds up the mountain to Albion Basin. At 10 miles you hit Catherine Pass trailhead. Because parking is limited the information booth will let you know if the parking lot is full at the Sunnyside Parking, the parking lot right across from the trailhead. If it is, there is an Albion Basin Shuttle on weekends and holidays. The shuttle runs every 20 minutes between the parking lot down near the checkpoint/booth, the Albion Basin Campground, and the Catherine Pass trailhead. This is a busy area and parking along the road is not allowed. If you are lucky enough to get a spot in the parking lot, count your blessings; otherwise you'll need to shuttle. **GPS:** N 40.58292' / W 111.61844'

The Hike

Sunnyside Parking and Catherine Pass trailhead sit at 9,400 feet in elevation at the very top of the road up Little Cottonwood Canyon. The trailhead is easy to find and right across from the Sunset parking area, which provides restrooms. The trail is clearly signed and takes off from the roadside up toward the pass to the east, passing under a ski lift and winding through interesting geology and fields of wildflowers in July and August.

At 0.2 mile the trail turns left and transitions from a single trail to what appears to be a section of dirt road for four-wheeled vehicles. There is a small arrow sign pointing the way. The trail is easy to follow and passes across and next to the stream, crosses a bridge, and winds its way up to Catherine Pass. At 0.8 mile the main trail continues east while side trails branch off to the west providing lookout points over Albion Basin below and the soaring peaks of Devil's Castle, Sugarloaf, and Baldy standing as sentinels over the basin. At 1.5 miles Catherine Pass sits at 10,195 feet, an 800-foot elevation gain from the trailhead. The pass is well signed and points you clearly toward the pass and Sunset Peak. It also opens up views into Big Cottonwood Canyon with a loud greeting from Catherine Lake down the other side. The view down this other side of the pass is Brighton ski resort during the winter. Just the

The trail to Catherine Pass

Top: You get to pass through this beautiful meadow on your way to Catherine Pass.
Bottom: Looking down from Sunset Peak over Lake Catherine and Lake Martha

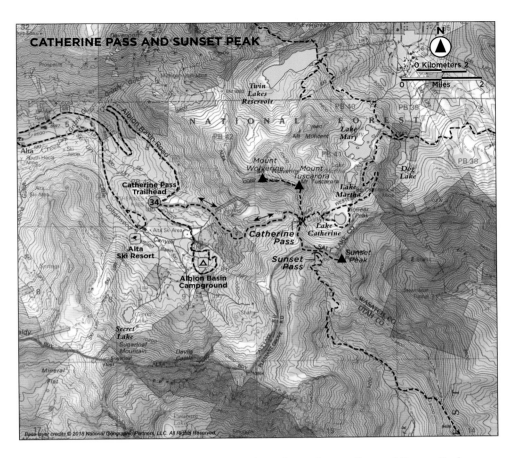

CATHERINE PASS AND SUNSET PEAK

beginning of the scenery, the climb up the ridge to Sunset Pass and Sunset Peak opens incredible 360-degree views everywhere you look. Lake Mary also appears off to your left as you climb. There are numerous side trails where you can get off the main trail to take in the views as you hike. The trail to Sunset Pass begins with switchbacks, hits a sandy section at 1.8 miles, and at 1.9 miles the trail forks. The right fork takes you around and over to the Sunset Pass, while the left fork takes you higher up the mountain, but joins back in with the main trail—it takes you higher for more scenic views. This section of the trail is part of the Great Western Trail, a 4,455-mile trail that runs through five western states and intersects with many of Utah's trails. From here you can see all the way south to Mount Timpanogos in Utah County. There are a number of side trails branching off to viewpoints. Stay on the trail that heads east toward the peak and travels the ridge. At 2.0 miles there is another fork, and the trails

Lake Mary was originally two lakes—Lake Phoebe and Lake Mary. The two were combined in 1915 when the dam was built.

meet up down the road. Follow the well-worn path along the ridgeline providing gorgeous views down both sides of the canyons. The path is a staircase of roots and rocks as it climbs its way up to the peak. At 2.1 miles the trail sharply horseshoes and climbs the last few yards to the peak. At 2.2 miles you will stand atop Sunset Peak and suddenly you can see all the Brighton Lakes, as well as Silver Lake. You can also see down the canyons to the south. It's hard to leave once you're on top. Return the way you came.

Miles and Directions

0.0 Begin at Sunnyside Parking and the Catherine Pass trailhead.

0.2 Trail heads east as it intersects with a wider gravel road.

0.8 Trail to Catherine Pass heads east, while offshoot trails head west for lookout points over Albion Basin.

1.5 Catherine Pass.

1.8 Sunset Pass.

2.1 Trail horseshoes sharply for the summit.

2.2 Sunset Peak.

4.4 Arrive back at the trailhead.

Hike Information

Local information: Albion Basin Campground: For reservations call (877) 444-6777; Albion Basin has been known not to open some years until July due to snowpack. Reservations are highly suggested as the campground is almost always full. It sits at the trailhead for another hike, Cecret Lake.

Local events and attractions: Albion Basin is renowned for its vivid summer wildflowers. The Wasatch Wildflower Festival is held here annually in late July (http://cottonwoodcanyons.org/events/wasatch-wildflower-festival/). A collaboration between the nonprofits Alta Community Enrichment, The Cottonwood Canyons Foundation, and The Snowbird Renaissance Center, it is also supported through the efforts of Alta Ski Area, Snowbird Ski and Summer Resort, Solitude Ski Area, Brighton Ski Area, and the US Forest Service.

35 Ferguson Canyon to Big Cottonwood Canyon Overlook

One of the lesser-known canyons of the Wasatch, Ferguson Canyon is a hidden gem. Access doesn't get easier—the trailhead is located right outside a Cottonwood Heights neighborhood—and the trail has the best of all worlds. Once inside the canyon the trail climbs beneath a lush canopy of shade trees as it parallels a stream fraught with moss-and-fern-adorned waterfalls. You'll enjoy granite cliffs and formations, a fun tree arch over the trail, and ultimately an overview that takes in the sweep of the Salt Lake Valley as well as an unobstructed view into Big Cottonwood Canyon. The trail is a steady and consistent climb—you'll feel like you've had a workout once you get back to the car.

Start: Ferguson Canyon trailhead
Distance: 4.0 miles out and back
Hiking time: About 2.5 hours
Difficulty: Strenuous
Elevation gain: 1,400 feet
Trail surface: Doubletrack gravel trail, rock stairs, stream crossings, silt hill, singletrack, boulders
Best season: Early summer through fall
Other trail users: None
Canine compatibility: Leashed dogs permitted. Owners must clean up after pets; doggie-refuse bags are available at the trailhead.

Land status: Cottonwood Heights, Uinta-Wasatch-Cache-National Forest—Twin Peaks Wilderness Area
Nearest town: Cottonwood Heights
Fees and permits: No fees or permits required
Schedule: Trail and trailhead closed 10 p.m. to 6 a.m.
Maps: USGS Draper, Dromedary Peak
Trail contacts: Trail maintenance, (801) 943-3190; Salt Lake Ranger District, 6944 South 3000 East, Salt Lake City 84121
Special considerations: Watch out for patches of stinging nettle next to the stream. The city is serious about keeping your dogs leashed and can ticket those who do not leash their dogs.

Finding the trailhead: Because it sits right in a neighborhood, the Ferguson Canyon trailhead has an address: 7743 South Timberline Dr., Cottonwood Heights 84121. From Salt Lake City take I-215 south to 6200 South (exit 6) and head east off the ramp toward the ski resorts in the left exit lane. Turn right and follow 6200 South until it becomes Wasatch Boulevard then continue 0.3 mile past Big Cottonwood Canyon to Prospector Drive (7535 South). Turn left onto Prospector Drive and then take a quick right. Follow the road 0.4 mile and turn left onto Timberline Drive (7780 South). The trailhead is on the right-hand side of the road, with a total of sixteen parking spaces on both sides of the trailhead. There are no facilities at the trailhead. **GPS:** N40 36.622' / W111 47.292'

The Hike

The Wild West is full of legends, one of which is the legend of Ferguson Mine. An early pioneer named Ferguson did some prospecting in the canyons east of what is now Cottonwood Heights. According to the legend, one day Mr. Ferguson came out with some gold ore and claimed there was a whole ledge of the stuff. He first reported his discovery to Brigham Young, leader and prophet of the Mormons who had settled Utah. Young asked him to go back and cover up the gold and forget it for the time being because a gold rush would end the isolation the Mormons came to the area for. Ferguson complied. Many years later Ferguson started up the mountain with his family to show them where the gold vein was but had a heart attack and died before he could reach the spot. The purported Ferguson Mine has never been found.

As you begin your exploration of Ferguson Canyon, you'll start out on a gravel doubletrack that leads up and out of the Cottonwood Heights neighborhood, all

Left: One of the waterfalls found along the climb up Ferguson Canyon
Right: Climbers on the rock climbing routes up Ferguson Canyon

the while enjoying open views of the surrounding neighborhood and even over the valley. The trail passes a water tank at 0.25 mile, and then the trail transitions into a singletrack as it quickly descends into Ferguson Canyon. The trail begins next to scrub oak and grasses, but as you enter the canyon the lush riparian area is filled in with ferns, mossy rocks, maples, cottonwoods, and oaks. Once in the canyon the trail parallels a stream that you will follow all the way upcanyon. The sounds of the stream and the supreme shade from the trees make this a peaceful if strenuous hike as you climb your way to the top of the canyon.

At 0.7 mile the trail passes next to granite slab walls, a favorite rock climbing spot. There is a good chance you'll run into climbers along the trail. The trail runs next to granite walls and formations all along this midsection for 0.1 mile. In the climbing area the trail appears to fork. The right fork is littered with rock "steps"; these are belay platforms for the climbers. The hiking trail continues to the left.

At 1.0 mile you make the first of several river crossings on logs. During spring the water will be higher, and it may be harder to keep your feet dry. It's possible the water may obscure the trail during spring runoff as the stream expands. In this case, just make your way up the stream. Just after this first crossing, the trail becomes a steep climb up a sandy section of the canyon. The trail climbs up this loose, light dirt for 0.1 mile passing a beautiful little waterfall on the right. At 1.25 miles the trail comes to the largest waterfall on the route and a second stream crossing that will take you to the south bank of the stream and another steep section as you continue to climb up Ferguson Canyon. Take time to enjoy the lush peace of the waterfalls. This hike is as much about the journey as the destination.

At 1.6 miles the trail horseshoes and turns north and begins the climb up and out of Ferguson Canyon. The last 0.4 mile contains a couple of switchbacks before the trees begin to open and give way to the view. Just 0.2 mile after starting the climb out, you get your first views out over Salt Lake Valley and the Great Salt Lake.

At 1.7 miles the trail comes to a three-way intersection; head right (east). There are two nice viewpoints before you reach the end of the trail. Enjoy the views that reach all the way to downtown Salt Lake City to the north and south to the Kennecott Copper Mine. The Oquirrh Mountains lie to the west, and the Salt Lake Valley spreads between them.

At the end of the trail (2.0 miles) you are treated to a view directly into Big Cottonwood Canyon. From here you can see the cars snaking their way up the canyon and the park-and-ride lot at the bottom of the canyon, as well as all the aforementioned sights. One of my favorite views from here is back down Ferguson Canyon, where you can gain an appreciation of all you have just hiked through: the water tank, the canopy of trees, and the steady climb you just conquered. It's fun to see your route from the bird's-eye perspective. The trail ends at the overlook. Return the way you came.

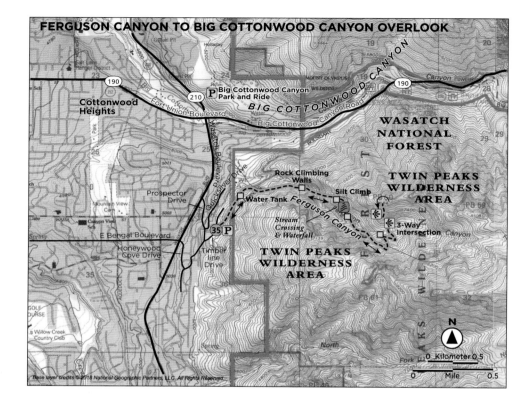

Miles and Directions

0.0 Start at the Ferguson Canyon trailhead.

0.25 Pass a water tank.

0.7 Reach the rock climbing walls.

1.0 Cross the river on logs and begin a steep, sandy climb up the trail.

1.25 Come to a waterfall and the second stream crossing.

1.6 The trail begins to climb out of Ferguson Canyon toward the overlook.

1.8 Reach a nice viewpoint.

2.0 The trail ends at Big Cottonwood Canyon overlook. Return the way you came.

4.0 Arrive back at the trailhead.

Hike Information

Local events and attractions: Wasatch Wildflower Festival: http://cottonwood canyons.org/events/wasatch-wildflower-festival/

Camping: Campgrounds can be found up Big Cottonwood Canyon to the north of Ferguson Canyon, or in Little Cottonwood Canyon to the south. See trail write-ups in those canyons to pinpoint a specific campground that works for you.

36 Mormon Pioneer Trail

The West was settled by the strong and hardy who survived the grueling work of pushing handcarts, driving wagons, and riding horses over 1,400 miles to reach the new territory. This hike follows a historic trail that was first cut by the emigrant Donner-Reed party; a year later the same route was followed by the Mormon pioneers who followed Brigham Young to their new Zion. The trail was then used by the Pony Express, miners, California gold seekers, the West's original telegraph line, and a host of other hardy pioneers, including 70,000 Mormons. A walk back through history, this trail climbs Little Emigration Canyon to Big Mountain Pass where Brigham Young was reported to have said, "This is the place. Drive on." Running next to a stream with old beaver ponds and regular wildlife sightings, including moose and deer, you can hike in 5 hours what took the Donner-Reed party 13 days and the Mormons 6.

Start: Mormon Flat
Distance: 9.6 miles out and back
Hiking time: About 5 hours
Difficulty: Moderate
Elevation gain: 1,400 feet
Trail surface: Dirt path, bridges, stream crossings, gravel
Best season: Summer through fall
Other trail users: Bikers and horses; nonmotorized use only
Canine compatibility: Leashed dogs permitted up to Big Mountain Pass; once you reach the pass you will be in watershed area where dogs are prohibited.

Land status: National Historic Trail
Nearest town: Jeremy Ranch
Fees and permits: Parking fee
Schedule: Gates to Big Mountain and Mormon Flat closed during winter
Maps: USGS Mountain Dell; National Mormon Pioneer route maps available from the National Park Service by calling (801) 741-1012
Trail contacts: National Park Service, Utah Office; (801) 741-1021
Special considerations: Hiking poles are handy for the stream crossings.

Finding the trailhead: From Salt Lake City take I-80 east to Jeremy Ranch (exit 141). Turn left off the exit ramp, cross under I-80, and then take your first left onto Rasmussen Road. Continue on Rasmussen and take the first right out of the roundabout onto Jeremy Ranch Road. Continue past the golf course and onto the dirt road for 4.3 miles where you will pass through a large gate with signs telling you that you are passing through private land. The Mormon Flat trailhead is at 5 miles. There are restrooms at the trailhead and fifteen parking slots. Parking is also available along the road. **GPS:** N40 48.921' / W111 35.099'

The Hike

What is now known as Mormon Flat—a trailhead, group campsite, and picnic ground—was once a defensive site of the Mormon militia where they built up stone walls that can still be seen on the ridge to the west. Ripe with history, this trail begins by crossing East Canyon Creek on a bridge and making its way 0.2 mile through a riparian area complete with willows taller than a human. In spring this area is occasionally swampy with water, and the crossing can be dirty. As you come out of the willows, you'll find the mouth of Little Emigration Canyon and another set of trail markers. Pass through the cattle-control gate and step onto the path that so many others before you have trod as they made history.

The trail up Little Emigration Canyon repeatedly crosses the stream as it makes its way to Big Mountain Pass. During spring, winter runoff increases the water you'll find along the trail. Be prepared for many stream crossings during that time. Water flow varies by the season.

At 1.7 miles come to a marker for Pioneer Camp 1. The Donner-Reed party were the first to camp here. They called it 1-Mile Camp and stayed for 3 or 4 days while they cut trail.

Old beaver dams can be found all along the central portion of the trail. Keep an eye out for moose also; the area is prime moose habitat. Moose deserve your caution and respect. They are strong and can be dangerous if they feel threatened. If water is high in spring, at 2.8 miles the trail appears to dead-end into a pond. Head to the left, making your way around the pond, and pick up the trail again on the far side.

Farther up the canyon the forest becomes denser and the trees grow taller; evergreens are more prolific, and the alpine environment becomes even richer.

At 4.2 miles the trail crosses a natural land dam that the stream cuts under. The trail crosses on top of this dam and then proceeds away from the stream for the last 0.5 mile—the steepest section of the trail. The pioneers had no idea that the steepest, most sustained climb of their journey would come on this last push into the Salt Lake Valley. In 1846 the Donner-Reed party crested this hill; on July 19, 1847, Mormon scouts Orson Pratt and John Brown first climbed the mountain; and on July 23, 1847, Brigham Young followed with his first group of religious emigrants. Today this last 0.5 mile climbs beneath a set of power lines.

Big Mountain Pass can also be accessed by driving up East Canyon, where there's an established trailhead with restrooms and benches for taking in the surrounding view, including that first sight of the Salt Lake Valley that let the pioneers know they had arrived. The trailhead also hosts a historic marker and sits across the road from tall satellite towers. The Great Western Trail runs beneath the towers.

From here you can do as the pioneers did, lock your wagon wheels with chains and slide down the mountain to Little Dell Reservoir (Option 2), or you can retrace your route to Mormon Flat trailhead. The continuation of the Mormon Trail to Little Dell Reservoir leaves Big Mountain Pass on the south side of the parking area. A sign marks the trail.

Mormon Pioneer Trail

The Mormon migration began in Nauvoo, Illinois, and the first group was 13,000 strong. Many pioneers died as they made their way across the country, pushing handcarts and driving wagons pulled by oxen. As you hike this trail, imagine the difficulty of cutting a path up this mountain. It took the Donner-Reed party 13 days to cut the route through Little Emigration Canyon.

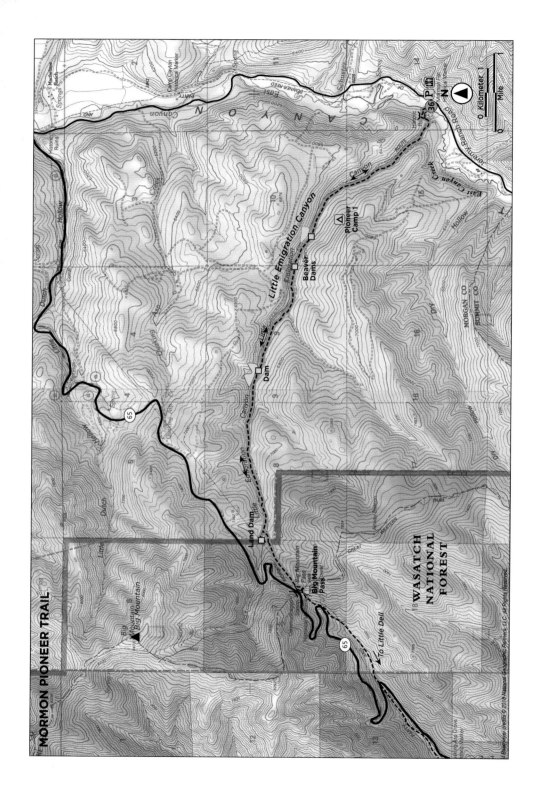

MORMON PIONEER TRAIL

Left: The Mormon Pioneer Trail summits at Big Mountain Pass
Right: Hikers enjoying the walk through the trees

Miles and Directions

0.0   Begin hiking from Mormon Flat trailhead.

0.2   Exit the riparian area; pass through a cattle gate and meet up with the historic trail.

1.7   Reach the site of Pioneer Camp 1.

4.2   The trail crosses the stream on a natural land dam.

4.8   Reach Big Mountain Pass. Return the way you came.

9.6   Arrive back at Mormon Flat trailhead.

Options

Option 1: To make this a one-way (4.8-mile) hike, leave a shuttle car at Big Mountain Pass. To reach the pass: from I-80 eastbound, take exit 134 UT 65 East Canyon. Turn left on UT 65 and go 8.4 miles to Big Mountain Pass. This road is closed seasonally from Nov through May; exact dates depend on snow pack.

Option 2: To hike the full Mormon Pioneer route down to Little Dell Reservoir, leave a shuttle car at the Little Dell recreation area parking lot. When you reach Big Mountain Pass, continue on the trail that heads south out of the parking lot. A wooden marker on the trail says "MORMON PIONEER TRAIL." This full route from Mormon Flat to the Little Dell trailhead is 9.1 miles.

Hike Information

Camping: Camping at Mormon Flat (capacity 100) is by reservation only. Picnic tables and restrooms. Call (800) 322-3770 for more information.

37 Lambs Canyon to Mill Creek Ridge

Lambs Canyon does not have the busy notoriety of the trails located in the larger canyons of the Wasatch, making it one of the most quiet and remote escapes with an easy-access trailhead. In a protected, narrow canyon, the trail winds beneath tall, straight evergreens and aspen accompanied by birdsong and the jangle of the stream. This trail climbs to the top of the canyon and looks down into Mill Creek Canyon on the other side of the ridge. Alpine beauty at its best, this lovely escape is one of my favorite hikes.

Start: Lambs Canyon trailhead
Distance: 4.2 miles out and back
Hiking time: About 2.5 hours
Difficulty: Moderate
Elevation gain: 1,450 feet
Trail surface: Packed-dirt and rock path
Best season: Summer and fall
Other trail users: None
Canine compatibility: Dogs prohibited
Land status: Uinta-Wasatch-Cache National Forest

Nearest town: Salt Lake City, Park City
Fees and permits: No fees or permits required
Maps: USGS Mount Aire; Trails Illustrated Wasatch Front (709)
Trail contacts: Salt Lake County Parks and Recreation, (385) 468-1800; Salt Lake Ranger District, 6944 South 3000 East, Salt Lake City 84121; Uinta-Wasatch-Cache National Forest, 8236 Federal Building, 125 South State St., Salt Lake City 84138

Finding the trailhead: From Salt Lake City follow I-80 east toward Park City, continuing through Parley's Canyon for 7.3 miles to the Lambs Canyon exit (exit 137). The trailhead is located 1.7 miles from the exit up Lambs Canyon on a narrow but well-maintained road. The trail starts on the right (west) side of the road. Parking and a restroom are available on the left (east) side of the road across from the trailhead. **GPS:** N40 43.274' / W111 39.48'

The Hike

Lambs Canyon Trail climbs up a tributary canyon that dumps into Lambs Canyon. From the trailhead the trail crosses a small bridge over the stream and then curves south, cutting through a rich alpine environment. After 0.25 mile the trail curves west and begins the climb west into the side canyon. Surrounded by tall subalpine fir, quaking aspen, and shrubs (even the buckbrush is big), the peaceful trail follows the stream for the first 1.0 mile before the spring disappears into the ground. During spring runoff the stream may continue farther up the canyon, but whether it is wet or dry, the streambed lies to the south of the trail the entire way up the side canyon.

Trail up Lambs Canyon ROBERT BUNKHALL

The trail climbs gradually to the top of the narrowing gulch and at 1.7 miles crosses the streambed, where it quickly hops to the south side of the canyon. The trail climbs out of the canyon on leisurely switchbacks up the face and then follows a straight stretch amidst tall, shady evergreens to the ridge overlooking Mill Creek Canyon. The overlook is a large, flat area with a trail junction sign. Enjoy views down Mill Creek Canyon into Salt Lake Valley and over the Great Salt Lake.

Lambs Canyon is a combination of land managed by the US Forest Service and private lands higher up the canyon. These private lands are gated off. At 6,300 feet, the mouth of Lambs Canyon sits higher than other Wasatch canyons, which means it has cooler daytime temperatures. This canyon is known for the variety of butterfly species that can be found here. Lambs Canyon is considered part of Salt Lake City's watershed, so dogs and horses are prohibited.

Lambs Canyon began to be used for its timber resources in the mid to late 1800s. Charles Decker installed the first steam sawmill in the territory here in 1864.

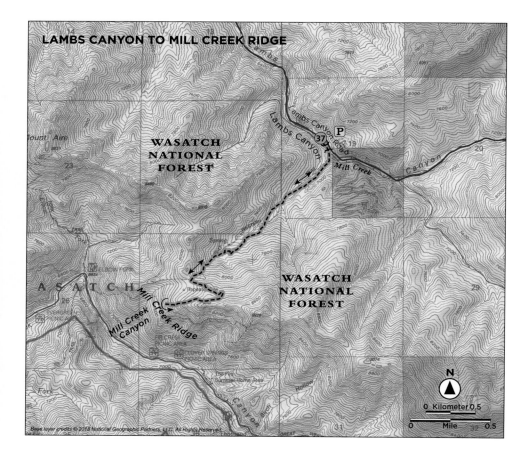

Miles and Directions

0.0   Start at Lambs Canyon trailhead.

0.25 The trail winds west and heads upcanyon.

1.7   Trail crosses to the south side of the canyon.

1.8   The view opens to the east.

2.1   Reach the ridge between Lambs and Mill Creek Canyons. Return the way you came.

4.2   Arrive back at the trailhead.

Option

From the ridge between Lambs and Mill Creek Canyons, you can continue into Mill Creek Canyon. The trail ends in Mill Creek Canyon at the Elbow Fork trailhead, where you will need to leave a shuttle vehicle, for a total 4.0-mile one-way hike.

The bridge crossing onto the Lambs Canyon Trail

Hike Information

Organizations: Wasatch Mountain Club, 1390 South 1100 East, Salt Lake City 84105-2443; (801) 463-9842; www.wasatchmountainclub.org

Mountain Trails Foundation, 1353 Park Ave., Park City 84060; (435) 649-6839; http://mountaintrails.org

Outdoor equipment: Recreational Equipment Inc. (REI), 3285 East 3300 South, Salt Lake City 84109; (801) 486-2100

South of Salt Lake City

Corner Canyon is a Draper City trail system located just east of Draper behind the LDS temple. Developed with funds from a community bond and supported and managed by the city with the help of hundreds of volunteer hours, this trail system offers a maze of options. In 2012, 2,400 additional acres of open space were purchased for expansion of the Corner Canyon trails system. New trails will be developed in Corner Canyon on a continual basis moving forward. There are currently over 60 miles of trails in the Corner Canyon trail complex. These three highlighted in the book are just a sampling.

Bell Canyon lies to the southeast of the Salt Lake Valley. The trailheads into Bell Canyon take off a few miles south of Little Cottonwood Canyon and are located on the east side of the Salt Lake Valley.

Utah County lies around the Point of the Mountain to the south, and though the trails are still in the Wasatch Range, they are near Provo, 30 minutes south of Salt Lake.

Spanish Fork Canyon is yet farther south. US 6 runs through Spanish Fork Canyon and is the major roadway that cuts east across the state toward Moab.

Corner Canyon

38 Ghost Falls

Ghost Falls can be accessed from every trailhead in the Corner Canyon system of linking trails, but when approached from the Ghost Falls trailhead, the hike is a pleasant downhill stroll, complete with shade, gurgling springs, and seasonal wildflowers. Short and sweet, with a scenic waterfall at the end, this trail is perfect as a family hike with youngsters or just a quick forested getaway.

Start: Ghost Falls trailhead
Distance: 1.5 miles out and back
Hiking time: About 45 minutes
Difficulty: Easy
Elevation gain: 250 feet
Trail surface: Dirt path and bridge
Best season: Spring through fall
Other trail users: Mountain bikers
Canine compatibility: Dogs prohibited (watershed area)
Land status: Regional park owned by Draper City
Nearest town: Draper
Fees and permits: No fees or permits required

Schedule: Park hours 6 a.m. to 10 p.m. The road to Ghost Falls trailhead is gated off during winter and remains closed while any snow remains.
Maps: Draper City trails map available at www.draper.ut.us/116/Trails-Open-Space, or in the Draper City Office at 1020 E. Pioneer Rd., Draper
Trail contacts: Draper City Parks and Recreation, 1020 East Pioneer Rd., Draper 84020; (801) 576-6500
Special considerations: Beware of poison ivy by the falls.

Finding the trailhead: From Salt Lake City head south on I-15 to the Bangerter exit 289 near Point of the Mountain. Head east off the exit and turn left in 0.5 mile at the second light onto 13800 South. Follow 13800 South for 1.7 miles to 1300 East. Turn right and go under South Mountain Bridge. On the other side of the bridge, turn left and continue 1.4 miles to a right turn into the Orson Smith trailhead. From here follow a dirt road for 2.6 miles to Ghost Falls trailhead. A high-clearance or four-wheel-drive vehicle is needed. **GPS:** N40 29.665' / W111 49.033'

The Hike

Ghost Falls is so named because no one knows where the water comes from. Natural springs in the mountain apparently spring to the surface and form the falls. The Draper City Parks Department and volunteers have turned what was once an old horse trail into a curvaceous, winding trail that runs beneath shady maples and scrub oak, dotted in spring with wildflowers. The trail is perfect for a hike with children—it is short and nicely shaded and ends at a beautiful waterfall.

Ghost Falls trailhead

Picnic tables, a pit toilet, and a trail kiosk are located at the trailhead. Right after you pass the picnic tables, the trail heads both up and down the canyon. The trail to the left (east) hooks in with Jacob's Ladder, while the trail that heads right and downhill takes you to Ghost Falls. This trail is different from most in the Wasatch in that you descend to your destination and then ascend on the way out. All trails have no more than a 10 percent grade, so the uphill remains pleasant and easy.

Nice springs and streams can be heard as you descend, but often you won't be able to see the water. Wild rose, wild onion, horsemint, and too many other wildflowers to name dot the landscape.

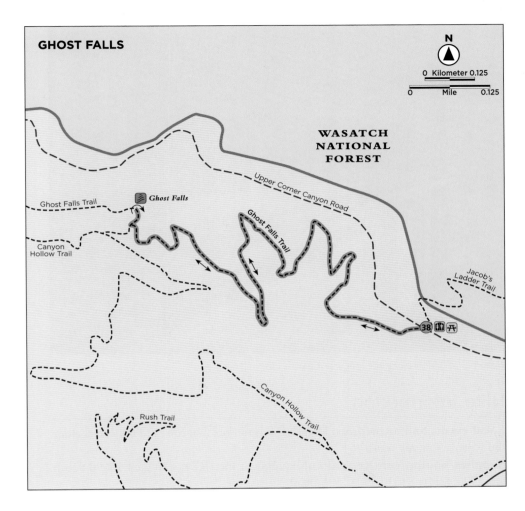

Just before the falls the trail hits a T junction (0.7 mile); you can see and hear the falls from here. Turn right to reach the waterfall at 0.75 mile. A Boy Scout cleared the area around the waterfall as an Eagle Scout project, and most of the plants and poison ivy have been cut away to provide a nice clear area for sitting on rocks and enjoying the falls or taking photos. Return the way you came.

Miles and Directions

0.0 Start at the Ghost Falls trailhead.

0.7 Come to a T intersection; head right to reach the falls.

0.75 Arrive at Ghost Falls. Return the way you came.

1.5 Arrive back at the trailhead.

As of 2017 there are 60 miles of trails in the Corner Canyon area, and more are being developed.

Beautiful fall colors along the bridge to Ghost Falls

Hike Information

Local events and attractions: Draper City sponsors trail runs and bike races along the Corner Canyon trails.

Supplies/equipment: Recreational Equipment Inc. (REI), 230 West 10600 South, Ste. 1700, Sandy 84070; (801) 501-0850

GREEN TIP
Throw a plastic bag in your pack so you can haul
out toilet paper.

39 Canyon Hollow/Ghost Falls Trail

This trail climbs the main canyon, parallel to Corner Canyon Creek, up to Ghost Falls. Intermixed with shaded singletrack, gravel road, and riverside travel, there is also a trail option that allows you to make the hike a lollipop. Ghost Falls, so named because no one is certain where the water comes from, is a beautiful cooling station and a highlight of the Corner Canyon trail system. Because the Corner Canyon trails sit at a lower elevation, the snow melts off these trails earlier than most and they are some of the first to be accessed in spring. This trail takes the Canyon Hollow Trail to Ghost Falls.

Start: Coyote Hollow trailhead
Distance: 2.8 miles out and back or 2.8-mile lollipop
Hiking time: 1.5–2 hours
Difficulty: Easy
Elevation gain: 280 feet
Trail surface: Dirt, gravel road, bridge
Best season: Spring through fall
Other trail users: Mountain bikers, horses
Canine compatibility: Dogs prohibited, watershed area
Land status: Regional park owned by Draper City

Nearest town: Draper
Fees and permits: No fees or permits required
Schedule: Park hours 6 a.m. to 10 p.m.
Maps: Trail maps are available at www.draper .ut.us/116/Trails-Open-Space or in the Draper City Office, 1020 E. Pioneer Road, Draper.
Trail contacts: Draper City Parks and Recreation, 1020 East Pioneer Rd., Draper 84020; (801) 576-6500
Special considerations: These trails are very popular with mountain bikers. Prepare to share the trails and be on the lookout for fast downhill riders.

Finding the trailhead: Coyote Hollow trailhead sits directly behind the LDS Draper temple. From Salt Lake City head south on I-15. Take the Bangerter exit 289 near the Point of the Mountain. Head east off the exit and turn left 0.5 mile later at the second light onto 13800 South. Follow 13800 South for 1.7 miles to 1300 East. Turn right and go under the South Mountain Bridge. Take a right on the other side of the bridge and go to Rambling Road/1220 East. Turn left onto Rambling Road/1220 East and follow the signs to the LDS Draper temple. When you get to Pinon Hill Lane, turn left and then take your first right then your first left down Gray Fox Drive. Coyote Hollow Court is your first right after that. The trailhead sits at the bottom of the circle. There are no restrooms. **GPS:** N40 29.606' / W111 50.344' For additional parking you can park at Red Rock trailhead, just west of Coyote Hollow on Mike Weir Drive across from South Mountain Golf Course. You can follow the Bonneville Shoreline Trail back to Coyote Hollow.

The Hike

Coyote Hollow is Corner Canyon's most popular trailhead. The land that is now Corner Canyon Regional Park was purchased by Draper City in 2005 to protect the land and watershed from the massive residential development taking place in the Draper foothills. The park's 1,021 acres are in the process of continued development, and pristine mountain trails continue to be added per the master plan. In 2012, 2,400 more acres of land were purchased by Draper City to continue with Corner Canyon trail development. Their master plan was redone in 2016. This trail system is open to all nonmotorized use, so everyone works together to be respectful to a variety of users as well as to the land.

Head east out of Coyote Hollow trailhead—365 feet later there is an intersection where the Canyon Hollow Trail and the Silica Pit go to the right and the Bonneville Shoreline Trail goes to the left. Follow the sign to the right staying on the Canyon Hollow Trail. At 0.13 mile the trail splits. Head right again toward the Silica Pit. At 0.3 mile you reach the Silica Pit. Cross through it. At 0.5 mile the Rush Trail, a downhill mountain bike trail, crosses the Canyon Hollow Trail. Watch for fast-moving bikes. Stay on the trail marked Canyon Hollow. At 0.6 mile the trail splits again. Continue straight ahead taking the right fork. A scenic view opens at 0.8 mile where the trees open up providing a view of the LDS Temple with its tall spire, the surrounding neighborhoods, and part of the valley below. At 0.85 mile the Hoof and Boot Trail, a foot traffic and horse-only trail, intersects from the right. At this point the trail opens up to a doubletrack dirt road for a hundred feet. Head up the road and follow the signs to Canyon Hollow. At 1 mile the Canyon Hollow trail comes to a T. Turning right will simply loop back around and take you back down to hook into the Canyon Hollow Trail down below. Turn left and continue up the canyon instead. At 1.06 miles the Hoof and Boot Trail intersects again from the right. The trail then crosses a bridge and at 1.25 the Hoof and Boot Trail intersects from the left. This foot and horse path crosses the Canyon Hollow Trail four times along this route. At 1.3 miles leave the Canyon Hollow Trail and head left toward Ghost Falls. In the next tenth of a mile you will cross two bridges. When you come to the third bridge you are at Ghost Falls (at the 1.4-mile mark). Enjoy the stream, the waterfall, and the rocks around the area that provide a place to sit and rest, picnic, or just enjoy the scenery. Return the way you came for a 2.8-mile round-trip hike.

Miles and Directions

0.0 Start at the Coyote Hollow trailhead.

365 feet Trail splits for Canyon Hollow and the Silica Pit.

0.13 Trail splits. Go left to continue toward the Silica Pit.

0.3 Trail crosses the Silica Pit.

0.6 Trail splits—continue straight ahead.

0.8 Trail opens up for a scenic view.

1.0 Trail comes to an intersection. Lead left and continue up the canyon.

1.3 Leave the Canyon Hollow Trail and take a left onto the Ghost Falls Trail.

CANYON HOLLOW/GHOST FALLS TRAIL

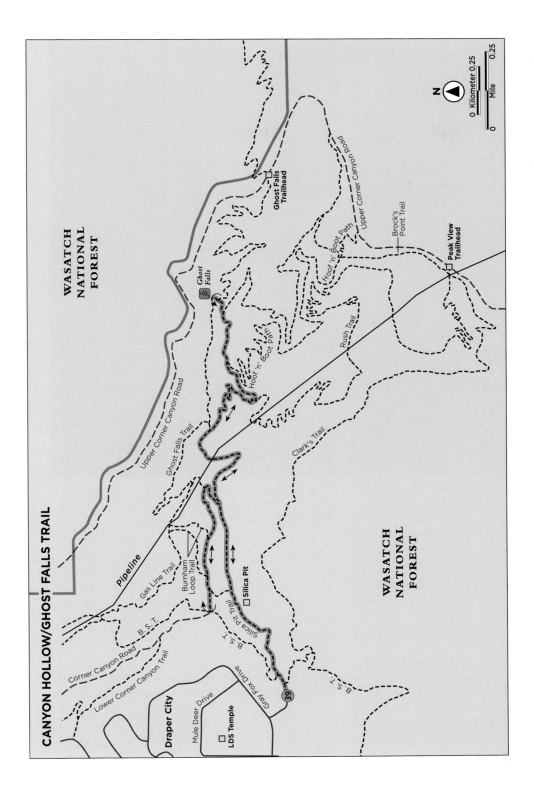

WASATCH NATIONAL FOREST

WASATCH NATIONAL FOREST

Draper City

LDS Temple

Mule Deer Drive

Gray Fox Drive

Corner Canyon Road

Lower Corner Canyon Trail

B. S. T.

Gas Line Trail

Pipeline

Burnham Loop Trail

Silica Pit Trail

Silica Pit

B. S. T.

B. S. T.

39

Clark's Trail

Rush Trail

Ghost Falls Trail

Upper Corner Canyon Road

Ghost Falls

Hoof 'n' Boot Path

Hoof 'n' Boot Path

Upper Corner Canyon Road

Ghost Falls Trailhead

Brock's Point Trail

Peak View Trailhead

N

0 Kilometer 0.25

0 Mile 0.25

Trail to Ghost Falls

1.4 Arrive at Ghost Falls. Return the way you came or take the lollipop option.

2.8 Arrive back at the trailhead.

Option

The Canyon Hollow to Ghost Falls hike can also be done as a lollipop. Instead of returning on Canyon Hollow trail, cross the bridge at the foot of the falls and continue on the Ghost Falls trail that heads west. The Ghost Falls trail is rockier and has less shade, but it allows for different scenery.

Hike Information

Local events and attractions: Draper City sponsors trail runs and bike races along the Corner Canyon trails.

Supplies/equipment: Recreational Equipment Inc. (REI), 230 West 10600 South, Ste. 1700, Sandy 84070; (801) 501–0850

Corner Canyon

40 Clark's Trail/Canyon Hollow Trail Loop

Clark's Trail is a beautiful hike up the mountain to the Peak View trailhead. Shaded trails occasionally open up to full, rich views of the surrounding Draper neighborhoods and expand to the Wasatch Front, Kennecott Copper across the valley, and down into Corner Canyon. A great combination of a beautiful shaded trail with panoramic views, you'll love this trail any time of day. It is the longest and prettiest loop in the park. As Clark's Trail tops out at Peak View trailhead, it cuts across to Brock's Point Trail and then hooks into Canyon Hollow Trail farther downcanyon for a nice loop around the Corner Canyon area. Just steps from a Draper neighborhood, the trail is easy to access.

Start: Coyote Hollow trailhead
Distance: 4.3-mile loop
Hiking time: About 3 hours
Difficulty: Moderate
Elevation gain: 670 feet
Trail surface: Packed dirt and gravel road
Best season: Spring through fall. Snow melts off the Corner Canyon trails earlier than most in the Salt Lake City area because the trail system sits at a lower elevation right next to town.
Other trail users: Mountain bikers (allowed uphill only on Clark's Trail but prevalent elsewhere), horses
Canine compatibility: Dogs prohibited, watershed area

Land status: Regional park owned by Draper City
Nearest town: Draper
Fees and permits: No fees or permits required
Schedule: Park hours 6 a.m. to 10 p.m.
Maps: Trail maps are available at www.draper .ut.us/116/Trails-Open-Space, or in the Draper City Office, 1020 E. Pioneer Rd., Draper.
Trail contacts: Draper City Parks and Recreation, 1020 East Pioneer Rd., Draper 84020; (801) 576-6500
Special considerations: These trails are very popular with mountain bikers. Prepare to share the trails, and be on the lookout for fast downhill riders.

Finding the trailhead: Coyote Hollow trailhead sits directly behind the LDS Draper temple. From Salt Lake City head south on I-15. Take the Bangerter exit 289 near the Point of the Mountain. Head east off the exit and turn left 0.5 mile later at the second light onto 13800 South. Follow 13800 South for 1.7 miles to 1300 East. Turn right and go under the South Mountain Bridge. Take a right on the other side of the bridge and go to Rambling Road/1220 East. Turn left onto Rambling Road/1220 East and follow the signs to the LDS Draper temple. When you get to Pinon Hill Lane, turn left and then take your first right then your first left down Gray Fox Drive. Coyote Hollow Court is your first right after that. The trailhead sits at the bottom of the circle. There are no restrooms. **GPS:** N40 29.606' / W111 50.344' For additional parking you can park at Red Rock trailhead, just west of Coyote Hollow on Mike Weir Drive across from South Mountain Golf Course. You can follow the Bonneville Shoreline Trail back to Coyote Hollow.

The Hike

Clark's Trail offers panoramic views as you stroll through a shaded forest dotted with wildflowers in spring and colorful leaves in fall. This popular trail naturally draws hikers and bikers.

As you leave the Coyote Hollow trailhead, quickly turn off to the right onto Clark's Trail, marked with a wood sign. Clark's Trail is a leisurely climb to Peak View trailhead at the top of the park. At 0.2 mile the trail comes to its first intersection—the Bonneville Shoreline Trail. Head to the left, over the bridge. From here the trees part and open to views of the surrounding neighborhoods and cities, including an incredible view of the castlelike LDS Draper temple.

The trail quietly winds its way up the mountain until at 1.7 miles you reach Peak View trailhead. The trailhead consists of a wide gravel gathering area, a kiosk with a map, and trails that head out from all sides. Cross to the northeast side and exit through the wooden fence. A wooden sign on the fence says "CANYON HOLLOW/ BROCKS TRAIL." From here the trail descends back into the canyon.

Coyote Hollow trailhead

Left: First turnoff onto Clark's Trail
Right: The Silica Pit

Brock's Trail meets up with Canyon Hollow Trail at 2.1 miles. Take the hairpin turn and follow the trail to the left. Brock's Trail continues to the right on its way to Upper Corner Canyon Road.

At 3.0 miles the trail to Ghost Falls intersects on the right. It is an extra 0.1 mile to the falls.

Continue down Canyon Hollow. Two hundred feet past the Ghost Falls turnoff the Hoof and Boot Trail, a foot and horse-only path, intersects the Canyon Hollow Trail. At 3.2 miles the trail crosses a bridge and the Canyon Hollow Trail turns down-canyon. Shortly after the Hoof and Boot Trail intersects the trail again and you cross a bridge where the Hoof and Boot Trail picks up on the other side as well. Stay on the main Canyon Hollow Trail and continue down the canyon. At 3.3 miles the trail splits. Either fork takes you farther down the Canyon Hollow Trail. The two trails link up a short way down the canyon, so pick your poison. At 3.4 miles Canyon Hollow Trail comes out of the trees

SILICA PIT

The "pit" is a big white gouge out of the side of the mountain where the community mined silica at the turn of the 20th century to make glass.

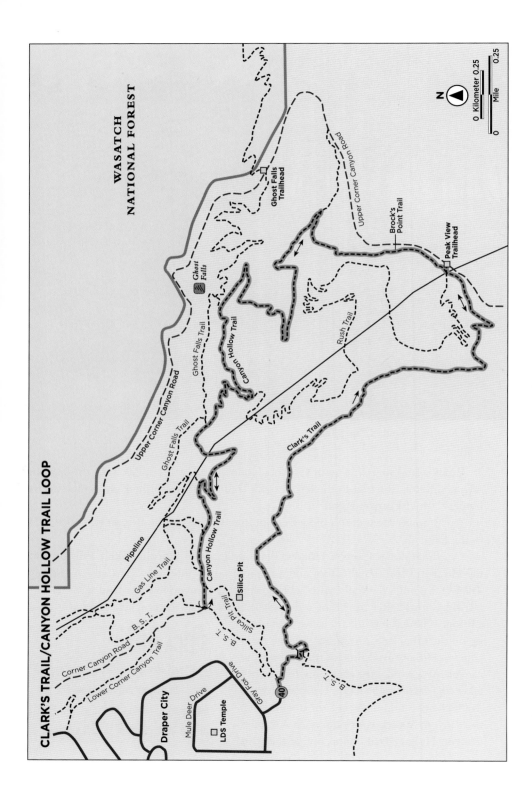

CLARK'S TRAIL/CANYON HOLLOW TRAIL LOOP

WASATCH
NATIONAL FOREST

Draper City

LDS Temple

Mule Deer Drive

Gray Fox Drive

40

Corner Canyon Road

Lower Corner Canyon Trail

B. S. T.

Pipeline

Gas Line Trail

Silica Pit Trail

B. S. T.

B. S. T.

Silica Pit

Canyon Hollow Trail

Canyon Hollow Trail

Ghost Falls Trail

Ghost Falls Trail

Upper Corner Canyon Road

Ghost Falls

Ghost Falls Trailhead

Clark's Trail

Rush Trail

Brock's Point Trail

Upper Corner Canyon Road

Peak View Trailhead

N

0   Kilometer   0.25

0   Mile   0.25

and heads down a dirt road. A hundred feet later the trail transitions back into single-track and the Hoof and Boot crosses Canyon Hollow Trail, yet again. At 3.6 miles the Memorial Cove hiking-only trail enters from the left, and at 3.8 the Rush downhill biking trail crosses the Canyon Hollow Trail. Watch for fast-moving bikes. Continue straight staying on the Canyon Hollow Trail. At 4 miles you reach the Silica Pit, a big white gauge out of the side of the mountain where silica was mined for glass. The path takes you right through the pit and back into the trees on the other side. At 4.25 miles the trail comes to a Y. Take the left path back toward Coyote Hollow trailhead. The right fork takes you to the Bonneville Shoreline Trail. At 4.3 miles you're back at the Coyote Hollow trailhead having completed the loop.

Miles and Directions

0.0 Start at Coyote Hollow trailhead.

100 feet Turn right onto Clark's Trail.

0.2 Reach intersection with Bonneville Shoreline Trail; head left and cross the bridge.

1.7 Arrive at Peak View trailhead; exit through the wooden fence on the northeast side.

2.1 Brock's Trail intersects Canyon Hollow Trail; turn left onto Canyon Hollow Trail.

3.0 The trail passes the turnoff to Ghost Falls.

3.2 The trail crosses a bridge and Canyon Hollow Trail turns downcanyon.

3.3 This confusing intersection is unsigned and appears to go straight. Both options connect to one another below, so either one will work.

3.4 Canyon Hollow Trail comes out of the trees and heads down the dirt road; a hundred feet later it rejoins the singletrack.

4.0 Trail crosses the Silica Pit.

4.25 Trail intersection—head left to get back to the trailhead.

4.3 Arrive back at the Coyote Hollow trailhead.

Hike Information

Local events and attractions: Draper City sponsors trail runs and bike races along the Corner Canyon trails. For more information visit their Facebook page or www.draper.ut.us.

Supplies/equipment: Recreational Equipment Inc. (REI), 230 West 10600 South, Ste. 1700, Sandy 84070; (801) 501-0850

GREEN TIP
Homemade trail snacks don't use unnecessary packaging.

Bell Canyon

41 Bell Canyon to Lower and Upper Waterfalls

Bell Canyon is a steep granite canyon dug out by a glacier that exposed some of the oldest Precambrian rock in the world. The canyon sits just south of Little Cottonwood Canyon and provides a steady, steep climb into a world of waterfalls, granite walls, and lush alpine environs. Along the way the trail affords views into the valley below, and the luscious waterfalls at the end are certainly worth the climb.

Start: Boulders trailhead
Distance: 5.0 miles out and back to the first falls; 6.2 miles out and back to both waterfalls
Hiking time: About 3 hours to lower waterfall; 4 hours to upper waterfall
Difficulty: Strenuous
Elevation gain: 1,580 feet to first waterfall; 2,350 feet to second waterfall
Trail surface: Sandy gravel, dirt, rocks and boulders
Best season: Spring through fall
Other trail users: None
Canine compatibility: Dogs prohibited
Fees and permits: No fees or permits required
Schedule: Trailhead closes at 10 p.m.

Maps: USGS Draper; Trails Illustrated Wasatch Front, Uinta National Forest
Trail contacts: Sandy City, (801) 568-2900, http://sandy.utah.gov/government/parks-and -recreation/city-trail-system.html; Uinta-Wasatch-Cache National Forest, 8236 Federal Building, 125 South State St., Salt Lake City 84138
Special considerations: Don't cross over streams during swift currents. Fatalities have occurred. The waterfalls can be dangerous if not respected. Trekking poles can help with the stiff climb up and descent on an often-rocky trail. No alcohol, fireworks, or motorized vehicles allowed. Watch out for rattlesnakes.

Finding the trailhead: From Salt Lake City take I-15 south. Merge onto I-215 east via exit 298. Follow I-215 for 5.5 miles to UT 190/6200 South. Take exit 6/6200 South toward the ski areas. Head east off the exit and follow the road which will change from 6200 South to Wasatch Boulevard, for 6 miles to the trailhead. Boulders trailhead is on the east side of the road at 10235 South Wasatch Boulevard. There are twenty parking slots. **GPS:** N40 33.900' / W111 48.2220'

Note: When the parking lot is full, overflow parking is available at the Salt Lake County parking lot just west of Wasatch Boulevard on the north side of Little Cottonwood Road.

The canyon also can be accessed from the Granite trailhead, just one block north and east of Boulders trailhead off Little Cottonwood Canyon Road, the light right before Boulder Trailhead off Wasatch Boulevard. At the stoplight just north of Boulders trailhead make a left and continue to Granite trailhead at 3470 East Little Cottonwood Road, complete with restrooms and twenty-three parking slots.

The Hike

Popular with hikers, the well-maintained trail to the waterfall is easy to follow, with the exception of a few intersections you'll want to hit correctly. Two trailheads access Bell Canyon: Boulders and Granite. This hike uses Boulders trailhead.

The trail begins in an urban neighborhood with a stroll through a landscaped section of trail, and then climbs a set of dirt-and-rock stairs as it exits the private residential areas to get you into the canyon. This first 0.25 mile is a steep uphill on rocky steps. Once at the top the trail drops down to Bell Canyon Creek where it empties from the canyon in a beautiful shaded space. After crossing the bridge you begin the climb up to Lower Bell Reservoir. As you climb, the view opens up over the Wasatch Front and out to Kennecott Copper Mine across the valley. At 0.3 mile the trail forks; one fork takes a more direct route, while the other is less steep, but both tie back in together. Taking either one works.

Within the first 0.5 mile you reach the fork in the trail right before the reservoir. Heading straight takes you to a corner of Lower Bell Canyon Reservoir. Fishing is

The stream on the way up the trail

Hiker enjoying the view of the first waterfall

allowed on a catch–and–release basis only, but because this is a Sandy City watershed, no swimming is allowed. The reservoir is stocked by the Utah Division of Wildlife Resources. An expected catch is primarily cutthroat trout. Anglers twelve years old and older must have a fishing license to fish. A small sign at this fork signifies that the trail up Bell Canyon continues to the left.

The wider trail heads left and takes you up and around the north side of Lower Bell Reservoir. The trail from Granite trailhead joins the trail here on the north side of the reservoir. The trail continues around the north side of the reservoir on the doubletrack dirt road. From this point you can see across the Wasatch Front and the Salt Lake City skyline. A tenth of a mile later (0.7 mile) a singletrack dirt trail intersects from the right (south); this trail goes around the lower reservoir, not up Bell Canyon. Stay on the wide trail for another 0.1 mile to where a dirt singletrack enters from the left (northeast). A wooden trail marker indicates that this trail leads up Bell Canyon.

A half-mile later the trail leads to a beautiful intersection with the stream. Easy access to the stream here allows for cooling off or just enjoying the stream close up, but during high runoff keep your distance. To continue up Bell Canyon, follow the trail on the north side of the stream and farther to a bridge that crosses over to the south side. There is a trail marker here that indicates it is 0.9 mile to the first waterfall, but my GPS showed it was actually 1.3 miles to the first falls from this sign. At 1.4 miles the trail splits, but the left trail is simply taking you closer to the stream for a view. Continue straight to get to the falls.

At 1.5 miles you enter the Lone Peak Wilderness Area and the Wasatch National Forest. The trail becomes large boulder steps and climbs for another mile up to the turnoff for the first waterfall. At 2.4 miles the trail forks and you've finally made it to the turnoff for the waterfall; head left. There is a sign pointing your way to the waterfall. The trail winds around the mountain and takes you to the first waterfall at 2.5 miles (**GPS:** N40 33.651' / W111 46.234').

The waterfall cascades down granite next to a lovely shaded slope. The area is popular for picnicking, cooling off, and photography. The area around the falls is badly eroded by foot traffic, but the waterfall is gorgeous and invigorating. The base of the falls sits at 6,695 feet.

If you wish to continue to the second set of falls, come back to the intersection and take the right fork and continue up the mountain. As you make your way up the next 0.5 mile to the upper falls, stay on the trails closest to the stream. The trail continues on a vertical ascent along the same staircase of boulders. At 3 miles the trail runs into the stream and a large slab of granite off to the right. Continue up this slab to a singletrack trail off to the left (north) that leads into a wonderful wet, mossy grove for approximately 50 yards directly to the second falls (**GPS:** N40 33.527' / W111 45.688'). Return the way you came.

Miles and Directions

0.0   Start at the Boulders trailhead.

0.3   Trail splits but both meet up farther up the trail.

0.5   The trail forks. A wooden sign leads you left (north) to continue around the north side of Lower Bell Reservoir. (**Option:** Continue straight to the reservoir itself. Fishing is allowed on a catch-and-release basis only.)

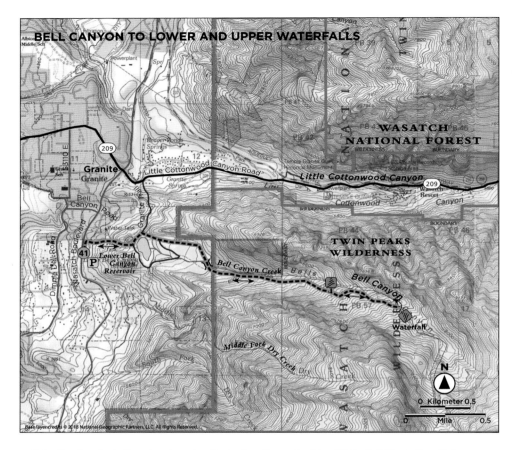

0.6 The Granite trailhead route enters the trail on the north side of Little Bell. The trail up Bell Canyon continues on the doubletrack dirt road that curves around the north side of the reservoir and heads east.

0.7 A dirt singletrack intersects from the right (south). Stay on the dirt road.

0.8 Come to the wooden trail marker that indicates the exit from the dirt road to the single-track trail on the left (northeast).

1.2 The trail meets up with the stream in a grove-type area. Stay on the trail as it leads up the north side of the stream and quickly crosses a bridge.

1.5 Enter the National Forest and Lone Peak Wilderness Area.

2.4 Come to a fork in the trail; turn left to reach the first waterfall.

2.5 Reach the lower falls. Return to the intersection and continue straight up the mountain to the upper falls.

3.0 The trail runs into the stream. To continue to the upper falls, head east up the granite bulge next to the trail about 50 feet, where you will find a singletrack off to the left (north) that will take you the remaining 0.1 mile to the upper falls.

3.1 Reach the upper waterfall.

6.2 Arrive back at the trailhead.

Hike Information

Organizations: Wasatch Mountain Club; www.wasatchmountainclub.org
Supplies/equipment: Recreational Equipment Inc. (REI), 230 West 10600 South, Ste. 1700, Sandy 84070; (801) 501–0850

HOW TO CHOOSE A BACKPACK

Carry capacity: How long will your backpack trips be? If you plan to engage in longer trips, you will need a pack that can carry more. If you'll be taking only weekend trips, you may not need as much room. If you carry an ultralight sleeping bag, sleeping pad, tiny camping stove, etc., you won't need the same pack capacity as someone with more traditional gear.

When will you be backpacking? If you will be backpacking during colder months or at higher elevations, you may need extra space to accommodate more clothing, a warmer sleeping bag, and a sturdier tent.

The importance of fit: While carry capacity is important to make sure your pack fits your needs, nothing is more important than choosing a pack that fits YOU. A well-fitted pack will allow you to carry more gear, take longer treks, and avoid the pain of an ill-fitted one.

The first and most important factor is your torso length; be sure you know it before you start shopping. Using a flexible measuring tape, measure the distance between your C7 vertebra (the bone that sticks out on your upper spine) and your hipbones.

Once you know your torso size, match your size into the fitting chart for the pack you're interested in. Packs usually come in small, medium, or large or have an adjustable suspension that allows the pack to be modified to fit your frame.

Most waist belts accommodate a wide range of sizes, with only simple adjustments needed to tighten or loosen the hip belt. The hip belt needs to support 80 percent of the pack's weight when you wear it, so be sure it's comfortable to you.

42 Mount Timpanogos from Aspen Grove

Mount Timpanogos is the second-highest peak in the Wasatch Range and has been one of Utah's most popular hiking destinations for almost a century. This hike provides a twisting alpine trail past waterfalls, glacial lakes, a herd of mountain goats, summer wildflowers, a summit notch on your belt, and 360-degree views across valleys, mountain ranges, cities, and lakes. Despite the length and the steep, challenging push for the summit, there is no question why this hike is a Utah classic.

Start: Aspen Grove/Timpanogos trailhead
Distance: 14.4 miles out and back
Hiking time: About 9 hours
Difficulty: Strenuous due to length and steep exposed climbing on the last portion of the trail
Elevation gain: 4,840 feet
Trail surface: Blacktop, rock, dirt, and talus
Best season: Midsummer through midfall. Snow melts here late in spring due to the high elevation, and water beneath the snow creates dangerous snow bridges during spring runoff. The snow is usually gone by July. During winter this area is prone to avalanches.
Other trail users: Horses
Canine compatibility: Leashed dogs permitted
Land status: Mount Timpanogos Wilderness Area; Uinta-Wasatch-Cache National Forest

Nearest town: Alpine
Fees and permits: Fee required to access Aspen Grove/Timpanogos trailhead
Schedule: The information/fee booth at the trailhead has varying hours depending upon the season.
Maps: USGS Timpanogos Cave, Aspen Grove
Trail contacts: Pleasant Grove Ranger District, (801) 785-3563
Special considerations: Groups no larger than fifteen are allowed on the trail. Trail cutting is prohibited due to erosion. Campfires are prohibited within the Mount Timpanogos Wilderness Area. Camping is prohibited within 200 feet of trails or water sources.

Finding the trailhead: From Salt Lake City take I-15 south toward Las Vegas/Cheyenne. Take the UT 52/800 exit (272) toward US 189. Turn left onto UT 52 and follow for 3.7 miles where the road merges onto Provo Canyon Road. From the mouth of Provo Canyon head 6.8 miles to the turnoff to Sundance ski resort/UT 92. Turn north and travel 4.5 miles past the Sundance ski area and past the BYU Aspen Grove Alumni Center to the Aspen Grove/Timpanogos trailhead, just past the Forest Service fee booth. The trail takes off from the west side of the huge parking lot. **GPS:** N40 24.276' / W111 36.315'

The Hike

As your feet hit the trail you cannot see your destination. In fact, Mount Timpanogos doesn't come into view until you hit 10,000 feet and have traveled almost 6 miles along the trail. The Timpanogos Wilderness Area is filled with soaring peaks and dramatic rock faces. The large rock face seen from the trailhead is Roberts Horn. The tallest peak on the left is Elk Point. On the right, Lame Horse Point towers. As you leave the trailhead you begin the path that will take you to the upper echelons of alpine beauty.

Early on the path there is a water faucet for final water bottle refills, and within the first 0.25 mile you reach a fork in the trail. During summer or spring, when runoff is high, the right fork takes you to a bridge that helps in crossing the hard-rushing water but connects back with the main trail in less than 0.1 mile. If you can hear the roar of the river, take the right fork, but be careful you don't end up heading north on the Lame Horse Trail, which will take you to the Alpine Loop trailhead. If you don't hear the rush of water, take the left fork, staying on the main trail, and continue west.

In 1984 Congress designated just over 10,750 acres as the Mount Timpanogos Wilderness Area, managed by the US Forest Service. At 0.3 mile you officially enter this wilderness area.

Timpanogos is rich in history. From the World War II–era bomber that crashed on the mountainside in 1955, to the annual "Timp Hike" made popular by Eugene "Timp" Roberts, an athletic director at Brigham Young University in the early 1900s, to the Native American tribes the area was named for, entire books have been written on the area's history.

In summer the trail is patrolled by TERT, or the Timpanogos Emergency Response Team. This team of volunteers provides emergency assistance and is often found setting up shop around Emerald Lake at the base of The Glacier. TERT also regulates trail use and reports destructive use.

You come to the first waterfall just before the 1.0-mile mark, and the second quickly materializes around the next turn. This section of the trail is rich and lovely

Eugene Roberts, an athletic director at Brigham Young University in Provo, started taking small groups to the summit of Timpanogos in 1912 in the first of fifty-nine such hikes. This first group consisted of nineteen college students and teachers, and the trip was such a success that the event grew larger every year until in 1970 more than 7,000 people participated, with 3,500 reaching the summit. Traditions were established, such as the Friday-night campfire program held each year before the Saturday hike. Walking sticks, called "Timp sticks," were given out; even fireworks came into play. Many photos of these early-20th-century forays can be found in the BYU photo archives.

The environmental nightmare that such a large group created caused the US Forest Service to end the annual trek that had made its way through 60-plus years of history. Today the trail is still very well traveled. Many still attempt the summit, with fewer making it to the top, but group size is limited to fifteen persons.

Mount Timpanogos as seen from the saddle

in the lush green of a healthy alpine environment. The unnamed stream that drains Primrose Cirque is the source of these falls. At 3.5 miles the trail begins diverging into side trails on a regular basis. Most of these are shortcuts that have been worn into the mountainside by hikers seeking to cut the trail length. Try to stay on the main trail when possible to keep from adding to the erosion. All trails lead up the mountain.

At 9,200 feet of elevation the wildflowers begin to thicken. During the earlier spring runoff there will be more water in the creeks, more streams cutting their way down the mountains, and more waterfalls. Later in the season the wildflowers become more prolific.

You hit Primrose Cirque, named for the primrose wildflower that covers the area, at 4.0 miles. At 4.5 miles the trail appears to continue to the north. Instead follow the path to the south under a steep rock face. The trail becomes clearer as you get past this section.

At 4.8 miles the path forks. Stay to the right. The left fork follows a talus trail into a grove of trees—a fine diversion if you want to rest.

Hidden Lake, sometimes not much of a lake at all, lies at 5.0 miles. This is a popular camping spot, as there is water to be filtered and you can camp in the cirque.

Pack something to keep you warm on the summit. Even on summer days the summit is windy and often cold. Bug repellent, sunscreen, and plenty of water and snacks are a must for this strenuous hike.

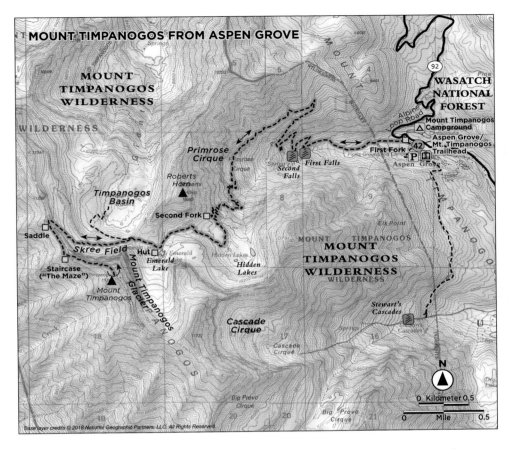

MOUNT
TIMPANOGOS
WILDERNESS

WILDERNESS

Primrose
Cirque

Roberts
Horn

Timpanogos
Basin

Saddle

Skree Field   Hut   Emerald
Emerald   Lake
Lake

Staircase
("The Maze")

Mount
Timpanogos

Second Fork

Hidden Lakes
Hidden
Lakes

MOUNT   TIMPANOGOS
MOUNT
TIMPANOGOS
WILDERNESS
WILDERNESS

Cascade
Cirque

Cascade
Cirque

Second
Falls
First Falls
First Fork

Elk Point

Stewart's
Cascades

WASATCH
NATIONAL
FOREST
Mount Timpanogos
Campground
Aspen Grove/
Mt. Timpanogos
Trailhead
Aspen Grove

Big Provo
Cirque

Big Provo
Cirque

N

0   Kilometer 0.5

0   Mile   0.5

From here you have limited tree line, so beyond this point there is a loss of privacy for camping or bathroom stops.

Shortly after Hidden Lakes you hit the 10,000-foot mark and get your first glimpse of Timpanogos. There is an aluminum shack sitting on the summit. From this point you can look back down the way you have come and see into Heber Valley and Deer Creek Reservoir.

Emerald Lake sits at the base of the snowfield often referred to as "The Glacier." A stone hut sits near the lake. This hut was built in 1959 and used to contain pit toilets. The toilets have been dismantled, but the hut is still used by TERT, the stray hiker who forgot his tent, and others who need it. A herd of mountain goats also frequents this area. Although they are used to the many hikers they see, wildlife should never be harassed. Give them their space.

Many hikers descend the summit by glissading down this snowfield for a quick and thrilling exit. Many hikers also are injured here; if you choose this route, make sure you know what you are doing.

Scenery along the Timpanogos Trail MIKE SCALORA

As you continue past Emerald Lake, you begin the most difficult part of the trail. At 5.9 miles the trail opens to the north. From here you can see into American Fork Canyon and over to the highest peaks in Little Cottonwood Canyon, including Pfeifferhorn and Red Baldy. From here you can also look down into the cirque and see the trails merging from the Timpooneke trailhead.

At this point the trail changes to and continues among talus to the summit. You will need sure footing and good ankle support. At 6.0 miles the trail forks in the talus. The right fork takes you down onto the Timpooneke Trail and into the cirque below; the left continues across the talus field. Stay left, crossing the snow if needed. When the talus is hard to follow, look for cairns and just keep heading to the northwest.

When the trail finishes the traverse across the talus, it begins a stiff climb up boulders and dirt to the saddle. At the top of the climb, follow the trail to the left to reach the saddle. The saddle sits at 11,050 feet and could be a destination in itself. Expansive views over the entire Utah Valley and down the other side into American Fork Canyon to the north and Heber Valley to the east make this a great place to stop and enjoy the fruits of your hard work.

From the saddle head south to a rock staircase that takes you up the mountain toward the summit. Known as "The Maze," the staircase requires sure footing. The mountain is covered with talus, and the approach is exposed; tread carefully. Continue climbing up the talus on trails that are decipherable but varied. A traverse across the mountain brings you just below the summit ridge. Switchbacks then take you up the

side of Timpanogos to the grand summit and an aluminum building signed by those who have reached the summit in past years. The reward of the summit makes the struggle well worth it.

The 360-degree views from the summit of Timpanogos must be experienced to be appreciated. Looking down the east side of the summit, you can see directly into Emerald Lake below, and in every direction the view of the world opens to you.

Miles and Directions

- **0.0** Start at the Aspen Grove/Timpanogos trailhead.
- **0.2** Come to a fork that will allow you to cross the stream at high water if you are hiking during the spring. No need to use the fork unless the water is high.
- **0.3** Enter Mount Timpanogos Wilderness Area.
- **0.4** Previous high-water fork merges back onto the main trail.
- **0.9** Come to the first waterfall.
- **1.2** Come to the second waterfall.
- **3.5** Shortcut trails formed by hikers cutting up the mountain begin.
- **4.0** Reach Primrose Cirque.
- **4.5** The trail forks. Head south/left.
- **4.8** The trail forks. Head south/right.
- **5.0** Reach Hidden Lakes.
- **5.7** Come to Emerald Lake and The Glacier. Look for mountain goats here.

One of the waterfalls along the first section of the trail

The Dangers of Altitude Sickness: If you come from sea level to altitudes above 8000 feet, you could be in danger of developing symptoms of altitude sickness if you don't give your body time to acclimate to the decreased pressure of the air around you—the barometric pressure. At higher altitudes there is less oxygen in the surrounding air. Symptoms often improve when you descend. If you are coming in from out of town and are used to lower elevations, give your body time to adjust to the thinner air around you.

6.0	The trail forks in the talus. Stay left and continue along the talus. Descending takes you to Timpooneke.
6.6	The trail begins a steep climb to the saddle.
6.7	Come to the saddle.
6.9	Reach the rock staircase called The Maze.
7.2	Reach the summit of Mount Timpanogos. Return the way you came.
14.4	Arrive back at the trailhead.

Options

Option 1: There are 17 miles of maintained trails accessed from two trailheads in the Timpanogos Wilderness Area: Aspen Grove/Timpanogos (where the featured hike begins) and Timpooneke. Mount Timpanogos can be reached from both trailheads. The Timpooneke Trail meets up with the Aspen Grove Trail just below the saddle before the summit. The Timpooneke route brings you up through a steep glaciated valley and a staircase of five flat benches. The Timpooneke trailhead is located in the Timpooneke Campground, 5 miles farther up UT 92, and sits at 7,360 feet of elevation.

Option 2: Return from the summit via a glissade down The Glacier. To take this route, from the summit travel south across the ridge for 0.6 mile to the top of The Glacier, then glissade to the bottom. Be aware that many people have sustained injuries in this area, so take appropriate care.

Hike Information

Local events and attractions: Sundance ski resort, owned by Robert Redford, offers lift-assisted hiking and mountain biking in the summer months. The resort also offers artistic programs and outdoor theater. During winter the resort has downhill skiing, a Nordic center, and ongoing environmental programs. For information call (877) 831-6224 or visit www.sundanceresort.com.

Scenic drive: The Alpine Loop begins near the Aspen Grove/Timpanogos trailhead and winds up the mountain into American Fork Canyon. Considered one of the most scenic drives in the state, especially in fall, it has been designated as a Utah scenic byway.

Camping: Mount Timpanogos Campground sits at an elevation of 7,600 feet and is located just a few hundred feet past the Aspen Grove/Timpanogos trailhead. Sheltered by aspen and fir trees, the campground has vault toilets and drinking water. Reservations are suggested on busy summer weekends. Campers also must have a recreation pass. Passes can be purchased as you enter the Alpine Loop from either end or from one of the self-service fee tubes located at major trailheads. No trailers or RVs longer than 20 feet. This park has first-come, first-served sites. For reservations call (877) 444-6777 or go to www.recreation.gov. Theater in the Pines is a group campground located on the south side of the Aspen Grove/Timpanogos trailhead. Reservation only; call (877) 444-6777.

43 Stewart's Cascades (Stewart Falls)

The Timpanogos area is rife with waterfalls, but Stewart's Cascades, also known as Stewart Falls, are the easiest to access and possibly one of the most scenic. Popular with families, this pleasant, easy trail is often shaded and ends in a beautiful two-tiered waterfall that plunges 200 feet down the mountain. Fall colors are vibrant in this area, but the falls flow with greater intensity earlier in the year. Fir, aspen, and maple surround you in an alpine environment that makes for a dazzling day hike.

Start: Aspen Grove/Timpanogos trailhead
Distance: 3.8 miles out and back
Hiking time: About 1.5 hours
Difficulty: Easy
Elevation gain: 310 feet
Trail surface: Gravel and dirt path
Best season: Summer and fall; winter avalanche hazard
Other trail users: Horses
Canine compatibility: Leashed dogs permitted
Land status: Uinta-Wasatch-Cache National Forest; trail mostly on Sundance Resort property

Nearest town: Provo
Fees and permits: Fees required to access Aspen Grove trailhead
Schedule: The hours posted at the information/fee booth at the trailhead vary by season. The trail is never closed. If you arrive and no one is manning the booth there is a self-serve payment required.
Maps: USGS Aspen Grove
Trail contacts: Pleasant Grove Ranger District, (801) 785-3563

Finding the trailhead: From Salt Lake City take I-15 south toward Las Vegas/Cheyenne. Take the UT 52/800 exit (272) toward US 189. Turn left onto UT 52 and follow for 3.7 miles where the road merges onto Provo Canyon Road. From the mouth of Provo Canyon, head 6.8 miles to the turnoff to Sundance ski resort/UT 92. Turn north and travel 4.5 miles past the Sundance ski area and past the BYU Aspen Grove Alumni Center to the Aspen Grove/Timpanogos trailhead that sits just past the US Forest Service fee booth. The trail takes off on the right side of the restrooms on the west side of the huge parking lot. **GPS:** N40 24.25' / W111 36.315'

The Hike

Stewart's Cascades Trail leaves from the southwest side of the parking lot on the trail just north of the restrooms. A trail marker 130 feet up the trail directs you left to Stewart's Cascades, Trail 56. The trail quickly turns southeast and climbs into a forest of tall evergreens. The view from this corner looks back over lush Primrose Cirque.

At 0.35 mile the trail forks, with the left fork descending to the BYU Alumni Center and the right fork continuing to Stewart's Cascades. As the trail progresses you pass a big water tank on the left where the BYU Alumni Center stores their water.

Stewart's Cascades MIKE SCALORA

   The trail winds through old evergreens and young aspen groves and tall, lush ferns during spring and summer. At 1.4 miles the trail forks; continue straight. As you continue around the mountain, Sundance Resort becomes visible, with ski runs cutting through the trees. Privately owned homes cut into the mountains and beautiful

In the early 1900s the Stewarts, a family of Scottish immigrants, settled the canyon now known as Sundance. The second generation of Stewarts saw the potential of the surrounding mountains as a ski resort and opened Timphaven in the 1950s. The resort had a chairlift, a rope tow, and a burger shack. In 1969 actor Robert Redford bought Timphaven and surrounding lands from the Stewarts. Redford then proceeded to build what is now known as Sundance Resort, a place for skiing, environmental conservation, and artistic exploration. Heard of the Sundance Film Festival? The Sundance Institute? As the resort's website explains, "Sundance has many shapes, many moods, and many possibilities...."

foliage that covers the area. The last section of the trail becomes rockier. The trail to Stewart's Cascades runs through areas that can be ravaged by avalanches during the winter months. You will see evidence of past slides.

The trail reaches an elevation of 7,200 feet before descending 300 feet to the upper falls. Rocky slabs provide a lookout point over the falls. Continue down the trail marked "Sundance" to the lower falls, where you can enjoy the full scope of the falls. After enjoying the area's scenic beauty, return the way you came.

Miles and Directions

0.0 Start at the Aspen Grove/Timpanogos trailhead.
130 feet Come to the sign for Stewart's Cascades; turn left.
0.35 The trail forks; go right.
0.5 Pass a BYU water tank off to the left.
1.4 The trail forks; continue straight.
1.65 Pass a giant rockslide.
1.8 Come to the viewpoint for the upper falls.
1.9 Reach the base of the lower falls. Return the way you came.
3.8 Arrive back at the trailhead.

Option

During summer and fall, hikers can ride Sundance Resort's chairlift to mid-mountain (7,150 feet), where a pleasant downhill stroll brings you in from the south to Stewart's Cascades at 6,800 feet.

Hike Information

Local events and attractions: Sundance ski resort, owned by Robert Redford, offers lift-assisted hiking and mountain biking in the summer months. The resort also offers artistic programs and outdoor theater. For information call (877) 831-6224 or visit www.sundanceresort.com.

Scenic drive: The Alpine Loop begins near the Aspen Grove/Timpanogos trailhead and winds up the mountain into American Fork Canyon. Considered one of

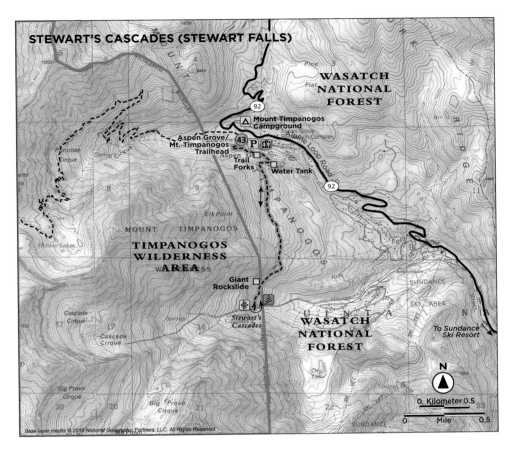

the most scenic drives in the state, especially in fall, it has been designated as a Utah scenic byway.

Camping: Mount Timpanogos Campground sits at an elevation of 7,600 feet and is located just a few hundred feet past the Aspen Grove/Timpanogos trailhead. Sheltered by aspen and fir trees, the campground has vault toilets and drinking water. Reservations are suggested during busy summer months. Campers also must have a recreation pass. Passes can be purchased as you enter the Alpine Loop from either end or from one of the self-service fee tubes located at major trailheads. No trailers or RVs longer than 20 feet. This park has first-come, first-served sites. For reservations call (877) 444-6777 or www.recreation.com. Theater in the Pines is a group campground located on the south side of the Aspen Grove/Timpanogos trailhead. Reservation only; call (877) 444-6777.

GREEN TIP
Rechargeable batteries reduce one source of toxic garbage.

Utah County

44 Squaw Peak

Utah Valley holds one of Utah's most populous counties as well as some of its most historic cities and sites. Pioneers quickly settled Utah Valley after arriving in Salt Lake in the mid-1800s. Settlement wasn't easy, and Squaw Peak is rumored to be named for one of the conflicts between Mormon settlers and the Ute tribe, which ended the life of Big Elk's wife in Rock Canyon. From the valley, the view of Squaw Peak looms jagged, rocky, and impregnable, but the trail is not as difficult as it may appear. In fact, the elevation gain is the hike's only challenge. The well-used, easy-to-follow trail ends with stunning views.

Start: Rock Canyon Park trailhead
Distance: 7.6 miles out and back
Hiking time: About 5 hours
Difficulty: Difficult
Elevation gain: 2,737 feet
Trail surface: Pavement, rock, dirt, stream crossings, bridges
Best season: Summer and fall; snow often in Rock Canyon until early summer
Other trail users: Rock climbers, mountain bikers, horses, and trail runners
Canine compatibility: Leashed dogs permitted

Land status: Uinta-Wasatch-Cache National Forest
Nearest town: Provo
Fees and permits: No fees or permits required
Schedule: Rock Canyon Park is closed from 11 p.m. to 5 a.m. but access to the trail does not close.
Maps: USGS Bridal Veil Falls
Trail contacts: Provo Parks and Recreation, (801) 852-6606
Special considerations: No motorized vehicles. Take plenty of water and insect repellent. Restrooms at the trailhead.

Finding the trailhead: From Salt Lake City head south on I-15 toward Provo for 46 miles. Take exit 269 onto UT 265 (University Parkway) and head east for 3.2 miles. Turn left onto 2230 North, which becomes 2200 North. After 1.1 miles turn left onto North Temple Drive. Follow the road east for 0.9 mile to the mouth of Rock Canyon. The trail starts at the east end of the parking area. **GPS:** N40 15.870' / W111 37.804'

The Hike

Popular with students at Brigham Young University as well as area high school students, Rock Canyon is often populated with hikers and rock climbers who are enjoying the limestone and quartzite that make up the amazing rock for which the canyon is named. Hikers looking for more of a challenge head up First Left Fork for the hike to Squaw Peak. Rock Canyon trailhead has two parking lots (upper and lower),

Squaw Peak as seen from the trailhead

restrooms, and interpretive signs on the area's flora, fauna, geology, and history. This trailhead is also an entry to the Bonneville Shoreline Trail, so it is easily one of the busiest recreational areas in the valley.

The trail to Squaw Peak can be defined in three parts. The first is the hike up Rock Canyon, the second is the climb up First Left Fork, and the third is the climb to the summit. The most difficult aspect is the steady climb up First Left Fork, but the trail is forested and easy to follow. The summit provides 360-degree views of Utah Valley that include Utah Lake, Brigham Young University, the LDS Provo temple, and LDS Missionary Training Center. Owned and operated by the Church of Jesus Christ of Latter-Day Saints, Brigham Young University is internationally renowned. Founded in 1875 as Brigham Young Academy, it has become one of the nation's largest and

In 1934 the Civilian Conservation Corps (CCC) helped build debris basins to catch the trees, mud, and rocks that flowed out of Rock Canyon. Overgrazing had decimated the area flora and resulted in massive erosion. After many efforts over the years to stabilize the canyon, the watershed is back in place and the canyon is healthy. Water is now diverted into pipes, providing 5 percent of Provo's potable water.

best known private universities. The mind-boggling view down into Rock Canyon includes dramatic rock formations pushed up almost vertical because of their location along the Wasatch Fault. The view of Cascade Mountain to the east, Timpanogos to the north, and Provo Peak to the southeast combine to provide the summit reward.

The trail leaves the parking area on the east, following the gravel road that heads into Rock Canyon. From here you can see Squaw Peak high above to the left. A short way up, the road forks; stay right. The road cuts through Gambel oak and passes beneath fascinating geology, including a cave to the left (north) and rock climbing walls. Smaller trails intersect the main road up Rock Canyon, but stay on the main gravel road/trail, crossing the stream and wooden bridges as they appear. The first

Left: Wildflowers in the meadow, mid hike
Right: Squaw Peak Trail

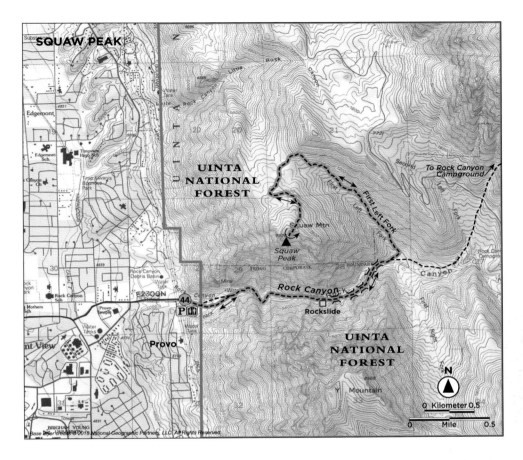

bridge appears at 1.1 miles. At 1.8 miles the turnoff for First Left Fork is off to the left. This turnoff is not easy to see. A 060 flexible brown Forest Service trail marker on the main gravel road marks the trail forward. The marker is the indicator that you are at the turnoff for Squaw Peak—First Left Fork.

First Left Fork is a singletrack dirt trail that intersects the main road from the left. A medium-size rock with the words "Squaw Peak Trail" painted on it sits at the opening of the trail. The trail heads northeast up First Left Fork under a canopy of trees. The trail is a beautiful climb through groves of aspen, oak, and maple. It is well shaded in many places, but most of your elevation gain is experienced in this section of the trail—more than 1,000 feet in just over 1.0 mile, with no switchbacks. At the top of the fork, at 3 miles, the trail enters a meadow and swings southwest, where the trail levels out a bit for some easy strolling. The trail then climbs to the ridge that overlooks Utah County below. Views open of Utah Lake to the west and Buffalo Peak to the east. The last 0.5 mile of the climb is up Squaw Mountain to the peak—a rocky summit with large tabletop rocks for sitting and enjoying the view. From here you can look down into the sharp dropoff of Rock Canyon to the southeast, where you can really gain an understanding of how the canyon got its name; Provo and Utah County to the west; Cascade Mountain (10,908 feet) to the east; Mount Timpanogos (11,749 feet) to the north; and Provo Peak (11,068 feet) to the southeast. Enjoy the view and then return the way you came.

Miles and Directions

0.0 Start at the Rock Canyon Park trailhead.

0.3 Come to a rock climbing slab with sport routes off to the right side of the trail.

0.4 You can see a cave up to your left.

0.45 The paved trail transitions into gravel. A green gate crosses the road here; the trail goes around it to the left. The rock face around the gate is called "The Kitchen" and is a popular rock climbing area.

1.1 Come to the first of five consecutive bridge crossings. There may or may not be water, depending on the time of year.

1.8 Reach the First Left Fork; turn left off the main trail. Look for the rock at the trail junction that says SQUAW PEAK.

3.0 Trail opens to the meadow.

3.3 The trail hits the ridge.

3.8 Reach Squaw Peak. Return the way you came.

7.6 Arrive back at the trailhead.

Hike Information

Camping: Hope Campground sits at 6,500 feet, 5 miles up Provo Canyon on Squaw Peak Road. Twenty-four single campsites and two double sites sit among maples, scrub oak, and fir. For reservations call (877) 444-6777 or go to www.reserveamerica .com or www.recreation.gov.

Rock Canyon Campground is located just upcanyon from the Squaw Peak hike, but the reservation-only group campsite is accessed via Squaw Peak Road. The primitive campground has no running water, so bring your own. Sitting above Utah Valley at 6,500 feet, the forested campground offers plenty of shade, meadows, and wildflowers. For more information or reservations, visit www.reserveamerica.com or call the park at (801) 885-7391. Campground host is located at Hope Campground.

Rock Canyon trailhead is home to an amphitheatre, restroom, and pavilion. To rent the picnic pavilion, go to 311.provo.org or call (801) 852-6000. A seven-day notice is needed for reservations. You may reserve the pavilion between 8:30 a.m. to 2:30 p.m. or 3:30 p.m. to 9:30 p.m.

GREEN TIP
Don't pick the wildflowers; leave them for others to enjoy.

Spanish Fork Canyon

45 Diamond Fork Hot Springs: Fifth Water Trail

Diamond Fork Hot Springs has several man-made rock pools at the base of a waterfall in which to enjoy a relaxing soak. The hot springs bubbling from the ground are naturally cooled by the waterfall that runs directly into the pools from the east side. This beautiful waterfall, rich in green moss, provides a stunning backdrop for the pools. The hike is great year-round, and the springs provide a variety of soaking temperatures. The path to the pools follows along the creek the entire way, and the beautiful rolling trail is a joy in itself.

Start: Three Forks trailhead
Distance: 5.0 miles out and back
Hiking time: About 2.5 hours plus soaking time
Difficulty: Easy
Elevation gain: 632 feet
Trail surface: Dirt and rock path
Best season: Year-round; snowshoes may be needed in winter
Other trail users: Bikers
Canine compatibility: Leashed dogs permitted
Land status: Uinta-Wasatch-Cache National Forest
Nearest town: Spanish Fork
Fees and permits: No fees or permits required
Schedule: Once the road is no longer passable by car in winter (a gate is closed across the road 3 miles from the Three Forks trailhead), you can park along the road before the gate and snowshoe the extra 3 miles into the trailhead.
Maps: USGS Rays Valley
Trail contacts: Spanish Fork Ranger District, (801) 798-3571
Special considerations: Cows are allowed to graze in the area during summer, so watch your step. Beware of rattlesnakes during warmer months as well. Carry insect repellent, and remember that if you stay in hot pools for an extended time your body can become dehydrated, so take plenty of water. Consider carrying an extra garbage bag to help keep the place tidy. This trail struggles with high usage, and forgetful bathers leave all kinds of things.

Finding the trailhead: From Salt Lake City travel south on I-15 to the exit for US 6/Spanish Fork/Price (exit 258). Head east off the exit into Spanish Fork Canyon for 11 miles and then turn off the main highway to the north, toward Diamond Fork Campground. A sign on the highway indicates the unobtrusive side road. Travel on Diamond Fork Canyon Road for 10 miles to the Three Forks trailhead—a sign marks the spot. There is a pit toilet at the gravel parking area. The trail leaves from the east southeast side of the parking lot. **GPS:** N40 05.072' / W111 21.307'

Fishing is a primary outdoor activity in the Diamond Fork area.

The Hike

A soak in Diamond Fork Hot Springs makes for a fun day trip to get away from the hustle and bustle of life. Located up Diamond Fork but along the Fifth Water Creek, the natural hot springs go by both names. There are two sets of pools. The trail reaches

Fifth Water Creek

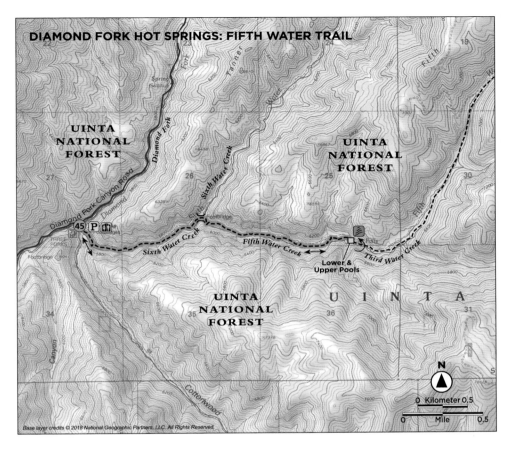

the lower pools first, which are cooler and colored by minerals. The upper pools, 100 feet up the trail, are nearer the hot spring source and are warmer than the lower pools.

The trail to the hot springs leaves the parking area through a gate on the southeast. The trail almost immediately forks, with the right fork crossing a bridge and the left heading up the north side of Fifth Water Creek. Take the left fork and head straight up near the creek. The trail continues along the left side of Fifth Water for the next 1.2 miles, where it crosses over Sixth Water on a bridge and heads right, up the Fifth Water tributary for the final 1.3 miles to the hot springs.

The well-used trail is easy to follow, with fascinating conglomerate rock formations and walls along the way. The sound of the streams serenades the hike, and as you get closer to the hot springs, the sulfur smell marks the spot.

The pools are blue and green; the rocks are covered in a white buildup. Small waterfalls pour into the lower pools, while a 20-foot waterfall stands sentinel over the upper pools. The area is natural and generally unmonitored, and there are no changing areas or restrooms. Pack out everything you bring in, as well as anything the less considerate have left behind.

Left: Hiker at the waterfall pouring into the hot pots
Right: Bathers at the Diamond Fork Hot Springs

After a nice soak—which is fun both night and day and really shines in winter—return the way you came.

Miles and Directions

0.0 Start at Three Forks trailhead.

40 feet Reach the first fork at the beginning of the trail; take the left fork and follow the path up the north side of the stream.

1.2 Come to the bridge that crosses Sixth Water Creek; cross and continue up Fifth Water Creek.

2.5 Arrive at the lower hot pools. The upper pools are 100 feet up the trail. Return the way you came.

5.0 Arrive back at the trailhead.

Hike Information

Camping: Diamond Fork Campground, located 6 miles up Diamond Fork Canyon, is managed by the US Forest Service. Open May 15 to October 15, the campground sits at an elevation of 5,200 feet and has vault toilets, picnic tables, drinking water, and fishing for brown, cutthroat, and rainbow trout. There are sixty-eight sites available. The campground sits amidst cottonwood trees and towering red rock. For reservations call (877) 444-6777 or go to www.recreation.gov.

GREEN TIP
Carry an extra bag with you to haul out trash
others have left behind. If you see someone else littering,
muster up the courage to ask them not to.

West of Salt Lake City

The Oquirrh Mountains form the western border of Salt Lake Valley, but if you drive around the Oquirrh Range and across the valley to the next range of mountains to the east, you will come to the Stansbury Range. The Stansburys hold only a few select trails, but one of the favorites is the climb to Deseret Peak, the tallest in the Stansbury Range.

46 Deseret Peak

Deseret Peak, tallest peak in the Stansbury Mountains west of Salt Lake City, affords views over the Skull Valley to the west and Tooele County to the east that you can get from no other location. Besides a tallest-summit notch, the first section of the trail winds through a beautiful forested area to the saddle and then opens to a rocky, bare ascent to the summit. Douglas fir, alpine fir, and aspen are common on the north-facing slopes, while juniper, sagebrush, and grass cover terrain at higher elevations—a mixed bag of desert and alpine trekking. A full-day adventure, the hike to Deseret Peak is not as crowded as trails in the Wasatch Range, making solitude another benefit.

Start: Top of Loop Campground; Mill Fork trailhead
Distance: 8.0 miles out and back
Hiking time: About 5.5 hours
Difficulty: Strenuous
Elevation gain: 3,550 feet
Trail surface: Dirt, talus, and sandy gravel
Best season: Late summer and fall; snow possible on upper sections of the trail until late June
Other trail users: Horses
Canine compatibility: Dogs permitted

Land status: Deseret Peak Wilderness Area; Uinta-Wasatch-Cache National Forest
Nearest town: Grantsville
Fees and permits: No fees or permits required
Maps: USGS Deseret Peak East, Deseret Peak West
Trail contacts: Salt Lake Ranger District, 6944 South 3000 East, Salt Lake City 84121
Special considerations: The saddle, ridges, and summit are often windy. Be prepared by carrying a jacket to keep warm; throw in the bug repellent too.

Finding the trailhead: From Salt Lake City drive west on I-80 for 20 miles to UT 36 (exit 99). Drive south toward Tooele for 3.5 miles to Mills Junction. Turn west onto UT 138 and drive 11 miles, through Grantsville, to West Street/400 West and a sign directing you to South Willow Canyon. Turn left and continue for 6 miles and then turn right onto South Willow Canyon Road. After about 3.3 miles the road is no longer paved; continue on the dirt road. Two miles up the dirt road, the trail forks for the Boy Scout Camp. Go straight at this junction and in 1 mile pass beneath rock walls that line the roadside. Follow the road for another mile to the top of Loop Campground and the Mill Fork trailhead. The trailhead has pit toilets, a trail marker, and parking for ten cars. **GPS:** N40 28.978' / W112 36.404'

The Hike

Utah is one of only two states that hold three distinct geological zones: the Colorado Plateau, the Rocky Mountains, and the Great Basin. The Great Basin occupies western Utah and is often called the "west desert." Vast desert valleys cut with occasional mountain ranges stretch westward, but these cannot be seen from the Wasatch Front. The Stansbury Mountains, the range that flanks the west side of Tooele County, is

Road to the trailhead William Barba

the most accessible of Utah's Great Basin ranges and thus holds the best collection of hiking trails in the basin. Deseret Peak, the tallest peak of the range, sits at 11,030 feet.

The value of the area was noted, and the Deseret Peak Wilderness Area was added to the Utah Wilderness Act of 1984. The area now includes 25,212 acres, all managed

SALTAIR—RESORT/CONCERT HALL/AMUSEMENT PARK

Saltair, designed by Richard K. A. Kletting, Utah's foremost architect at the turn of the 20th century, was built on the shores of the Great Salt Lake as a place of "wholesome recreation." The Mormon Church wanted to provide a resort that would be enjoyed by the residents of the state and all who came to Utah: a typical amusement park with roller coaster, merry-go-round, Ferris wheel, midway games, bicycle races, rodeos, bullfights, swimming at the lake, fireworks, and dancing on the world's largest dance floor.

Envisioned as the "Coney Island of the West," Saltair opened on Memorial Day 1893 and hit its peak in the early 1920s, attracting close to half a million visitors each year, but this 32-year stint was to be the resort's heyday. In 1925 Saltair burned to the ground, and though many attempts were made to resurrect the resort, they have been curtailed by fire, flood, and salt corrosion. Today Saltair has a concert stage where local and national artists occasionally play.

by the US Forest Service. Enjoyed by hunters in fall, hikers in summer and early fall, and backcountry skiers in spring and winter, Deseret Peak and the surrounding chutes have a personality that smacks of the semiarid wilderness it occupies. Located in the zone between the Great Basin and the Rocky Mountains, the climb to Deseret Peak sports both mountain and desert feels. To reach the top of the limestone escarpment that is Deseret Peak, one travels forested paths as well as naked, rock-strewn hillsides past little more than crooked old juniper trees.

Mill Fork trailhead sits at the top of Loop Campground. The trail leaves the parking area from the southwest corner and meanders up South Willow Canyon for 0.7 mile, where you come to a streambed and two important forks in the trail, one right after the other. Two trails take off on the other side of the stream. The right fork, the most obvious one, heads up and to the southwest; the left fork is 100 feet below and heads down. Cross the stream and follow the left fork, taking the lower trail. The second fork, which is signed, immediately appears. Follow the signs and again take the left fork to continue to Deseret Peak. (The right fork goes to South Willow Lake.) The trail climbs up Mill Fork and at 1.8 miles exits the tree cover and enters a meadow where you get an open view of the steep, rocky cliffs and mountains around you. The meadow is full of dead trees from an old fire, beetles, and avalanche debris. The trail winds its way through the meadow and continues up and out of Mill Fork to the saddle at 10,000 feet.

At the saddle is a barren four-way intersection with signs pointing to Deseret Peak, Antelope Canyon, Bear Fork, and back the way you came to Loop Campground. Take the right (northwestern) trail up the rocky south-facing mountain, which leads near the chutes and a giant, jagged cliff face; traverses two talus piles; and finally reaches the summit.

Upper section of the Deseret Peak Trail William Barba

View from the Deseret Peak summit WILLIAM BARBA

The summit affords 360-degree views of Skull Valley to the west and the Skull Valley Goshute Indian Reservation adjacent to the wilderness area; the Great Salt Lake and Stansbury Island to the north and east; and the Oquirrh and Wasatch Ranges and Tooele County to the east—a view you can't get from any other vantage point. Deseret Peak allows a peek into the vast west desert and an isolated area void of cities and crossed by very few roads. After enjoying the view, return the way you came.

Miles and Directions

0.0 Start at Mill Fork trailhead.

200 feet Enter Deseret Peak Wilderness Area.

0.7 Cross a stream and come to two forks, one right after the other; take the left fork at both.

1.8 Exit the tree cover and enter a meadow.

3.3 Reach the saddle at the top of the canyon and a four-way intersection. Head right (northwest) along the trail.

3.9 Come to a dominant jagged cliff face along the path.

4.0 Reach Deseret Peak. Return the way you came.

8.0 Arrive back at the trailhead.

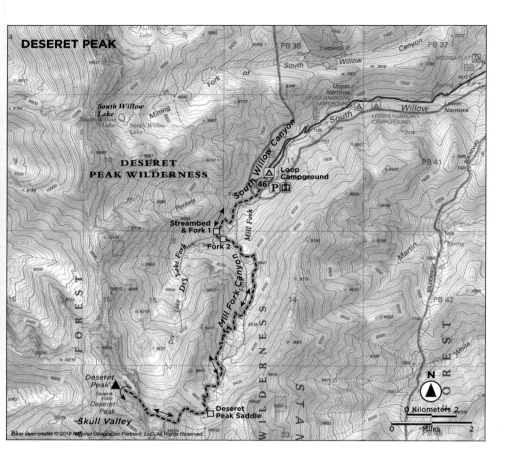

Option

The trail to Deseret Peak can be hiked as a loop. From the peak the loop continues north on the summit ridge before it drops down below the ridge onto the west side on paths that are less defined and not well maintained. Confused hikers can find themselves heading down the wrong drainage, but many enjoy the loop aspect that eventually makes its way back into Mill Fork Canyon.

Hike Information

Local events and attractions: The Upper Narrows, a spot along the road where the walls of the canyon narrow down to the roadbed, are home to a dozen climbing routes. The creek flows at the base of the limestone cliff, requiring some maneuvering to get on the routes. A stick-clip is helpful for getting started.

> The Stansbury Mountains are the centermost of three prominent north–south mountain ranges including the Oquirrh Mountains to the east and Cedar Mountains to the west.

View from the saddle WILLIAM BARBA

Camping: There are five US Forest Service campgrounds located in South Willow Canyon: Cottonwood, Loop, Upper Narrows, Lower Narrows, and the Boy Scout campground. Each campground has fewer than ten sites (fee required) available with fire rings and picnic tables, but water and garbage receptacles are not provided. Please pack out all trash. A number of campsites are nestled near Willow Creek. Camp in designated sites only. Reservations can be made for Upper Narrows campground at www.reserveamerica.com.

GREEN TIP
When driving, don't let any passenger throw garbage
out the window. Keep a small bag in the car that you can
empty properly at home.

Appendix: Resources

Clubs and Trail Groups

Davis County Hiking Meet-Up Group: www.meetup.com/DavisCountyHiking/
Leave No Trace: www.lnt.org
Mountain Trails Foundation: Park City, http://mountaintrails.org
Sierra Club: Utah Chapter, http://utah.sierraclub.org/
Wasatch Mountain Club: 1390 South 1100 East, Ste. 103, Salt Lake City 84105; (801) 463-9842; www.wasatchmountainclub.org

Further Reading and Resources

Brinkerhoff, Brian, and Greg Witt. *Best Easy Day Hikes Salt Lake City.* Globe Pequot Press, 2009.

Guide to Farmington Trails. Farmington Trails Committee, 2016.

A History of Sivogah to Draper City 1849–1977, vol. 1–3. The Draper, Utah Historical Society.

Ikenberry, Donna Lynn. *Camping Utah.* Globe Pequot Press, 2001.

Keller, Charles L. *The Lady in the Ore Bucket.* The University of Utah Press, 2001.

Prettyman, Brett. *Fishing Utah,* Second Edition. Lyons Press, 2008.

Winters, Randy. *Wasatch Eleveners.* The University of Utah Press, 2006.

Online guide to the backcountry yurts of Utah: www.YurtsofUtah.com.

Online guide to winter snowshoe trails of the Wasatch Range: www.SnowshoeUtah.com

Hike Index

About the Author

Lori J. Lee is a 31-year resident of Utah and has written for the Outdoor Recreation industry for the past 20 years. She is the author of three previous guidebooks: *Wild Weekends in Utah, The Best Snowshoe Trails of the Wasatch,* and *Yurts of Utah.* She has been published in national, regional, and local magazines including *Back-packer, Sea Kayaker, Camping Life, Outdoor Utah Adventure Guide, Her Sports,* and *Cross-Country Skier.*

Lori has been a guest trail guide host on Park City TV and hosted "Lori's Mountain Report" on KALL 700's *Utah Outdoor* radio show. Lori currently resides in Bountiful, Utah, where she is often out exploring the trails on foot, snowshoes, skis, and her bike.